Lacan and the New Wave in American Psychoanalysis

THE SUBJECT AND THE SELF

Edited by
JUDITH FEHER GUREWICH
and
MICHEL TORT

in collaboration with
SUSAN FAIRFIELD

OTHER

Other Press

New York

The editors gratefully acknowledge permission to print "'Someday' and 'If Only' Fantasies," by Salman Akhtar, published in the *Journal of the American Psychoanalytic Association*, 1996. Used by permission of International Universities Press and the *Journal of the American Psychoanalytic Association*.

This book was set in 11 pt. Berkeley Book by Alpha Graphics of Pittsfield, New Hampshire.

ISBN-13: 978-1-892746-03-0

For information write to Other Press LLC, 2 Park Avenue, 24th Floor, New York, NY 10016. Or visit our Web site: www.otherpress.com.

Library of Congress Cataloging-in-Publication Data

Subject and the self.
    Lacan and the new wave in American psychoanalysis : the subject and the self / edited by Judith Feher Gurewich and Michel Tort in collaboration with Susan Fairfield.
       p. cm.
    Originally published: The subject and the self. Northvale, N.J. : Jason Aronson, c1996.
    Includes bibliographical references and index.
    ISBN 1-892746-03-4 (pbk.)
    1. Lacan, Jacques, 1901—Congresses. 2. Self—Congresses.
3. Self psychology—Congresses. 4. Psychoanalysis—Congresses.
I. Gurewich, Judith Feher. II. Tort, Michel. III. Fairfield, Susan.
[BF109.L28S88 1999]
150.19'5—dc21   99-26605

Contents

Part III: The Subject and the Self: Conclusions

Acknowledgments

The chapters of this book were originally papers presented at a Franco-American conference held in Paris on November 5 and 6, 1994, under the auspices of the Laboratory for Basic Psychopathology and Psychoanalysis of the University of Paris VII. First and foremost, therefore, we wish to extend our gratitude to Professeur Pierre Fédida, who as Director of the Laboratory made this endeavor possible. We are also grateful to M. Yves Mabin of the Ministry of Foreign Affairs and to Christian Delacampagne, the Cultural Attaché in Boston of the French Embassy in the United States, for the generous financial contribution that helped to defray the expenses of the American participants. We extend our thanks to the French Ministry of Higher Education and Research for the use of their auditorium, and to the Assets Management Society, Sanofi Pharma, Inc., Upjohn, Inc., Roche, Inc., Gruenenthal and Beaufour Ipsen, Inc. for their sponsorship.

We also wish to extend our thanks to Professeur Agnès Oppenheimer of the University of Paris V and the Paris Psychoanalytic Society for her astute comments as director of discussion.

We are grateful to *The Journal of the American Psychoanalytic Association* for permission to reprint the paper of Salman Akhtar, M.D., "'Someday' and 'If Only' Fantasies," originally delivered in a slightly different form at the Paris conference.

Finally we wish to acknowledge our profound appreciation to Susan Fairfield, not only for translating the French papers and the discussions but for applying her outstanding editing skills to the manuscript as a whole.

Contributors

Salman Akhtar, M.D., F.A.P.A., is Lecturer on Psychiatry, Harvard Medical School, and Professor of Psychiatry at Jefferson Medical College in Philadelphia. A Training and Supervising Analyst at the Philadelphia Psychoanalytic Institute, he is the author of *Broken Structures: Severe Personality Disorders and Their Treatment* (1992) and *A Quest for Answers: Understanding and Treating Severe Personality Disorders* (1995) and the author or editor of more than 100 other scientific publications. Dr. Akhtar has also published four volumes of poetry.

Marcianne Blevis, psychoanalyst and psychiatrist, is Director of the Department of Psychoanalytic Psychotherapies at the Hôpital Ste.-Anne and is a Member of the Cercle Freudien in Paris. The co-founder of the psychoanalytic journal *Patio,* she has published numerous articles in journals of psychoanalysis, aesthetics, and art.

Monique David-Ménard, psychoanalyst, is a Member of the Société Freudienne de Psychanalyse and is Vice President of the Collège International de Philosophie, where she directs a program in Philosophy and Psychoanalysis. She is the author of books and articles including *Hysteria from Freud to Lacan: Body and Language in Psychoanalysis*, trans. Catherine Porter (Ithaca, NY: Cornell University Press 1989) and *Les constructions de l'universel* (Paris: P.U.F. 1996).

Joël Dor, psychoanalyst, is a Member of the Association de Formation Psychanalytique et de Recherches Freudiennes: Espace Analytique. He is in charge of lectures and is Director of Research in the Department of Training and Research in Clinical Human Sciences at the Université Denis-Diderot, Paris VII, where he teaches psychopathology and psychoanalysis. Widely published on the theory and practice of psychoanalysis, he is the author of *The Clinical Lacan* and *Introduction to the Reading of Lacan: The Unconscious Structured Like a Language* as well as the author/co-author of two books forthcoming from Other Press: *Structure and Perversion* and *Lacanian Psychoanalysis: Theory and Practice*.

Pierre Fédida, psychoanalyst, is a Member of the Association Psychanalytique de France and the International Psychoanalytic Association. He is a Professor in the Department of Training and Research in Clinical Human Sciences at the Université Denis-Diderot, Paris VII, where he directs the Laboratory for Basic Psychopathology and Psychoanalysis. The Co-Director of the *Revue Internationale de Psychopathologie*, he has published numerous articles and books, including *Crise et contre-transfert* (Paris: P.U.F. 1992) and *Site de l'etranger* (Paris: P.U.F. 1995).

Judith Feher Gurewich, Ph.D., practices psychoanalysis in Cambridge, MA. She is affiliated with the Boston Psychoanalytic Institute and is a Member of the Association de Formation Psychanalytique et de Recherches Freudiennes: Espace Analytique in Paris. Dr. Gurewich is the Director of the Lacan Seminar at Harvard University's Center for Literary and Cultural Studies. She has published a number of papers on various topics in psychoanalysis and the social sciences in French and American journals and is the editor of "The Lacanian Clinical Field" series, published by Other Press.

Jacques Hassoun, psychoanalyst and psychiatrist, is a founding member of the Cercle Freudien in Paris. He has directed scientific meetings throughout the world and regularly lectures and offers clinical supervision in Montreal and New York. Among his many books are *Les Indes Occidentales* (Paris: Eclat 1987), *Fragments de langue maternelle* (Paris: Point Hors Ligne 1993) and *La cruauté mélancholique* (Paris: Aubier 1995).

Nicholas Kouretas, M.D., is a graduate of the Boston Psychoanalytic Institute and a member of the American Psychoanalytic Association. He is on the faculty of the Psychoanalytic Institute of New England, East, and is an Assistant Professor of Psychiatry at Harvard Medical School. He has lectured and published on subjects related to psychoanalytic epistemology and theory.

Arnold H. Modell, M.D., is Clinical Professor of Psychiatry, Harvard Medical School, and a Training and Supervising Analyst at the Boston Psychoanalytic Institute. He is the author of *Object Love and Reality* (1968); *Psychoanalysis in a New Context* (1984); *Other Times, Other Realities* (1990); *The Private Self* (1994); and many articles.

Juan-David Nasio, psychiatrist and psychoanalyst, is Director of Studies at the Université Denis-Diderot, Paris VII and Director of the Séminaires Psychanalytiques de Paris. He is the author of many books, including *Les yeux de Laure* (Paris: Aubier 1987), *Enseignements de sept concepts cruciaux de la psychanalyse* (Paris: Rivages 1988), and *Hysteria from Freud to Lacan: The Splendid Child of Psychoanalysis* (Other Press 1998).

Malkah T. Notman, M.D., is a Training and Supervising Analyst at the Boston Psychoanalytic Institute. She has written extensively on the psychoanalytic psychology of women and issues related to reproductivity. She is Clinical Professor of Psychiatry at Harvard Medical School and Director of Faculty Development at The Cambridge Hospital Department of Psychiatry.

Anna Ornstein, M.D., is Professor of Child Psychiatry and Co-Director of the International Center for the Study of Psychoanalytic Self Psychology, University of Cincinnati Department of Psychiatry. The author of many publications on Self Psychology, she is a Training and Supervising Analyst at the Cincinnati Psychoanalytic Institute.

Paul H. Ornstein, M.D., is Professor of Child Psychiatry and Co-Director of the International Center for the Study of Psychoanalytic Self Psychology, University of Cincinnati Department of Psychiatry. He is a Training and Supervising Analyst at the Cincinnati Psychoanalytic Institute. He has written extensively on the topic of Self Psychology.

Michel Tort, psychoanalyst, is a Professor and Chair of the Department of Training and Research in Clinical Human Sciences at the Université Denis-Diderot, Paris VII. He is Program Director at the Collège International de Philosophie and is the author of several books, including *Le désir froid* (Paris: La découverte 1992) and the forthcoming *Le nom du père incertain*, and of numerous articles.

Daniel Widlöcher, psychoanalyst and psychiatrist, is currently Vice President of the International Psychoanalytic Association. He is a Member of the Association Psychanalytique de France; Professor of Psychiatry, Université Pierre et Marie Curie, Paris VI and the Groupe Hospitalier Pitié-Salpêtrière; Director of the French National Health and Medical Research Institute division of Behavioral Psychopathology and Pharmacology; and Co-Director of the *Revue Internationale de Psychopathologie*. Dr. Widlöcher is the author of many books on child psychopathology, psychoanalysis, and biological psychiatry, including *Traité de psychopathologie* (Paris: P.U.F. 1994) and *Psychanalyse et psychothérapies* (Paris: Flammarion 1996).

Joan J. Zilbach, M.D., is a Training and Supervising Analyst at the Boston Psychoanalytic Society and Institute and is on the faculty of Harvard Medical School and of the Fielding Institute in Santa Barbara. She is the author of numerous articles and books focusing on child and family therapy and on the psychoanalytic psychology of women.

Who's Afraid of Jacques Lacan?

JUDITH FEHER GUREWICH, PH.D.

WHY *THE SUBJECT AND THE SELF*?

The chapters of this book were originally papers presented at an unusual conference held on November 3 and 4, 1994, in Paris. French analysts who had made varying use of the thought of Jacques Lacan were asked to discuss papers delivered by American analysts who represent various schools of thought prevalent in the United States today. The topic originally selected for the conference had been borderline states, chosen not only because of its actuality but also because the American-born concept of borderline states had been met with a certain resistance by Lacanian analysts, who remain wedded to Freud's diagnostic nosography of neurosis, perversions, and psychosis.

Both literally and metaphorically, then, borderline states seem to represent the line of demarcation between American and Lacanian psychoanalytic perspectives. Whereas in the United States major trends in psychoanalytic theory have gradually abandoned Freud's hypothesis of the sexual origin of psychic ailments and have moved towards a different understanding of what causes human suffering, French psychoanalysts influenced by Lacan have developed theories that have kept alive Freud's discovery of the unconscious and of its sexual underpinnings. Because of this major discrepancy between the two sides of the Atlantic, it seemed worthwhile to ask whether borderline states are an invention or, instead, a true discovery of an entirely new ailment. (This point is discussed in my opening remarks to the conference.) As the conference unfolded, however, it became apparent that the concept of borderline psychopathology only marginally informed the exchanges that took place and that this concept could no longer serve either to bridge or to highlight the differences of perspectives that were being presented. Therefore when the organizers of the conference became the editors of the present book, we decided that *The Subject and the Self* would be a more appropriate description of the two psychic domains that were being compared.

"The subject" is a direct allusion to the subject of the unconscious, a concept that underlies Lacan's reading of Freud. For Lacanian analysts the subject of the unconscious is the only subject of concern. The "Lacanian" unconscious has taken on a complexity akin to that of the concept of the self in current American psychoanalysis, insofar as it obeys specific laws and principles that the analyst must decipher. The Lacanian subject of the unconscious "speaks" a language that reveals a mode of desiring of which the conscious subject is unaware. In that sense the status of the ego, its fragility or strength, falls outside the Lacanian analytic field. The ego is the barrier that needs to be broken through in order to have access to a desire that operates behind the subject's back. Coming to terms with this unconscious desire enables the patient to lessen the grip of his ego's defenses without having the latter become a focus of analytic treatment.

The theoretical divide between the subject of the unconscious and the ego is no longer prevalent in American psychoanalysis. This is not to say that the unconscious has disappeared from the psychoanalytic scene but rather to suggest that in elaborating the concept of the self many authors—through different avenues—seem to have merged the conscious and unconscious strivings of the individual. The self stands for a richly layered composite that far exceeds the Freudian notion of the ego as the agent of the reality principle. The transference reveals the ways in which primordial intersubjective relations have influenced the shaping of the patient's self and its vicissitudes: such an approach no longer relies on Freud's Oedipus complex or on instinct theory to explain the genesis of psychopathology.

In hindsight, therefore, our subtitle, *The Subject and the Self*, conveys the editors' sense of the overall import of the conference and indicates how both theoretical perspectives have continued their dialogue with Freud either through a deepening of his insights or through explicit or implicit denunciation of his failures.

If the differences and similarities between the French and American approaches are well represented in the introductory remarks, the discussions, and the conclusions, it nevertheless remains the case that American readers unfamiliar with the clinical Lacanian approach may at times be at a loss while reading certain of the discussions. To give such readers a head start that the courageous American presenters did not have, I shall therefore try to provide an outline of some basic Lacanian concepts. Not all of these papers require elucidation, and this discrepancy in clarity of exposition among the various Lacanian discussions already says something about Lacan's approach. Lacan felt that Freud's clarity and didactic talent had ultimately led to distortions and oversimplifications, and his own notoriously "impossible" style was meant to serve as a metaphor for the difficulty of listening to the unconscious. Cracking his difficult writings involves not only the intellectual effort of the reader but also his or her unconscious processes. Comprehension will dawn as the reader-analyst recognizes in his own work what was expressed in sibylline fashion in the text. Some of Lacan's followers continued this tradition, fearing that clear exposition would leave no room for the active participation of the reader. Others felt that, although Lacan's point was well taken, it was not necessary to prolong indefinitely an ideology of obscurantism liable to fall into the same traps as the ones Lacan was denouncing in the first place.

One of the great difficulties for an American analyst trying to figure out the Lacanian genre is the way these theorists explain their own rather far-out ideas as if they were coming straight from Freud. It was apparent throughout the conference that the French discussants were often under the mistaken impression that referring to Freud as the denominator that was common to both parties was the best way to reach out to American analysts. This approach was misleading, to say the least; Lacanian analysts seem to have forgotten that Lacan's famous "return" to the founder of psychoanalysis cannot be taken at face value. Lacan's Freud and the American Freud are far from being transparent to each other. Lacan had dismantled the Freudian corpus and rebuilt it on entirely new foundations, so that the new edifice no longer resembled the old. At the same time he had always downplayed, with a certain *coquetterie*, his position as a theory builder because he was intent on proving that he had remained, despite all odds, true to Freud's deepest insights. Since Lacan was very insistent on keeping

Freudian concepts as the raw material of his theory, Lacanian analysts of the second generation have followed in their master's footsteps and have continued to read Freud scrupulously in order to expand with new insights this large structure that had been laid out. Moreover, complicated historical circumstances have fostered their isolation so, that their acquaintance with recent psychoanalytic developments outside of France has been limited. Lacan's critical views on ego psychology and selected aspects of object-relations theory have continued to inform their vision of American psychoanalysis and have left them unaware that certain of their misgivings about these schools of thought are shared by some of their colleagues in the United States. This apparently undying allegiance to Freud, therefore, does not necessarily mean that Lacanians are frozen as if they had not moved beyond what is commonly called "id psychology."

Lacan's theory developed over a span of fifty years; it is therefore futile even to try to explore it in depth. To refer the psychoanalyst reader to secondary sources on Lacan that are available in English would not necessarily serve the purpose either, since these books were in large part destined for academicians who had found much appeal in Lacan's extensive use of linguistics, anthropology, and philosophy. There have been very few tools that would enable a clinician to get a firm grasp on Lacanian theory; indeed, there have been very few books in English that provide a systematic, clear, and didactic explanation of this theory, and there are none that describe the clinical implications of what is unique in Lacan's reading of Freud. This situation has recently changed, however, with the publication of *The Lacanian Clinical Field* series by Other Press. More books are being added to this series every year. Among the authors are some of the discussants in the present conference. Thus the American clinician who develops an interest in the Lacanian clinical approach now has at his or her disposal the kind of work that can finally shed some light on the insights of this obscure and elusive figure of the French psychoanalytic scene.

Introducing Lacan is a task that bears some resemblance to Sisyphus' ordeal. Indeed, Lacanian theory introduces into the psychoanalytic corpus entirely new concepts whose function becomes apparent only once their relevance to analytic practice is made clear. Yet giving a definition of these terms without providing a rationale for their existence is a futile exercise, because readers may understandably feel that they are being asked to grapple with ideas that they will not be able to connect to their habitual mode of thinking. They may feel that they are forced to swallow a meal that they had no appetite for in the first place. On the other hand, the strategy that consists in introducing the context that has led to the emergence of this new terminology may also be confusing, because ideally the reader should already know "the grammar" in order not only to understand "the language" but also to enjoy the story that this new language narrates. The only solution I have found to this vicious circle is to provide the reader with a glossary (following this Preface) of the Lacanian terms that I will progressively introduce here. A look at this glossary may provide an overview of the concepts that will be elucidated in the text.

LACAN "WITH" AND "BEYOND" AMERICAN PSYCHOANALYSIS

With this in mind, I think that what may be useful now for the American reader would be to situate Lacan's thought within the general frame of psychoanalytic theory. Despite what has been said about Lacan's obscurantism, elitism, and intellectualism, his work remains deeply grounded in a dispute that has been raging in psychoanalytic circles since the '20s—a dispute between drive theory and what would become object-relations theory, between a *one-body psychology* and a *two-body psychology*, and, more recently, between intrapsychic perspectives and intersubjective or interpersonal ones. Lacan's theory addresses every one of these issues in an attempt to introduce into the Freudian corpus the concept of the Other.[1] This concept is meant to place Freudian theory in a context that brings to the fore the intersubjective structure of the human psyche.[2] The Other refers not only to the primordial other—the mother—and her role in shaping the subjectivity of her child, but also to the otherness of language in the sense that the unconscious has its roots in the discourse of this Other. In a manner that differs from the approach of object-relations theory, Lacan attempted to create a theoretical framework that would resolve the ques-

---

1. The "Other" with a capital "O" refers to the other of the unconscious, while the "other" with a lowercase "o" refers to the other as experienced in reality or in fantasy. This distinction will become clearer in what follows.

2. It is important to note, however, that Lacan's concept of intersubjectivity refers exclusively to what, as we shall see, is the intersubjective structure of the unconscious; it therefore bears no similarity to what American psychoanalysis means by intersubjectivity, that is, the empathic understanding between one self and another.

tion of what is primary in the elaboration of psychic life: the input of the drives or the input of the Other? Within his perspective it is no longer necessary to struggle with the nature/nurture debate or to wonder about the predominance of pre-oedipal or oedipal dynamics in the constitution of human subjectivity. The classical dichotomies between inside/outside and self/other disappear and with them our usual understanding of human development.

What Lacan demonstrates is that the psychic life of the individual develops in an intersubjective structure that is *not intuitively or phenomenologically graspable* because such a structure is not merely composed of the drives or affects on the one hand and the social milieu on the other hand.

LACAN AND STRUCTURALISM

Understanding what Lacan means by the Other—this intersubjective structure that cannot be phenomenologically grasped—requires that we make a small excursion into a world of ideas that emerged in France in the '60s and that is commonly called structuralism. The structuralist movement has left its mark both on the cognitive sciences (as in the work of Piaget, for example) and on the humanities (for example, Lévi-Strauss' anthropology, Saussure's and Jakobson's linguistic theory). Structuralism breaks with our usual way of thinking about objects. Its goal is to reveal how objects or their elements are related according to systems that are not immediately apparent. We must no longer describe things in terms of their nature or their specific properties, for what is important is to discern these underlying relations.

The idea of exposing hidden relations between objects independently of what they represent on the surface—that is, their manifest content— seems particularly akin to Freud's hypothesis about the functioning of the unconscious as described in *The Interpretation of Dreams*. Lacan found in the work of Saussure, the founder of structural linguistics, and in the work of the formalist Roman Jakobson, the founder of phonology, the elements he needed to reconceptualize Freud's definition of the unconscious. Lévi-Strauss' seminal structural anthropology, on the other hand, provided Lacan with a new interpretation of Freud's (1913) foundational myth of the prohibition of incest. With the help of these different theoretical approaches Lacan was able to extract from Freud's work an entire array of laws defining the functioning of human subjectivity.

One of the great contributions of the structuralist position—a position that the world of literary criticism in the United States has widely utilized—has been to rethink the genesis and the status of the human subject. It is of course no news to American psychoanalysis that people are unaware of the motives that animate them. Much less congenial is thinking of the individual as a structure without a core, without an authentic self ready to emerge under enabling circumstances. Lacan has often been accused, I think wrongly, of being an antihumanist precisely because the structural underpinnings of his theory lead him to view the human subject as shaped not by the laws of the instincts but by other laws, laws that do not emerge from the individual's constitution but that operate beyond him, laws that constitute individuals in their humanity and in their sexuality.

What are these laws? How do they operate? How can we conceptualize an individual whose subjectivity is entirely dependent on structures to which he can have no access? Is there a connection between these ideas and Freud's idiosyncratic *one body psychology*?

From structuralism Lacan borrows the idea that the individual does not start his career in the world as a subject but becomes shaped by structural forces that are not graspable phenomenologically. In order to account for such a difficult concept it is necessary to define a field that can accommodate these invisible laws without, of course, losing sight of the actual realm of human experience, for it is obvious that the individual's mental life is experienced within the boundaries of a private world: only psychotic people feel that their thoughts can be accessible to others. (This point, by the way, suggests that our ability to constitute a private world is far from being a natural process.) How, then, can we understand that the subject's psychic space is shaped by non-graspable forces?

The fact that we believe we are the sole engineers of our thoughts and feelings, that we believe we are autonomous and cohesive individuals in control of our actions, that we think we know why we seek analytic treatment, that we imagine that the analyst knows something about us that we don't know, that we feel that the analyst is casting judgment upon us— these aspects of experience are what Lacan calls *méconnaissance* or misrecognition. This *méconnaissance*—our usual way of being in the world— gives us access only to a realm of illusion in which our experience of "reality" is not layered but monolithic. But as the transference unfolds *méconnaissance* becomes more fragile. What we think, say, and see is less imbued with certitude: a dream, a slip of the tongue, a fantasy, a misplaced affect, an acting out makes us aware that another structure is operative, that an invisible puppeteer pulls the strings of our destiny. We realize that we not only speak but that we are also spoken by invisible laws that run through our discourse and our affects, shaping our conscious life, linking us to others in ways we cannot perceive or understand.

The essential point thus far is that Lacan breaks the illusory envelope that surrounds our experience of subjectivity. He uses the model of the Möbius strip as a vivid metaphor to describe how what is exterior to human subjectivity becomes not only interior but central. Exterior and interior are, as it were, in a continuum: what is interior can become exterior and vice versa.

THE OTHER AND STRUCTURAL LINGUISTICS

With this very sketchy understanding in mind, let us have a closer look at how Lacan has used structural linguistics to shape his concept of the Other. As I mentioned above, one of Lacan's goals was to integrate certain insights of object-relations theory into Freud's theory of the Oedipus complex. He wished to give an entirely new status to the Other so as to explain why drives, as theorized by Freud, cannot be the unmediated motor of human strivings. It is not as if we have, at the outset, a human subject who tries to get satisfaction in an other and through an other. On the contrary: for Lacan it is the Other who shapes the destiny of the drives. For him as for object-relations theory the Other is primary, and yet his conception of the Other cannot be exhausted by object-relations theory. The Lacanian Other goes beyond the notion of the other as actual—the real parent as in Winnicott—and beyond the notion of the other as an internal object or fantasy as for Fairbairn or Melanie Klein. Here is where we encounter those peculiar laws that traverse both the subject and his Other. This Other is no incarnation of the divine: it borrows its modus operandi from the realm of language as the structural linguists understand it.

What does structural linguistics bring to our understanding of the function of language that we did not know before? The fundamental notion (a rather counterintuitive one) is that language is not at the service of the things it apparently designates. Language is constituted to form a whole with its own laws and regulations. Words ("signifiers") are not selected to match pre-given things ("the signifieds"); they are selected in relation to each other according to the sounds and permutations that are available in a given language. This implies that the process of learning to speak has little to do with putting words to things. Learning a language requires that we absorb its structure, its grammatical rules, its pronunciation, the culture that informs it, and so forth. This process is unconscious when we learn our mother tongue, but we are made painfully aware of it when as adults we learn a foreign language from scratch.

For structural linguists, language and its structure are what makes the world meaningful. Intuitively we tend to believe that language simply conveys a meaning immanent in the thing. For structural linguists, however, meaning is an arbitrary effect of a set of rules. It is almost as if the word preceded the thing instead of the reverse. Of course linguists are neither philosophers nor psychoanalysts; their interest remains grounded in finding out what language is and how it operates. Lacan used these findings for his own purpose and devised his concept of the Other to explain the intersubjective structure of the unconscious. The unconscious of the subject is this Other. It is not the id but a structure that has borrowed from language certain operational modes such as condensation and displacement (corresponding to what linguistic theory calls metaphor and metonymy). The Other informs our psychic life in a fashion akin to the way the laws of language inform the way we speak. But these rules that organize the unconscious are not innate; they come from outside the individual. A simple way to put it would be to say that our unconscious finds its roots in the discourse of the first Other of our existence: the mother.

This is how it works. Even before a child is born he or she is already assigned a place in the world of language in the sense that he or she is expected by the parents and thus already symbolized in their minds. He may already have a name; she may already be the bearer of many of her parents' expectations. In that sense the parents' unconscious and conscious signifiers will be projected onto this imaginary child and will continue to surround the baby after its birth. How these signifiers of the desire of the Other will ultimately become the milestones of the child's unconscious will be explained shortly. At this point let us simply say that these signifiers— these words, sentences, affects, attitudes of the other—will become the landmarks of the child's existence much before the time she can impute her own subjective meaning to them. By the time the child learns how to speak, these signifiers will already have made inroads in what will become the subject's unconscious. We can understand at this point Lacan's famous dictum to the effect that the unconscious is the discourse of the Other, or, as he also put it, that the Other is the keeper of the signifiers.

It is important to emphasize that the chains of signifiers that structure the unconscious are not to be understood as chains of signification per se. The key words or sounds that have shaped our childhood life are not symbols (a horse is not necessarily a symbol of sexuality; a snake is not necessarily the penis as Freud would sometimes have it). These signifiers do not refer to the things they normally represent. The processes of dreamwork (Freud 1900)—condensation and displacement—determine these signifiers when they appear in a patient's discourse, causing a signifier to stand for another signifier (condensation) or to be replaced by an adjacent signifier in the associative chain (displacement). Free association is thus the best way for the patient to follow these landmarks and to see which reminiscences they may lead to.

This is a good place to make a brief parenthesis. Lacan has often been dismissed by American psychoanalysts because his keen attention to language supposedly causes him to ignore the realm of affects. This accusation is, I think, unfounded. Affects as "signifieds," as expressions of sadness, and so forth, must of course be acknowledged by the analyst, but they may not necessarily be productive material, because, to put it plainly, they don't lead anywhere. This does not mean that Lacanian analysts are not empathic, but they would define empathy as their ability to be precisely in tune with the patient's desire as it is represented in the key signifiers of his or her utterances. If, on the other hand, a mutative interpretation leading to the unveiling of an unconscious chain of signifiers produces an emotional outburst, such affects are understood as a natural outcome of the intervention and in that sense they don't deserve much explanation. An affect, however, can on occasion have the status of a signifier. For example, a given patient cries intermittently during her sessions. Yet her tears do not seem to be related to what she says, nor do they evoke in the analyst any reaction except a keen curiosity. It is as if those tears do not belong to the patient, as if she were crying on behalf of somebody else. It turns out that her tears are related to her mother's own sadness, a sadness the patient does not want to confront.

THE ACQUISITION OF LANGUAGE AND THE
BIRTH OF THE UNCONSCIOUS

How does the child's unconscious come into being? Following Freud, Lacan links the birth of the unconscious to the dynamics of the Oedipus complex, but his treatment of this issue offers an entirely new perspective on Freud's views. For Lacan the birth of the unconscious cannot be separated from the processes that lead to the child's acquisition of language. Yet we must be careful not to take this idea too literally, since Lacanian psychoanalysis does not subscribe to a linear, chronological model of human development. It is not the place of psychoanalysis to observe the growth of the child. Everything that can be said about the production of psychic life and human motivation is always retroactive and is always a construction or reconstruction. This explains why language and the rules that organizes speech are so crucial in Lacanian theory: the discourse of the patient speaking to the analyst is what defines the field of analytic inquiry. Infant research therefore remains marginal. For Lacanians, it is more appropriate to speak of structural moments of psychic development instead of stages or developmental lines. From this perspective the preoedipal period is a more or less fictive construct retroactively understood by the analyst on the basis of the patient's discourse as it unfolds in the transference.

Lacan conceives the preoedipal period as the phase of the child's life when, we can infer, the dependence on the Other (the mother) is total and there is no real distinction between self and other in the child's experience. For such a dependence to be severed the child must be able to come to terms with his mother's inevitable absences or unavailability, to tolerate a frustration that is incomprehensible. How can he organize his experience so as to replace what is missing? This is where Lacan situates both the child's entrance into language and the birth of the unconscious. Language and its structure provide an almost Darwinian solution to this failure of the environment, offering the child the support necessary to deal with the bewildering experience of loss. Yet the very processes that enable the child to find the words to name the loss also trigger the formation of the unconscious. The signifiers of the Other's desire—that umbilical cord of sounds, signs, and affects that unites mother and child—go under, so to speak, and become the hallmarks of the child's unconscious. In that sense language both separates and reunites the subject and his Other, for the dependency on the Other is both severed and perpetuated through these unconscious traces that will continue to inform the subject's desire throughout her life.

Let us first examine more closely how the subject and his or her unconscious come into being through the acquisition of language. I shall then turn to another dimension of the same process by discussing how Lacan links the child's entrance into language to the prohibition of incest and the oedipal dynamics.

Lacan calls upon Freud's (1920) example of the *fort/da* game of his 18-month-old grandson[3] and on Roman Jakobson's (1956) phonology to illustrate the way in which the acquisition of language goes hand in hand with the process of primal repression.[4] Jakobson showed that every language can be structurally reduced to twelve pairs of distinct vocal, physiological contrasts that he called bipolar phonematic oppositions. An example would be the opposition o/a in German. Therefore, when Freud's grandson was able to say *fort/da* to symbolize his mother's leaving and returning, he had at that point already unknowingly assimilated the differential features characteristic of the German language. In expressing joyfully, through words, his ability to control a loss, the child in this paradigmatic anecdote at the same time repressed the cause of his sadness, and his unconscious came into being. From this structural moment on, the unconscious becomes the repository of all the phonematic traces related to subsequent experiences of loss or lack. The signifiers of the mother's desire that were the landmarks of the child's world needed to be repressed so that he could situate himself without the actual mother's support.

This structural moment inaugurates for the child his subjective career in the world of signs. He can now put words to his wishes and his distress. And yet what psychoanalysis teaches us is, as Lacan said, that the subject does not know what he is saying when he speaks, because he does not know that when he speaks he replaces a loss with the whole structure of language. He is unaware of the fact that he has not chosen to become a speaking being but instead was forced to sever himself from the maternal

---

3. We all remember that the little boy was able to deal with his mother's absence by throwing and retrieving a spool as he exclaimed "*fort*," "*da*" ("gone," "here"). Freud points out that by taking the active role the child was able to master the situation so as to control symbolically the comings and goings of his mother.

4. Lacan's description of this process is unusually evocative and clear, yet it has led to certain misunderstandings because he appears to connect the acquisition of language to a specific age. The acceptance of his mother's departure did not definitively inscribe the 18-month-old child in the world of symbols; the example merely captures one aspect of this structural moment. The process of separating from the mother needs to be repeated again and again before it can be completely achieved—if it ever is. It would therefore be wrong to assume that such a process is age related. At 18 months the child has certainly not acquired the status of a subject in the Lacanian sense, namely a subject whose misconstrued sense of autonomy is undermined by a chain of unconscious signifiers that persist in alienating him from the desire of the other (see *infra*). He is still what Lacan calls a nonsubject (*assujet*).

enclave. He was forced, however, by necessity because the maternal "paradise" also contained the kinds of threats that Melanie Klein (1925) so powerfully described. The child does not know that the threats and longings that he was able to escape, thanks to the new signifiers that provide meaning to his life, will continue to disrupt his recently acquired conviction that he has control over his wishes and his aspirations. Grinding behind the discourse of consciousness another quasi-linguistic structure is at work, a quasi-language that speaks imperfectly but powerfully of these longings and threats and that undermines the illusory correspondence between discourse and its objects.

At this point we can better understand why Lacan calls upon the structural linguistics of Saussure (1916) in order to show how the structure of the unconscious and the structure of language have similar modes of operation. Lacan reinterprets Saussure's distinctions between language/speech and the signifier/the signified. For Saussure, speech is determined by a system of values (language) that operates beyond the individual's control. The relation between a concept and its acoustic image does not result from a particular affinity between a word and its referent but is determined by the other signs that compose a given language. In that sense the arbitrary relation between signifier and signified shows that language is an entity with its own laws and regulations that operate independently of the realm of existence that it represents. For Lacan the dividing line between the signifier and the signified (S/s) expresses the problematic relation between what is said consciously and what is barred from conscious discourse:

> [W]e can say that it is in the chain of the signifier that the meaning "insists" but that none of its elements "consists" in the signification of which it is at the moment capable.
>
> We are forced, then, to accept the notion of an incessant sliding of the signified under the signifier. . . . [1977, p. 153f.]

BETWEEN FREUD AND LÉVI-STRAUSS: THE SYMBOLIC ORDER AND THE LACANIAN SUBJECT

Lacan's reworking of Freud's *fort/da* adds an entirely new dimension to the theory of the prohibition of incest. First of all, one of the contributions Lacan brings to Freudian theory is an elaborate definition of the individual as subject. In that sense Lacan has enriched psychoanalysis with a notion of subjectivity as not innate but produced. Indeed, what is most powerful in Lacan's conceptualization of the human subject is his linkage of the Oedipus complex and of primal repression with what determines the actual socialization of the individual, namely the acquisition of language, itself the bearer of culture. This process of socialization that is linked to primal repression occurs through the imposition of a law—the prohibition of incest—which we can view as what triggers the processes that inscribe the child in the structure of language. It is at this point that Lacan adds a radically original element to Freud's theory of the Oedipus complex: he describes the unconscious as an intersubjective structure belonging to a realm that transcends the individual. He calls this realm the symbolic.

The concept of the symbolic was first proposed by the structural anthropologist Lévi-Strauss (1949) in his attempt to give Freud's myth of the murder of the primal father a scientific foundation. According to Freud, the prohibition of incest is the law that transformed the state of nature into culture. Lévi-Strauss, while noting the dubious credibility of this myth, nevertheless demonstrated that the origin of culture could indeed be attributed to various practices of social life concerning primarily the exchange of women, words, and goods. A close examination of these numerous social practices revealed how social life is itself organized by laws analogous to the ones that, according to Saussure and Jakobson, regulate the structure of language. In this sense language and culture are both shaped by a symbolic system that, so to speak, operates on an unconscious level. Thus for Lévi-Strauss social consciousness is produced by a symbolic system whose modus operandi as such is inaccessible to representation. Through his analysis of the permutations at work in the elementary structure of kinship, Lévi-Strauss was able to establish that the prohibition of incest constitutes the foundation of this symbolic system in the sense that it both separates and reunites nature and culture. On the one hand it separates a woman or a man from her or his biological family, but on the other hand it unites her or him with a member of another clan, thereby assuring the perpetuation of the species.

What is radically new in Lévi-Strauss' approach is the hypothesis that social practices have a purpose other than the one that is phenomenologically graspable, for at no time do the members of the group know what they are doing. When, for example, they enforce the law of exogamy their intention is not to promote the law of the prohibition of incest but merely to assure conditions of exchange between groups. What structural anthropology has achieved, therefore, is the deciphering, in social practices, of recurrent elements that reveal the hidden universal principles organizing the social whole.

This structural reading of the prohibition of incest as the foundation of social life inspired Lacan to resolve and re-articulate, within a new conceptual register, the two contradictory mythical kernels of Freud's theory: the myth of "Totem and Taboo" (1913) and the Oedipus complex.[5] These myths are contradictory insofar as in "Totem and Taboo" it is the murder of the father that gives rise to the law prohibiting incest, while in the Oedipus myth it is precisely the murder of the father that provides the condition for incest to occur. Thanks to Lévi-Strauss' concept of the symbolic, Lacan is able to confer theoretical legitimacy on Freud's dubious proposition that the prohibition of incest is passed on through phylogeny. Freud had drawn upon Lamarck's obsolete theory in order to explain why castration anxiety is such a powerful organizer of psychic life—and this independently of any parental threats accompanying the forbidding of masturbation. What Lacan sets out to prove is that oedipal fantasies attempt to reverse the inescapable law of the prohibition of incest, that necessary structure whose imposition on the individual is the condition of his or her subjectivity. In this sense the contradiction between "Totem and Taboo" and the Oedipus myth is resolved. The difficulty of having to leave the "biological" maternal realm and submit to the symbolic law creates in the individual an aspiration to undo the prohibition that has caused him or her to become a subject in the first place.

Yet for Lacan this prohibition does not concern sex per se. What is at stake is not the desire of the child to sleep with the mother. It is rather that the submission to the law of culture implies that the child has to be cut off from the maternal realm in order to become a speaking subject in its own right. Here is where Lacan applies Lévi-Strauss' understanding of the symbolic—briefly, a version of "Totem and Taboo" compatible with the find-

---

5. In order to avoid confusion it is important to note that the "social" prohibition of incest that Lévi-Strauss describes is not isomorphic with Lacan's own treatment of the question. Lévi-Strauss is interested in the origin of culture, not in the ways human subjectivity is produced. Lacan has been known to adapt for his own purposes the concepts he borrows, and he makes free use of Lévi-Strauss' reading of the prohibition of incest in his own theory of the law that separates the child from the realm of nature and inscribes him or her in the realm of culture. Another way to put it would be to say that Lévi-Strauss conferred a new validity on the myth of "Totem and Taboo," thereby allowing Lacan to reinterpret its meaning in order to shed new light on the Oedipus complex

ings of structural anthropology—to give a foundation to the Oedipus complex that is no longer perceived as involving a reference to the real actors of the primal scene. What Lacan intends to show is that the production of subjectivity is not purely dependent on oedipal fantasies. These fantasies are an effect of the processes that makes a human being a speaking being. So when Lacan links the prohibition of incest to the child's entrance into language, he means to emphasize that it is not the real father who is solely responsible for imposing the incest taboo. The incest taboo exists independently of the father's will; it is a function that is imposed on the child to assure its psychic survival. We can understand this idea better if we consider what occurs when the taboo fails to operate: when a child has not submitted to the prohibition of incest his discourse will reflect his inability to locate himself in relation to others and to the things that he designates. When, on the other hand, a human being is able to name what is missing—including his own selfhood, which is for each of us the most elusive of all things—this indicates that he has entered the intersubjective realm of social reality. A psychotic may speak, to be sure, but the language that carries him does not convey that he has been pinned down as a subject.

Entering language is, therefore, the very process that causes primal repression, yet what is being repressed are not the drives per se but the signifiers that were attached to them and that originated in the desire of the other. From a Lacanian perspective, then, it is impossible to distinguish between the drives belonging to the child and the signifiers of the other's desire that give them shape. The pre-subject and the other's desire are merged until the structural moment when the child enters language and is able to designate himself first with his own name and then with an "I." But this sense of autonomy that language provides is deceptive, because the subject's unconscious remains bound up with the signifiers of the other's desire. Language, therefore, both saves and deceives as it simultaneously causes the formation of the subject and his splitting.

CASTRATION AND THE NAME OF THE FATHER

Thus far we have seen that the child's entrance into language corresponds, on a structural level, to his or her acceptance of the prohibition of incest. But, the reader may ask, how can the prohibition of incest be operative when the protagonists seem to be reduced to the mother–child dyad? The third term that intervenes to separate them seems to be language alone—where is the father in this process? First we must say that the real father is to a certain extent a negligible entity as far as imposing the prohibition of incest is concerned. This is not to say that his presence is not a crucial factor in the development of the child, but only that he is not a necessary condition for bringing the child out of the mother's desiring field. The prohibition of incest is above all a *function*. To carry out its effects all that is required is that the mother be able to leave, to frustrate her child with regard to her desire and her presence. This is key. And the frustration may take place without the presence of a father, or it may fail to take place despite the presence of a father.

At the heart of Lacanian theory is the idea that the condition for becoming a subject is that the child recognize that its mother is not totally invested in it, that her desire can be captured by an "elsewhere." For the *fort/da* to occur it may be enough that the child experiences his mother's distraction. The child needs to feel that its position as a love object is not what exclusively captures its mother's desire; it must come to wonder: What does she want? Moreover, once this question becomes salient, the child must realize that it cannot be all of what she wants. This necessarily painful realization (which may eventually bring a sense of relief as well) will force the child to find another position in its world than that of being the exclusive object of the mother's desire. It must look for clues in order to situate itself in relation to this perplexing, absorbing question. This structural turning point is where Lacan makes use of Freud's concept of castration.

Castration refers precisely to this structural moment when the child realizes that his mother is lacking. What is she lacking? Certainly not the penis, as some reductive readers of Freud would have it. She lacks something that the child is unable to be for her. The child comes to realize that his mother is lacking because he is not what can fulfill her; he is not the sole object of her desire—something else is "bugging" her; there is something else or somebody else that she wants and that the child is not. This is precisely what Lacan calls castration: the realization that the mother is desirous beyond the child causes a rift in him or her, and it is this that propels the child towards language. It is in this way that the prohibition of incest is made operative.

The linkage of the child's entrance into language and the incest taboo that leads to castration is what Lacan calls the *Name of the Father* (*le Nom du Père*) or the paternal metaphor. This pun, which can be heard as both the no/*non* of the father and his name/*nom*, contains the two dimensions of what Lacan understands to be castration: the negative side that enforces the prohibition of incest (no, says the law, you may not be your mother's exclusive object of desire) and the positive side, the child's inscription in the generational order (as the son or daughter of a father and a mother), which locates the child in the social world, the realm of language. Lacan's expression "paternal metaphor" not only refers to the double meaning of the *non/nom* but also points toward language per se as a metaphor for what has been irreversibly lost when the child becomes a speaking subject. In speaking, subjects do not know that they are symbolizing, through language, the object of their primordial yearning.

For Lacan, then, castration is not merely the fear of losing or lacking the penis. It is a symbolic operation that cuts the imaginary bond between mother and child and grants the boy or the girl the ability to symbolize this loss through words. The fear of losing the penis or the frustration at not having it is, therefore, grounded not in our anatomical "destiny" but in the dynamics at work within the intersubjective realm in which mother, father, and child are inscribed.

It must be emphasized again that the "no" of the father is not necessarily imposed by the real father. The mother's discourse, behavior, and affects are usually the locus out of which such a prohibition emerges. What is profoundly new in this perspective is the fact that the child encounters in the Other a limit, a law. Yet this law is not invented by the Other. On the contrary, the Other himself or herself has been subjected to it, and it is as a proxy of that Law that this Other conveys the law to the child. The analytic situation provides many examples of the problems that arise when a parent believes that he or she is the author of the law, or when this law is passed on ambiguously. Readers will easily recall examples from their own practices, ranging from victims of sexual abuse by psychopathic or perverted parents to regular neurotics caught in double-bind messages.

THE PHALLUS, OR THE FOURTH TERM OF THE OEDIPUS COMPLEX

Thus far I have focused on giving the reader a sense of what Lacan means by the symbolic order, by castration, and by the Name of the Father. Yet I have approached somewhat indirectly Lacan's view of the outcome of oedipal dynamics. It was first necessary to provide the reader with the sense that the oedipal drama is already set in a context that precedes its real actors. Thus without a grasp of the function and meaning of the symbolic order it is hard to understand why for Lacan the Oedipus complex does not have three terms—the mother, the father, the child—but rather four terms: the mother, the father, the child, and the phallus, this last term being one that Lacan borrows from Freud and reinterprets within his own structural model of subjectivity.

The phallus is probably the most difficult concept to grasp in Lacanian theory because it is a "thing" that does not exist. Yet such a "thing" is also what will set in motion the whole process of the paternal metaphor through which the human animal will become a subject in his or her own right. One way to understand what the phallus is would be to compare it to the joker in a deck of cards. It can assume various incarnations, yet it is a mask behind which there is nothing. The phallus represents what is wished for but can never be attained. Following Freud, Lacan speaks of the baby who hallucinates the breast in order to bring about the image that carries the promise of a fulfillment that will never be attained again, since the mother gave what was needed before the child could have a sense of what satisfaction could be. After that, the hallucinated breast will never be isomorphic to the real one because the primitive need will now take the form of a demand—a cry. The concept of the phallus marks the distance between the need and the demand, a gap that can never be bridged. This is why Lacan calls the phallus the signifier of desire par excellence. The search for satisfaction that will be channeled through oral, anal, and genital paths is motivated by a desire that will always be only partially gratified, since its object, the phallus, can never be refound in its original state. This remainder of gratification that Lacan calls *jouissance* (enjoyment), since it is precisely what the individual seeks in sexual relations, will always be out of reach. This is an apparently unfortunate state of affairs—but one thanks to which the subject's desire will be saved from extinction, since he will continue to seek this object throughout his life, in all his pursuits.

As far as the oedipal quartet is concerned, the phallus stands for the mystery of what constitutes the mother's desire within the child's experience. Through a series of dialectical reversals mother, father, child, and phallus will come to occupy different positions, and the child will be led to discover his own position as a sexuated being.

The Enigma of Sexual Difference

We know that Freud's account of oedipal dynamics underwent many changes (cf. Freud 1925b, 1931). He gradually came to link castration anxiety and penis envy to the question of sexual difference, yet he was never able to theorize the issues of oedipal love and sexual difference to his own complete satisfaction. Lacan tried to augment Freud's insights by developing the concept of the phallus as the chief organizer of the subject's psychic life: oedipal dynamics are played out around the subject's position towards the phallus. While the child will first shift from being the phallus of the other's desire to losing that privileged place, the second shift will lead the child to take the position of the one who is presumed to have it in order to give it, or, alternatively, of the one who needs to come to terms with not having it in order to receive it. These shifts orient the individual towards a certain mode of desiring that will determine the sexual identity he or she will take on.

Yet as Freud himself pointed out, this division—between having and not having—does not necessarily correspond to anatomical sex. A biological woman can continue to behave as though she "has it," while a biological man may resist giving his penis the status of a phallic symbol. The issue of sexual difference is therefore distinct from the one of sexual identity. To be or not to be, to have or not to have the phallus, will have different consequences for a man and for a woman. Yet at the same time the types of desire produced by these positions operate outside the constraints of anatomy. It is in relation to these various positions of the subject towards the phallus that Lacan has reinterpreted Freud's differentiation of neurosis (phobia, hysteria, and obsessionality), perversion, and psychosis. The neurotic, the pervert, and the psychotic display, through their symptoms, distinctive modes of desiring that inform their psychic life. It is important to note that these structures of desire are not character types. They must be understood as various unconscious strategies used by the subject to deal with what Freud (1925b) called the *bedrock of castration*.[6]

Like Freud, Lacan formulated his theory on the basis of his patients' discourse, so that his insights cannot be disentangled from the transference in which a patient's discourse emerges. The discourse of an obsessional, an hysteric, a pervert, or a psychotic will therefore constitute the material that allows the analyst to discern a specific mode of desiring. This mode of desiring reflects the vicissitudes of the patient in making sense of what was expected of him or her as he or she was in the throes of the oedipal

---

6. A thorough discussion of the structures of desire as they operate in hysteria, obsessional neurosis, and perversions can be found in Joël Dor, *The Clinical Lacan*, Other Press, 1999.

situation. For Lacan, each individual must confront a dilemma. How can one figure out the meaning of sexual difference without losing one's bearings in relation to the Other's desire? What compromises must be made in order for an individual to find a place as subject without losing a loving parental support? These are the questions that a Lacanian analyst must keep in mind as he or she listens to the ways in which patients articulate the malaise that brought them into treatment. Such an approach is in sharp contrast to the American view of separation-individuation, in which sexual difference is not perceived as the organizer of subjectivity.

THE MIRROR STAGE AND THE BIRTH OF THE EGO

The reader may recall that at the beginning of this Preface I introduced Lacan's concept of *méconnaissance* or misrecognition. This refers to our mistaken conviction that we know what we are saying when we speak—mistaken, since as a result of primal repression (the paternal metaphor) we are unaware of how we have come to believe that we are autonomous and fully conscious beings, perfectly capable of determining why the outside world seems repeatedly to disappoint our expectations. For Lacan *méconnaissance* is the fundamental characteristic of our ego. This view, developed out of the Freudian theory of narcissism in which the ego is conceived as a libidinally invested object, radically distinguishes the Lacanian theory of the ego from its American counterpart. The mirror stage (Lacan 1949) must be perceived as a sort of allegory that draws on developmental psychology yet is not itself a developmental theory. Moreover, Lacan wrote his paper on the mirror stage in the late '30s, when he was still a member of the International Psychoanalytic Association, intending it as a sharp critique of ego psychologists who believed in strengthening the ego by analyzing the defenses. In the ego-psychological tradition the ego is viewed as distinct from the defense mechanisms that prevent it from assuming its function as the agent of the reality principle. The subject, according to this view, must shed these ego defenses in order to realize that he is his own worst enemy, setting up for himself those very situations that he abundantly complains about. The ego is therefore capable of regaining its discerning abilities and recognizing external reality for what it is. Lacan vigorously opposed this view. Many trends in contemporary psychoanalysis are likewise opposed to it, but the Lacanian theory of the ego is unique and deserves further exploration.

So far we have seen how the symbolic order connects the subject's unconscious to the Other as symbolic. A consideration of Lacan's theory of the genesis of the ego will introduce the flip side of the symbolic, which Lacan calls the imaginary. This is the realm of conscious life, the realm of the signified, the realm of reality as the subject perceives and experiences it. It is through the imaginary that the subject's ego (*le moi*, "the me") comes into being. While the unconscious is formed as a result of the human being's submission to the Other in the symbolic, the ego is the effect of the encounter with the other in the imaginary.

This primordial encounter with the image of the other, one that will subsequently shape the subject's own image of himself as ego, is what Lacan calls the mirror stage.[7] The ego is above all a construct, a defensive shield that has its origin in an image formed by the gaze of the other. The ego is thus not innate but produced. Its function is to ward off those unconscious strivings that attempt to undermine the subject's sense of wholeness and autonomy. The psychoanalyst, therefore, cannot form an alliance with the ego. On the contrary, he or she must discern in the discourse and affects of the subject certain leads that permit the tricking of the ego in such a way as to enable the subject's unconscious desire to emerge.

This is how Lacan recounts the hypothetical scenario of the mirror stage: when between the age of 9 and 15 months the baby sees itself in the mirror, it will experience a feeling of great joy and will soon try to get its bearings in relation to this specular image. Such behavior is not seen in the animal world. Very young animals do not identify with their images or express any satisfaction at the sight of their specular counterparts; instead they see these images as others to play with, avoid, or attack. The human baby identifies with the visual gestalt of its own body—an ideal and salutary image that contrasts with the distress it feels and that is bound to the inner and outer discordance of the little human being during the first six months of its life.

---

7. The reader who is somewhat familiar with introductory texts on Lacan may wonder why I did not, as it is commonly done, start my exposition with the mirror stage since, after all, in setting forth his theory of this stage Lacan refers to experimental data concerning the preverbal years. I have chosen to avoid this path because I do not wish to place Lacan's ideas within a developmental framework. The mirror stage, like the Freudian *fort/da*, must be understood in terms of anecdotal data that can explain what occurs in general during the analytical process, and in particular in the transference between the patient's ego and the analyst's ego.

Lacan explains this asymmetry between the human and animal responses by contrasting animal instincts with human drives. Human beings cannot make sense of the world in terms of instincts (drives) and images alone. The tendencies that guide animals towards the satisfaction of needs are inhibited in humans. Whereas newborn animals are able to function competently, the human infant's nervous system is underdeveloped during the first six months of life, as is shown by the lack of motor coordination. However, these effects of prematuration are balanced in the human being by the precocious development of visual perception, which expresses itself in the remarkable capacity of very young babies to recognize a human face. Because this faculty is overdeveloped in contrast to the general "retardation" of the human infant, Lacan considers the ability to recognize and identify with the imago of the human form to be a salutary tendency compensating for the underdevelopment of instincts due to prematuration at birth. The baby expresses joy because the mirror offers it a sense of unity and wholeness that it does not experience in its own body. This joy indicates that some recognition has taken place:

> [The mirror stage] is the original adventure through which man, for the first time, has the experience of seeing himself, of reflecting on himself and conceiving of himself as other than he is—an essential dimension of the human, which entirely structures his fantasy life. [Lacan 1953–1954, p. 79]

It may be useful to note that this propensity to identification, resulting in a true captivation of the child by the imago of the other, has been observed in situations other than the confrontation with the mirror. Lacan (1977) cites investigators at the Chicago School, according to whom a baby of not more than 8 months (i.e., at a time when it still feels undifferentiated from its surroundings and still suffers from motor uncoordination) will complete gestures initiated by another child as if the other were itself. For Lacan this phenomenon is a further indication that the mirror stage is an allegory of the genesis of the identificatory process leading to the formation of the ego.

The mirror stage, of course, also represents the relation between mother and child. It is in the mother's loving gaze that the child recognizes himself—outside himself—as the "apple of her eye," as her phallus. In that sense the mirror stage is the first structural phase of the paternal metaphor, the stage in which the issue for the child is "to be or not to be" the mother's phallus. The experience of "not being" is encountered when the child loses sight of this positive reflection: the joy of the mirror stage thus alternates with expressions of rage, anxiety, or avoidance of the mirror image. The pleasure at seeing one's own wholeness is countered by an experience of disintegration as the child feels a split between a self that is whole and external, and, on the other hand, its own inner sense of motor uncoordination. The reflected alter ego turns into a rival that the child either submits to or wishes to destroy (obviously the experience of sibling rivalry is salient here).

Such vacillation between love and hate, sympathy and jealousy, illustrates the fundamental ambivalence on which human subjectivity is founded, an ambivalence that can only end in frustration. The feelings of rage, inferiority, or impotence triggered at the sight of the imago of the other are represented in what Lacan calls the fantasy of the dismembered body, the body in pieces. Such fantasies, he notes, were remarkably portrayed by the sixteenth-century painter Hieronymus Bosch in his images of the evisceration, dismemberment, and dislocations of the human body. The images of the body in pieces also represent the feelings of dismemberment and uncoordination that Melanie Klein observed in young children's games, drawings, and dream accounts and that she viewed as prefigurations of the castration complex.

In their games children enact such scenarios by mutilating and tearing apart their toys or dolls; later in life these images appear in nightmares or hallucinations. Even when they are represented in language they replay the effects of the mirror stage in expressions such as "I'm falling apart," or "I'm going to pieces," or "I want to tear his eyes out." These are expressions of a desire for the aggressive disintegration of the individual in an other or in himself. Such fantasies are more acute and more permanent in psychosis. According to Lacan, the psychotic literally experiences a vacillation between self and other. He or she is incapable of mediating the effects of the mirror stage through the symbolic order. Images of the body in pieces represent the alternative to the feeling of wholeness that the mirror image provides. They are triggered at moments when human beings feel their unity threatened, a unity that they cannot take for granted because its origin is external.

This alternate phase of the mirror stage, then, involves the experience of the child confronted with the realization that he or she is not all that the mother desires. Such a reconstruction of the preverbal years suggests that without the support of language the small child loses all bearings in relation to his primordial other. It therefore explains how the operation of the paternal metaphor provides the solution to the problematics of the mirror stage.

In view of the paradoxical balance between prematuration and visual precocity, Lacan regards the human capacity to become an object to one-self as an adaptive response of the organism to its environment. It is from that perspective that Lacan reworks the Freudian concept of the ego, cast-ing it as the psychic representative not of the reality principle but of an "imaginary" reality. On the basis of the contrast between the baby's pri-mordial jubilation when it encounters the mirror (or mirroring other) and the fantasies of dismemberment, Lacan explains how the human being constitutes his identity at the price of a fundamental split between a pro-jected image of unity and an inner sense of fragmentation.

For Lacan, the split experienced in the mirror stage is not eradicated by the process of primal repression but is merely transformed. The subject's original experience of powerlessness does not vanish; it retreats into the unconscious, and from there it reminds the subject of the fragility of her or his ego image. The ego therefore needs constant reinforcement from other ideal images to confirm its sense of wholeness (a phenomenon of which the clinician is well aware). Yet at the same time such an experience of wholeness granted through another deprives the subject of access to those very feelings of anxiety that the identification with the other covers over. This is why Lacan writes that the subject constitutes itself at the price of its own suicide: it can survive only *through that other* and therefore loses itself just at the moment it finds itself.

As the reader may have guessed, the seesaw movements between omnipotence and impotence, between love and hate, are characteristic ego states that are replayed in the transference. They are particularly marked in more acute pathologies such as narcissistic and borderline disorders. The reader may also have connected Lacan's description of the mirror stage with certain aspects of Kohut's theory of the self, even though Lacan, like Freud and unlike Kohut, excludes the possibility of a harmonious relation between self and other. Indeed, it is the asymmetry of the mirror stage that give rise to ego defenses. Thus for Lacan there is no point in distinguish-ing between the ego and its mechanisms of defense. The ego itself is ge-netically a defense, a cover-up of the split that constitutes us as subjects. While through the process of primal repression—the paternal metaphor— the individual is able to bring his or her ego into the realm of symbols and therefore to grant it consistency thanks to the support of language, the unity of the ego will nonetheless be challenged each time the image of the other conveys not a sense of gratifying wholeness but rather a sense of lack and powerlessness. Because the specular image appears to the subject as an other with whom it identifies and with whom it is in competition, this dialectical process leaves its marks on all interpersonal relations, most particularly on those in which the subject finds itself vulnerable to shifting feelings of being recognized or being annulled. In a passage that reveals the almost infinite resonance of the mirror stage, Lacan suggests that all social relations, from sympathy to jealousy to competition to feelings of inferiority or superiority, to prejudices, persecution, defamation and slander, to the cold war and spying, all find their roots in the dialectical relations of the mirror stage (cf. Lacan 1977, pp. 16f.).

For Lacan, as we have seen, the ego is not the agency that represents the reality principle. The ego is constituted as a lure, a defense, a refusal to recognize the precariousness and illusoriness of the sense of integration that the mirror conveys. In other words, the ego is a construct that denies the very alienation that has caused it to come into being. Paradoxically, then, the more subjects affirm themselves as ego the more they alienate themselves. The most fundamental function of the ego is therefore misrecognition, *méconnaissance*. *Méconnaissance* is not ignorance; it is rather a structure of affirmations and negations in which the subject invests. It is most obviously exemplified in the process Freud (1925a) calls *Verneinung*. *Verneinung* is a negation that is also an admission: it reveals what has been negated. Thus negation is in some way constitutive of the negated content and permits the appearance of that content in consciousness. What remains of what has been repressed is a resistance to the content. As Lacan says:

> Misrecognition . . . cannot be conceived without correlative knowledge. If the subject is capable of misrecognising something, he surely must know what this function has operated upon. There must surely be, behind his misrecognition, a kind of knowledge of what there is to misrecognise. [1953–1954, p. 167]

It is important to note that *méconnaissance* serves a necessary function for the subject's adaptation to the environment. The shield of the ego is for the human being what the instinct of survival is for the animal.

We can see how the inscription of the subject into the symbolic brings about the distinction between neurosis and psychosis. For Lacan, while the neurotic may continue to be prey to the fundamental alienation that has shaped the gestalt of his ego, his ability to symbolize the loss of his mother's imaginary support will nevertheless provide a foundation for his subjectivity. The psychotic, on the other hand, is unable to bridge the gap between the imaginary and the symbolic. He or she remains the victim of the seesaw movement of the mirror stage.

This lengthy description of the genesis of the Lacanian ego has delineated what Lacan calls the imaginary, the interpersonal realm that structures our experiences as we live it. Yet we must promptly add that the imaginary is never divorced from the symbolic. The symbolic never appears in its pure form, nor does the imaginary: these two registers are always intertwined. The imaginary is to the signified what the symbolic is to the signifier. We have seen that the signified—signification—does not exhaust the function of the signifier. This distinction appears clearly in the way Lacan conceptualizes the analytic situation. The imaginary transference is the relationship established between the analysand's ego and that of the analyst. While many affects, projections, identifications, and so on can be produced between these two egos, such an imaginary transference does not get to the unconscious signifiers that have produced these "signifieds." The transference that Lacan calls symbolic, on the other hand, will connect the patient's unconscious with the analyst's unconscious (the famous Freudian metaphor of the telephone receiver). Such a transference—and it can occur only intermittently—allows the signifiers of the patient's unconscious desire to emerge thanks to the analyst's desire to clue in to these signifiers. A dialectical movement is at work. The patient's ego assumes that the analyst knows something about him or her of which the patient is unaware. Under the sway of that imaginary belief, the patient will start to talk and, without knowing what he or she is saying, will utter certain words that will attract the attention of the analyst. The analyst, for her part, is (one hopes) aware that she does not know the patient's unconscious strivings. Yet her own desire is clued in, not on consciously wanting to make the patient feel better—this would be her ego speaking—but onto the signifiers of the patient's discourse that resonate for her within her own desiring listening position. It is evident that such attunement will necessarily be interrupted, since one cannot, even as an analyst, suspend at all times the demands of one's own ego. Nevertheless the symbolic transference is the goal toward which Lacanian psychoanalysis strives.

THE SYMBOLIC, THE IMAGINARY, AND THE REAL

Thus far we have explored some of the ways in which the imaginary and the symbolic structure the subject's psychic reality. The imaginary corresponds loosely to what contemporary American psychoanalysis has labeled the interpersonal realm, while the symbolic accounts for the intersubjective nature of our unconscious, which is, according to Lacan, structured like a language. Yet although these two categories describe the deep relations that link the self to its other, they do not account for the whole of psychic life. They do not leave room for what is in excess of our ability to give representation to our experiences. This excess is what Lacan calls the real. If we go back to our discussion of the *fort/da*, we can locate the real as that "thing" that these two signifiers attempt to control by giving it some signification. Yet this example also illustrates that the utterance cannot do justice to the experience of loss and anxiety that the child attempts to control. This is the fate of language in general: our words can never adequately express our experience of the world. Similarly, our subjectivity cannot find in the chain of signification in which we are inscribed words that can account for who we "truly" are. There is always something that escapes us. Therefore the category of the real is precisely what can explain the function of the symbolic and the imaginary realms. Since we are premature animals, our relation to the world is necessarily mediated by the imaginary and symbolic Other, and therefore our needs remain alienated by the Other's desire on which we depend. Such an alienation brings about our own desire to find that missing piece of the real that the knotting of the imaginary and the symbolic has failed to capture.

The real serves yet another function in Lacanian psychoanalytic theory. It refers to stimuli that take us by surprise, that overwhelm us with affects we cannot identify, that call into question the place that we occupy in the other's desire—to those experiences that force us to shift our understanding of the world. Consider the example of childhood phobias. From a Lacanian perspective, the phobic object serves to replace an incomprehensible anxiety with the fear of a specific object. Lacan finds the genesis of the child's phobia in an inability to make sense of "the real" of sexual difference. This brings us back to the dynamics of the Oedipus complex and to the crucial moment when the child comes to realize that his mother's desire is invested elsewhere than in what he wants to be for her. Such a realization calls into question the foundations of his existence. Normally the signifiers of his mother's desire provide an indication that another (usually but not necessarily the father) is able to provide the solution to what the child now comes to experience as a frightening enigma: "What does she want, and what is it about me that is not good enough?" This is also the time when the child begins to experience intensified sexual feelings, feelings that he normally assumes he can share with his mother as he does not yet experience himself as fully separate from her. Yet as is often the case in childhood phobias, if the mother shows some ambivalence toward the father and gives some indication that the enigma of her "lack" cannot find a solution, the child's foundations collapse and he is thrown into the angst of the real (as agoraphobia perfectly illustrates). The phobic object, therefore, operates as a safety valve permitting the child to find a point of reference in the outside world that prevents him from falling into the abyss of desubjectivation.

The complicated issue of sexual abuse can also be better understood in the light of the Lacanian concept of the real. Any stimulation that is experienced as being in excess of what a subject can metabolize constitutes a traumatic encounter with the real. Such an encounter is neither painful nor pleasurable; it is above all stunning in the sense that it shatters the ways the patient had organized his subjective world. Psychoanalysis may enable the patient to find the signifiers that can bind this experience in a chain of signification. As a result, the patient's ego will no longer need to deploy defense mechanisms in a futile attempt to control the trauma.

How does the category of the real fit within Freudian theory? We have seen so far that the symbolic order relates to the intersubjective structure of the unconscious and that the imaginary accounts for the formation of the ego. The real refers to the drives insofar as they can never be experienced in a pure biological form because the child's need is always mediated by the Other's desire. The real, therefore, is the fuel of human motivation but, as such, it can never find representation. As need becomes demand—through the process of identification with the desire of the other—there is always a remainder in the subject's demand that cannot be answered by the other because there is no original striving that can find expression outside of the intersubjective domain in which it is expressed. The imaginary can never adequately signify the symbolic, nor can the symbolic give structure to whole of the real. Human desire, therefore, owes its existence to the constant pursuit of what we mistakenly believe can eradicate the split that has caused us to become human.

Lacanian psychoanalysis does not need to remain idiosyncratic. The concepts of the symbolic, imaginary, and real can serve as an alternative model to enrich the understanding of the analytic situation in new ways. Take enactment for example. Enactment is a good illustration of an imaginary connivance between patient and analyst, both being trapped by the effects of the mirror stage, in which the distinction between self and other is temporary blurred. The interpretation that may follow such an enactment exposes the intersubjective structure of the unconscious, where the analyst's desire encounters the unconscious signifiers of the patient, signifiers that in turn may reveal the origin of the anxiety—the real—that has caused the enactment in the first place. Such an interpretation thereby gives a symbolic status to an experience of the real that previously could find a means of expression only in the imaginary.

The point of this exercise is not simply to replace one analytic lingo with another but to show how Lacanian theory not only leaves room for new psychoanalytic formulations but brings again to the forefront the atemporal traces of our human fate stored precariously away in the folds of what Freud has called the unconscious.

I hope that these preliminary remarks will gave the American clinician a taste of the richness and the clinical relevance of a body of work that up to now has been largely ignored by the psychoanalytic community in the United States. As editor of this volume, I particularly hope that this schematic overview will make the papers of the French discussants more accessible to an American readership.

REFERENCES

Freud, S. (1900). The interpretation of dreams. *Standard Edition* 4/5:1–626.
———— (1913). Totem and taboo. *Standard Edition* 13:1–161.
———— (1920). Beyond the pleasure principle. *Standard Edition* 17:7–64.
———— (1925a). Negation. *Standard Edition* 19:235–262.
———— (1925b). Some psychical consequences of the anatomical distinction between the sexes. *Standard Edition* 19:248–258.
———— (1931). Female sexuality. *Standard Edition* 21:225–243.
Jakobson, R., and Halle, M. (1956). Two aspects of language and two types of aphasic disturbances. In *Fundamentals of Language*, pp. 53–87. The Hague: Mouton.
Klein, M. (1932). *The Psycho-Analysis of Children*. London: Hogarth.
Lacan, J. (1949). The mirror stage as formative of the function of the I as revealed in psychoanalytic experience. In *Ecrits: A Selection*, trans. A. Sheridan, pp. 1–7. New York: Norton, 1977.
———— (1953–1954). *The Seminar of Jacques Lacan. Book I, Freud's Papers on Technique 1953–1954*. Trans. J. Forrester, ed. J.-A. Miller, New York: Norton, 1975.
———— (1977). *Ecrits: A Selection*, trans. A. Sheridan. New York: Norton.
Lévi-Strauss, C. (1949). *The Elementary Structures of Kinship*, trans. J. H. Bell, ed. R. Needham. Boston: Beacon, 1969.
Saussure, F. de. (1916). *Course in General Linguistics*, ed. C. Bally and A. Sechehaye with A. Reidlinger, trans. W. Baskin. New York: McGraw Hill, 1966.

Glossary of Selected Lacanian Terms

JUDITH FEHER GUREWICH, PH.D.

Castration, symbolic: For Lacan the child's submission to the prohibition of incest is linked to his or her entrance into the structure of language. The human being's capacity to symbolize is dependent on his or her acceptance of a loss, the loss of an imaginary complementarity with the mother. This loss consists in giving up one's privileged position as the mother's phallus in order to situate oneself in the social world as someone who "has the phallus" or "does not have it."

Desire is the margin that separates the speaking subject from a primordial object that is lost and cannot be refound because it remains beyond the reach of words. Such an object constitutes the cause of desire and is the bearer of the subject's unconscious fantasies. Lacan also defines desire as what remains unfulfilled in the subject after his need, channeled through his demand, has been addressed

Ego: In Lacanian theory the ego originates in the mirror stage (see *Imaginary*, below, and Preface). It is not the agent of the reality principle but the seat of the subject's narcissistic investment. Lacan characterizes the ego as a shield whose function is to fend off the disruptions of the subject's unconscious desire and to search in the other's gaze for confirmation of its existence.

Imaginary: The Imaginary is the realm of subjective experience per se, the world as it appears to the subject. Lacan explains the genesis of the imaginary in the mirror stage, the archaic experience in which the child encounters his or her reflection in the gaze of the (m)Other. From that moment on, both the child's perception of the world and his fantasies will be informed by the experience of such a gaze.

Lack (manque à être) refers to the loss entailed by symbolic castration. For Freud, the resolution of the Oedipus complex is dependent on the boy's fear of castration and the girl's penis envy, whereas for Lacan, both sexes must undergo the same painful but necessary process that symbolic castration entails.

Name of the Father (le nom du père) can be heard as both the no/*non* of the father and his name/*nom*. This pun contains the two dimensions of what Lacan understands by symbolic castration: the negative side that enforces the prohibition of incest (no, says the father, you may not be your mother's phallus, the exclusive object of her desire) and the positive side, the child's inscription in the generational order (as the son or daughter of a father and a mother), which locates the child in the social world, the realm of language. (See also *Paternal Metaphor*.)

Other: The Other (also called the Symbolic) refers to what is beyond the "real" or "imaginary" significant others; that is, what is exterior and anterior to the subject but determines it nevertheless. It is the locus of psychoanalysis. The subject's unconscious "speaks" a language that has its roots in the Other.

Paternal Metaphor: The paternal metaphor not only refers to the double meaning of the *non/nom du père* but also points toward language per se as a metaphor for what has been irreversibly lost when the child becomes a speaking subject. In speaking, the subject does not know that he or she is symbolizing, through language, the object of his or her primordial yearning. The paternal metaphor is a symbolic operation that cuts the imaginary bond between mother and child and grants the boy or the girl the ability to symbolize this loss through words. Therefore, the fear of losing the penis or the frustration at not having it is grounded not in our "anatomical destiny" but in the dynamics at work within the intersubjective realm in which mother, father, and child are inscribed.

Phallus: The organizing principle of the dynamic of the subject's desire. It is the signifier par excellence in relation to which the subject will assume his or her sexual identity. If, in the individual's fantasy world, the phallus acts as an imaginary object that the subject will first want to incarnate and then move on to have (or to seek in a romantic partner), within the symbolic order—that is, in the unconscious realm—the phallus operates as the signifier of a loss, the symbol of the lack of complementarity between the sexes. Lacan makes a clear distinction between the penis and the phallus.

Real: The real is reality in its unmediated form. It is what disrupts the subject's received notions about himself and the world around him. Thus it characteristically appears to the subject as a shattering enigma, because in order to make sense of it he or she will have to symbolize it, that is, to find signifiers that can ensure its control.

Signifier: An element of discourse, operative at the conscious and unconscious levels, which represents and determines the subject. The signifier does not designate a fixed referent (a signified) but always refers to other signifiers. That is to say, the relation between a (signified) concept and its acoustic image (signifier) does not result from a particular affinity between a word and its referent but is determined by the other signs that compose a given language. In that sense, the arbitrary relation between signifier and signified shows that language is an entity with its own laws and regulations that operate independently of the realm of existence that it appears to represent. For Lacan, the bar or dividing line between the signifier and the signified (S/s) expresses the problematic relation between what is said consciously and what is barred from conscious discourse.

Subject: The subject is the human being as constituted by the knotting of what Lacan calls the Real, the Imaginary, and the Symbolic. This triad breaks down the classical dichotomies between nature and culture, individual and society, and inner and outer reality. The Real, the Imaginary, and the Symbolic together weave the subject's reality at all times. These categories are always intertwined and are never processed by the subject in their pure or isolated form. Only a psychotic outbreak can undo the knotting of the triad. More specifically, the subject in Lacanian theory refers to the subject of the individual's unconscious desire

Symbolic: The symbolic order is the order of language and culture, the synchronic structure in which the child is unknowingly inscribed. It is a constraining structure imposed on the child through the *Law of the Name of the Father*. The repression that this law entails causes the formation of the unconscious. This concept of the symbolic was first proposed by the structural anthropologist Lévi-Strauss, who demonstrated how the permutations at work in the elementary structures of kinship not only establish the prohibition of incest as the law that transforms nature into culture, but also reveal that language and culture are both shaped by a symbolic system operating on an unconscious level.

Part I

Borderlines:
Between French and
American Psychoanalysis

2

The New Disorders of the Unconscious

JUDITH FEHER GUREWICH, PH.D.

Can we broach the idea that, following in the footsteps of their American counterparts, the patients of French psychoanalysts have exchanged their neuroses of yesteryear for a new psychic ailment known as the borderline state? According to therapists in the United States, this new spiritual disorder, in the middle ground between psychosis and neurosis, does not fall within the scope of the Freudian discovery. There is no longer any question, in accounting for its origins, of invoking undue sexual repression or the transformations of an unresolved Oedipus complex. The postmodern era, in this view, has a new concept of what causes human distress. Guilt, sexual inhibitions, and emotional setbacks are losing momentum. We must no longer search within the recesses of the unconscious for persistent residues of oedipal love. What the borderline patient is in pursuit of is, rather, the libido, the vital energy, that his disappointing family environment had left unawakened.

It is in this way that today's tragic man has replaced yesterday's guilty man: so states Heinz Kohut, the founder of one of the predominant movements in contemporary American psychoanalysis. This new tragic figure is far from being professionally or socially ineffective; in fact, he makes good use of the social stereotypes so abundant in American life. But be-

neath this normal (and sometimes quite sophisticated) exterior, the borderline patient suffers from uncontrollable rages, inner emptiness, and lack
of self-esteem, and he is usually unable to form lasting affective relationships. Each attempt he makes to establish an intimate relationship with
another person sends back to him an image of himself that he finds unbearable. Thus he seeks in solitude a semblance of authenticity to provide himself with an illusion of an inner life that will not be imperiled by the gaze
of the other.

The analysis of borderline patients reveals a childhood marked by a
lack of gratifying responses and by the scarcity of usable ideals. Their yearnings and their needs were ignored by a parental gaze that was indifferent
or even cruel. Because of this, they are unable to internalize a self-image
stable enough to allow them to get involved in life. This new pathology—
which undoubtedly reflects the attempt of the psychic system to cope with
the inadequacies of a society in the midst of upheaval—has allowed American psychoanalysis to rid the term *narcissism* of its pejorative connotations
and to highlight, instead, its structural effects. For what is missing in borderline patients is a secure narcissistic foundation. Heinz Kohut, in particular,
insists on the fact that a positive sense of self depends on the loving gaze of
the other, usually the maternal selfobject. What matters, then, is to distinguish healthy narcissism from the pathological variety in order to define a
therapeutic approach that can shore up the patient's fragile self-esteem.

It is no longer a question of overcoming the resistances of a patient
who wants neither to learn about the desires that motivate him nor to
struggle to discover the unconscious roots of the sexual fantasies that are,
we know, so conspicuous by their absence. And there is something else: a
number of these borderline patients seem to have been the victims of the
very sexual abuse that Freud ascribed to the imagination of his hysterics.
Now if the trauma is real, as Freud himself believed at the outset of his
discovery of the unconscious, its destructive effects cannot be undone by
an interpretation addressed to (for example) a repressed wish to indulge
forbidden desires. Besides, from what today's American psychoanalysts tell
us, this abuse, whether sexual or otherwise, is subject more to disavowal
or dissociation than to true repression. The borderline patient projects
painful childhood experiences, and he is on the lookout for their return
each time the demands of another seem to threaten an already shaky sense
of self.

Having set aside depth psychology, the new trends in American psychoanalysis promote a therapeutic approach characterized by empathy. This

involves putting oneself in the patient's place, sharing his experiences, emotions, and childhood setbacks in order to be able to name for him what is too painful, or even impossible, for him to express. Far from being impassive and silent like their colleagues in previous generations, today's analysts take an active part in the treatment as they try to provide the understanding, the support, that their patients lacked in childhood and adolescence.

The treatment of borderline patients is far from easy, American analysts say. The transference that such patients develop often leads them to give vent to such rancor and ingratitude towards the analyst that the latter finds himself reenacting the patient's childhood trauma, playing the part of either the aggressor or the victim. In both cases he is often obliged to acknowledge and interpret his own negative reactions towards the patient. This countertransference analysis, which may be done out loud, lets the patient relive certain troubled primordial relationships and come to understand the protective role of his aggressive impulses. With the help of the analyst, he can gradually develop a sense of self that he feels is positive enough to allow him to find meaning in life and to form deeper relationships with others.

In our Franco-American colloquium these so-called new psychic disorders and their treatment will be described by American analysts who have taken part in the formulation of the new diagnostic categories, and who, for the first time in the history of the discipline, will have as partners in dialogue French analysts who have made varying use of the thought of Jacques Lacan. The stakes in such a meeting, clinically and theoretically, are high. Indeed, we may well ask how the French psychoanalysts are going to explain the etiology of these so-called new disorders. For in putting the borderline states in a category other than the Freudian neuroses, psychoses, and perversions, the new American movements call into question the very fundamentals of psychoanalysis, especially those that entail giving voice to the subject's unconscious structure of desire.

French psychoanalysis has evolved in a different direction from its American counterpart. While in the United States psychoanalysis has progressively moved away from drive theory and from what is commonly called a *one-body psychology*, the tendency in France has been to reread Freud under a new lens. Creating this new lens was the task Lacan set himself for over fifty years. His methods, his ideas, and his controversial style caused him and his followers to become more and more estranged from mainstream psychoanalysis (especially in the United States), even though his theory has been extremely popular in the Latin countries of Europe and in South America.

Will the French analysts retort that "the more things change, the more they remain the same," and that the recent "discoveries" of the Americans are nothing more than a new phase of their ongoing misunderstanding of the work of Freud? This is the misunderstanding that Lacan poked such fun at in the '50s, when he accused his American colleagues of having transformed psychoanalysis into a science of adaptation that put Freud in the service of the ideals of free enterprise. Will the French analysts explain, in their own style, that while social change can certainly influence symptoms (there are, for example, fewer hysterical conversions and more depressive states nowadays), the unconscious psychic structures discovered by Freud—hysteria, obsessional neurosis, phobia, fetishism, voyeurism, paranoia, and so forth—nonetheless continue to be unvarying landmarks in psychoanalytic diagnostics?

We must recognize that the opening up of a dialogue between French and American analysts calls for a considerable effort on both sides and, as the Americans would say, for a certain amount of empathy. The fact is that the analysts from across the Atlantic tend to be unfamiliar with the theoretical models with which Lacan approached the works of Freud. The inroad Lacan has made in the United States is to all intents and purposes limited to the humanities departments of certain universities, to scholars, that is, who want to turn to account the cultural implications of a psychoanalytic approach broadly influenced by linguistics, anthropology, and philosophy. This divergence towards the academic world has given Lacanian thought an elitist aura that American analysts, trained for the most part in medical schools, can find intimidating. The more pragmatic American approach tends to stress clinical experience. To make themselves understood by their American colleagues, therefore, French analysts must place themselves on the level of clinical discourse in order to show how Lacanian analysis can shed a different light on the etiology of borderline disorders. What might be involved here, for example, is pointing out that the vicissitudes of unconscious desire are at the root of the destructive effects of wounded narcissism. Despite the difficulty of the task—it is hard to examine from the angle of clinical problematics fifty years of theoretical elaborations—the French can hope for an attentive and interested hearing on the part of their transatlantic colleagues. This is because the obstacles in the way of a Franco-American dialogue on the subject of psychoanalysis may gradually be disappearing. Today's American analysts do not automatically genuflect before the concepts that informed the ego psychologists' perspective from its beginnings—precisely those concepts that Lacan criticized. They prefer to be guided by clinical experience and observation in order to end up with new theoretical models that can account for their discoveries.

But in the opposite direction, given how widespread these new pathologies are in the United States, the question arises for French analysts as to whether this new psychic disorder put forward by their counterparts in the New World may also be about to take over their own couches. Guided by what seems to be the American head start, will they, too, find that their listening and their countertransference have changed as some of their patients come to resemble those described by their American colleagues? Without going so far as to abandon their fidelity to the Freudian models, will French analysts find themselves having to spell out new theoretical formulations in order to explain what irregularities of the oedipal dialectic might be linked to the distinctive symptomatology of borderline states?

3

The Development of the Concept of the "Borderline" in Psychoanalytic Diagnosis and Treatment

NICHOLAS KOURETAS, M.D.

INTRODUCTION

Almost every introduction to the concept of the borderline state (or the borderline disorder) begins with remarks about how problematic, confusing, and at times even embarrassing this concept has become. This predicament is understandable when we consider that the borderline concept originated in a strange admixture of inclusive and exclusive criteria (those of neurosis and psychosis), and that it was refined in the context of manifest theoretical tensions as well as latent personal investments in them. Hence to trace the development of a term which has come to function as the umbrella for a number of different psychopathological entities is a daunting task that will inevitably involve condensation, simplification, and sacrifice of subtlety and nuance.

Since borders are delineated by the two lands they divide, we can think of a geographical analogy for at least the early origins of the concept (Leichtman 1989). The lands, descriptive psychiatry and depth psychology, have at varying times either joined forces or considered each other with suspicion. And, although the term "borderline" is undoubtedly associated with psychoanalysis (the most elaborate expression of depth psychology), the clinical conditions it represents must have existed before psychoanalysis.

DESCRIPTIVE PSYCHIATRY

The first enlightened modern psychiatrist, Philippe Pinel (1801), described the *manie sans délire*, a subcategory of one of the four types of insanity. This *excitement without delirium* is the closest to what we would today call a severe personality disorder in a regressed state.

A quarter of a century later, John Pritchard (1835) added a new clinical syndrome that he called *moral insanity*, a form of psychopathology that did not entail cognitive impairment. Originally his term covered many individuals whom we would now call borderline, though later it gradually became restricted to psychopathic characters.

In 1890, thirty-five years after his groundbreaking description of *manic depressive illness (folie circulaire)*, Jean-Pierre Falret observed another type of madness, the *folie hystérique*. It is fascinating to recognize in his description of splitting, impulsivity, and affective lability many of the traits of today's borderline.

The two great descriptive psychiatrists who were both born the year after Freud, Emil Kraepelin (1905) and Eugen Bleuler (1911), were also intrigued by that middle territory between plain psychosis and unconventional normalcy. And in the narrow confines of this paper, the names of Ernst Kretschmer (1925), and Kurt Schneider (1923) ought to be mentioned. Both made significant contributions to the study of personality disorders but are largely ignored in the modern bibliography.

We may observe two trends in the early attempts of descriptive psychiatrists to come to terms with the diagnosis and understanding of severe personality disorders: first, the tendency to view these disorders as premorbid forms (or *formes frustes*, or good-outcome cases) of the main psychoses, particularly schizophrenia; second, and more intriguing, the tendency to approach with a broad outlook the entire spectrum of personality disorders and then to narrow the focus of clinical research to those with strong psychopathic traits and antisocial behaviors. It is as though, lacking the interpersonally derived data made available through the psychodynamic approach, the academic psychiatrist-clinician had no alternative but to restrict himself to the more loud and persistent antisocial behaviors (Stone 1986).

Finally, there is Karl Jaspers' *General Psychopathology* (1913, 1923, 1946), that *grand oeuvre* of phenomenological psychiatry, long neglected in the Anglo-Saxon world (it was translated into English fifty years after its first edition). Here we find, with surprise, the description of two personality types, the _self-insecure_, who would correspond to the narcissistic personality of our time, and the _incurable personality_, who would approximate what we would call the severe borderline.

The adjective "incurable" reveals the limitations of the descriptive-nosographic approach. With few exceptions, this descriptive approach remained dormant till the late '60s.[1] At that time in the United States the proliferation of mental-health centers, the availability of psychotherapists, and the pressing need to become more rigorous in psychiatric diagnosis resulted in a renewed undertaking of empirical studies, this time with the collaboration of psychoanalysts.[2] Space does not permit me to go into details of the descriptive approach, other than to underscore that, in recent years, empirical research on the comorbidity of the borderline disorder has shifted its focus from schizophrenia to affective disorders. This by no means suggests that the association with affective disorders is clear and definite; many borderlines never develop a clear affective disorder and their nuclear symptoms do not change when treated with antidepressant medication.

DEPTH PSYCHOLOGY: PSYCHOANALYSIS

In psychoanalysis, the term _borderline_ was first used, once, by Wilhelm Reich in his 1925 monograph on the "impulse-ridden character." With what would amount to a premonition of ideas to come, Reich noted the marked ambivalence, the primacy of pregenital aggression, the definite ego and superego defects, and the primitive narcissism that characterize these patients.

Though the concept of the borderline is present in the work of all the British object-relations theorists, from Melanie Klein to Fairbairn, Winnicott, Bion, and Balint, as a term and as a clinical diagnostic category, it is, in

---

1. There are two studies from the United States, one by Gregory Zilboorg (1941) on ambulatory schizophrenia and the other by Hoch and Polatin (1949) on pseudoneurotic schizophrenia. Both describe a diverse and unstable group of patients: some psychopaths or sexual perverts, others ineffective and unobtrusive people, with pananxiety, panneurosis and pansexuality; many were extremely sensitive to criticism and prone to rage. It is clear from the titles of their papers that both Zilboorg and Hoch and Polatin consider this diverse group to be a good-outcome variant of schizophrenia.

2. With the study of Roy Grinker and colleagues (1968) the empirical approach was given a new impetus and became more sophisticated; see Kety (1975), Gunderson and Singer (1975), Perry and Klerman (1978), Spitzer and Gibbon (1979).

birth and development, purely American. It is this American context that my paper addresses. In an effort to be schematic, and at the risk of over-simplification, I would distinguish three periods of evolution of the borderline concept in the United States.

First Period

I would call the years from 1938 to 1953 the period of unexpected realizations. During this time psychoanalysts recognized with surprise that many of their office patients did not benefit from the classic technique; occasionally such patients even became worse, developing transient psychotic states. While some (A. Stern, H. Deutsch) contributed elaborate clinical descriptions, others (P. Greenacre) turned their attention to the pathogenesis of the disorder.

Most reviewers agree that the actual term *borderline* was established in the psychoanalytic literature by Adolphe Stern in his 1938 paper "Psychoanalytic Investigation and Therapy in the Borderline Group of Neuroses" (Stone 1986). Succinctly but in detail Stern described the borderline condition under the following ten headings: narcissism, psychic bleeding, inordinate hypersensitivity, psychic and bodily rigidity, negative therapeutic reaction, constitutionally based feelings of inferiority deeply embedded in the personality, masochism, a state of deep organic insecurity or anxiety, use of projective mechanisms, and difficulties in reality testing, particularly in the area of personal relationships.

Stern thought that, for the borderline, narcissism is the substrate from which defenses originate on the basis of needs, whereas for the psychoneurotic, anxiety arises in connection with psychosexual impulses. Three years later, in an effort to shed light on the pathogenesis of these conditions, Phyllis Greenacre (1941) proposed the idea of constitutional predisposition to anxiety, which she called basic or elemental anxiety:

> I believe this organic stamp of suffering to consist of a genuine physiological sensitivity, a kind of increased indelibility of reaction, which heightens the anxiety potential and gives greater resonance to the anxieties of later life. The increase in early tension results first in an increase in narcissism and later in an insecure and easily slipping sense of reality. I referred (in an earlier paper) to an increase in the sense of omnipotence which may occur to overcome or balance the preanxiety ten-

sion state of the organism, and to an increased mirroring tendency arising partly from the imperfectly developed sense of reality. This tendency is the antecedent of the tendency towards overfacile identification. Libidinal attachments are urgent but shallow. The patient is not well individuated, with the libido quickly and urgently invested and withdrawn. [p. 618]

Helene Deutsch did not use the term borderline, but her 1942 description of the "as-if" personality foreshadows Winnicott's concept of the false self, Erikson's concept of ego diffusion, and many of Kernberg's diagnostic criteria for borderline psychopathology (identity diffusion, poor sublimatory potential, emptiness, impulsivity, etc.). She called attention to the disturbance of object relationships; the lack of warmth; the excessive formality; the quality of always acting as though on stage but without any enthusiasm; the absence of conviction as to one's true substance, leading to adaptation via superficial identification with others; and defectiveness in sublimatory activities, since no endeavor seems more real or engaging than any other.

Second Period

The second period in the development of the borderline concept started in the early '50s with the classic paper of Robert Knight on "Borderline States" (1953), and the subsequent two all-day panel discussions held by the American Psychoanalytic Association. I shall call this *the period of the elusive consolidation*, and I'll explain why.

During this time, mainstream American psychoanalysis felt threatened by the innovations in psychoanalytic technique proposed by Franz Alexander and his Chicago colleagues; these were parameters of technique that came under the rubric of the "corrective emotional experience." As a result, the early '50s were characterized by the concerted effort to redefine psychoanalysis and to differentiate it from psychotherapy, so as to avoid what Freud (1919) had warned against as "[alloying] the pure gold of analysis freely with the copper of direct suggestion" (p. 168). This was a time of closing of the ranks. It was hoped that an overarching theoretical construction, based on the paradigm of ego psychology, would explain and contain all forms of psychopathology. Consequently all clinical observations were filtered through the model of the tripartite mind, and all therapeutic interventions were molded, elaborated, and verbalized in terms of id, ego, and superego. This represented a wished-for consolidation of clinical knowledge and theory in psychoanalysis.

Thus it is the basic assumptions of ego psychology that are reflected in Knight's paper on "Borderline States," in which he maintained that, as a result of constitution, traumatic events, and disturbed human relationships, the ego of the borderline patient is fragile and hence unable to maintain its functioning. If left to its own devices, the ego of the borderline patient gravitates toward autistic thinking, which is indicative of the schizophrenic tendencies underlying it.

Knight insisted on a careful diagnostic assessment of the ego functions of the prospective analysand, and he cautioned against interpreting the few defenses left to the ego of the patient. On the whole, he felt that psychoanalysis was contraindicated. Although Knight disapproved of the term "borderline," his understanding and description were so resonant with the mandated ego-psychological postulates of the decade that his paper ended up promoting both the term and the category of the borderline as distinct from the psychoses.

Inspired by ego psychology, but feeling the need to move beyond the confines of the consulting room and the restrictive overdetermination of the first six years of life, Erik Erikson (1950) proposed a synthesis of sequential life tasks leading to integrity and emotional health. He amplified and enriched the concept of identity and its pathological counterpart, identity diffusion; years later, Otto Kernberg would assign to the latter the status of a cardinal and pathognomonic constellation of symptoms.

Third Period

Otto Kernberg's work ushers in the third period (1967–1975) of the development of the borderline concept. I will resort to a musical analogy and call this the period of the re-orchestration of the score. But before describing this third period, I would like to discuss some particular aspects of the nature of the score that was so much in need of re-orchestration. I am referring to the intellectual hegemony of ego psychology in the United States.

Particularities of North American Psychoanalysis

Every country creates the psychoanalysis it needs. Analysts do not function in a vacuum; they relate to the philosophical currents and struggle with the intellectual controversies of their times, and, wittingly or not, they participate in the conventions of the native culture. The psychosocial environment of the United States when the immigrant analysts arrived there in the '30s and '40s was very different from the one they were coming from. In the decade preceding World War II, American culture was permeated by a belief in a civilized morality and a coherent system regulating social and religious norms, defining behavior, prescribing a unique regime of sexual hygiene, and stipulating models of manhood and womanhood. At the same time, there existed a fierce passion for business, upward mobility, and acquisition of wealth.

The American world view presumed that willing something can render it actual (W. James); that truth is a consensus formed by a community of inquirers over time (C. Peirce); that nature is a plastic medium predisposed to human mastery (J. Dewey); that life progresses toward the better since its meaning, always contingent, awaits the future and shuns the past; and, finally, that life's overarching purpose is endless action leading to progress (Diggins 1993).

The immigrating Jewish analysts were highly educated and cultured scholars and scientists who had been driven out of their homes by an ominous fanaticism. They were grieving for two losses: that of their home, family, and country, and, from 1939 on, that of their spiritual father, Freud. When we consider that the reaction to object loss consists of introjection and preservation of the object by psychological means, then we can understand why Freud's last theoretical legacy (which, coincidentally, was being expanded by the only other living psychoanalyst bearing his name, Anna Freud) became all the more venerable and treasured. Among other tenets, this model, called the tripartite or structural model of the mind, entailed the idea of human adaptation involving autoplastic modification of the self and alloplastic modification of the environment, and the idea of a conflict-free sphere of the ego.

On the clinical level psychoanalysis accordingly defined itself as the means of freeing the ego from its crippling defenses and rendering it more adaptive to the environment. On the scholarly level psychoanalysis strove to become a psychology of normal development, with the ego being the field of empirical observation and hypothesis testing. Thus psychoanalysis, transferred across the ocean, could become a positive and positivistic science in the land of pragmatism.

In the period between the two world wars American academic psychiatrists lacked the educational background of their European colleagues, with its emphasis on the philosophical inquiries of phenomenology and existentialism. Nevertheless, most of them had been inoculated by the teachings of Adolph Meyer at Johns Hopkins University and were eager to have more systematic psychodynamic training. The newly arrived Middle European analysts promised to fulfill that desire and were put in a position of respectability and esteem. Thus externally derived expectations of authoritativeness were added to the inner psychological imperative of grieving for what had been lost. The price was considerable: two key elements of psychoanalysis, ambiguity and potential for subversiveness, suffered. It is interesting to note that intricacies involving language and (to a lesser extent) the unconscious did not become the focus of interest and passionate involvement as they did for European analysts. How could, for example, a foreign-born analyst who needed to maintain the authority attributed to him risk the ambiguity inherent in word play?

Kernberg's Main Theoretical Thesis

Kernberg emerged in American psychoanalysis in the late '60s with a series of papers on character pathology (Kernberg 1967, 1975, 1984). He posited a specific, albeit broad, realm of psychological functioning that was flanked on the one side by the neurotic personality organization and on the other by that of psychosis. He considered this neither a nosological entity nor a temporary state wavering between neurosis and psychosis but a stable and specific psychological structure that he called borderline personality organization.

Kernberg established the line between neurotic and borderline conditions by contrasting the defense of splitting—characteristic of borderline personality organization—with the more advanced defense of repression, indicative of neurotic functioning; he distinguished borderlines from psychotics by the capacity of the former to test reality. Under borderline personality organization he included all the clinical manifestations of severe character pathology, that is, the antisocial personalities, the self-mutilators, the severe addicts, the polymorphous perverts, the "as-if" and the prepsychotic characters (schizoid, paranoid, cyclothymic), and so forth.

Kernberg distinguished three sets of criteria, or features of the borderline personality organization: descriptive, genetic-dynamic, and structural. The descriptive criteria are chronic, diffuse anxiety; polysymptomatic neurosis; polymorphous perverse sexuality; the "classical" prepsychotic personality structures; impulse neurosis; addictions; and "lower level" character disorders. Genetic-dynamic elements include specific condensation of genital and pregenital conflicts; a precocious development of oedipal conflicts from the second and third year on; and the contamination of oedipal object images by oral and anal rage. The structural criteria are nonspecific manifestations of ego weakness (poor tolerance of frustration and anxiety, lack of impulse control, inadequate sublimation); the predominance over repression of splitting and the allied archaic defense operations of idealization, projective identification, denial, omnipotence, and devaluation; pathological internalized object relations; and primary-process thinking in unstructured situations.

Devising a specific approach to assessment that he called the *structural interview*, Kernberg shifted the diagnostic emphasis from the evaluation of symptoms to that of the structural determinants of character. He reformulated the development of internalized object relationships as follows. In early development, the ego has two essential tasks to accomplish: the differentiation of self-images from object-images and the integration of both self- and object-images under the influence of libidinal drive derivatives. In the future borderline the first task is attained, but the second one, the integration of libidinally determined and aggressively determined self- and object-images, fails because of the pathological predominance of primitive pregenital oral aggression. The resulting lack of synthesis of contradictory self- and object-images interferes with the integration of the self-concept and the establishing of a total object relationship and object constancy.

The need to keep good self- and object-images from being contaminated by aggressive influences leads to an active process of keeping apart introjections and identifications of opposite quality—that is, to splitting. Splitting, then, is a fundamental cause of ego weakness. Since splitting also requires less countercathexis than repression, a weak ego easily falls back on splitting and a vicious circle is created whereby ego weakness and splitting reinforce each other. This leads to seriously compromised oedipal and postoedipal identifications and, eventually, to identity diffusion (Meissner 1984).

Kernberg based his special form of modified psychoanalytic psychotherapy on this reciprocal and mutually reinforcing relationship between splitting and ego weakness. He believed (as had Knight [1953] and Frosch [1964] earlier), that borderline patients do not tolerate the regression brought about by psychoanalysis, nor are they helped by supportive psychotherapy. The latter leads to a precarious dissociation of the negative transference, which never gets worked through but is instead enacted on other persons while the treatment relationship remains shallow.

According to Kernberg, the borderline develops a primitive transference that reflects numerous dissociated or split-off aspects of the self and distorted and fantastic dissociated or split-off object representations. He therefore advocated a series of technical modifications involving frequent (three times a week) face-to-face interviews as well as systematic working through of the negative transference in the here and now, without attempting its genetic reconstruction. He felt that a complete transference neurosis should not be permitted to develop, nor should the transference be resolved by interpretation alone. But if the negative transference, along with its parallel manifestations in the patient's actual milieu, is systematically analyzed, then the splitting operations are weakened, the ego is strengthened, and a gradual integration of good and bad self- and object-representations takes place.

Kernberg's theoretical integrations and technical suggestions fertilized the field and brought together empirical-descriptive approaches, developmental research, and clinical case studies to an unprecedented degree.[3] This work culminated in the inclusion of the borderline concept as Borderline Personality Disorder in the official manual, *DSM-III*, of the American Psychiatric Association (Akhtar 1992). Thus in only 40 years this bland and nondescript word, "borderline," had journeyed all the way from Stern's account of a few difficult patients in his Manhattan practice to an established diagnostic category covering hundreds of thousands of outpatients in every private office, mental-health clinic, and training facility in the country.

By reformulating the borderline concept, Kernberg helped to bring about two changes in American psychoanalysis. First, ego psychology, which had drifted into claiming the status of a science of normal development and psychosocial adaptation, was invigorated and enriched by new insights into preoedipal development. Second, the Kleinian contribution to object-relations theory was introduced into the broad mainstream of psychoanalytic discourse. Although many psychoanalytic theorists in the United States had been aware of and involved in object-relations theory and its clinical applications, their work was in general seen as antithetical to the canons of ego psychology. While retaining the economic meta-

---

3. At times, Kernberg's comprehensiveness and articulateness can lead to the impression that his tightly woven conceptualizations are totally the product of his own inspiration. But the fact is that he has always expressed his indebtedness to Melanie Klein, Fairbairn, Bion, Mahler, and, above all, Edith Jacobson.

psychological hypothesis based on drive theory, Kernberg initiated an effort at integration of the two approaches by addressing himself to the diagnostic obscurities and the treatment impasses of the borderline patient, and by working ceaselessly on the theoretical interface—that is, on the structural derivatives of object relations.

By the early '80s, however, a number of authors had become critical of Kernberg's ideas. Some felt that his formulations have an unqualified specificity, whereas borderline patients represent such a heterogeneous group that no developmental defect, nuclear conflict, or structural abnormality can serve as the central point around which an explanatory theory can be woven. To aim at precision and systematization was thought to be counteranalytic. Other critics remarked that the *structural interview*, with its use of clarification, confrontation, and early interpretation of the transference, disturbs the establishment of a genuine therapeutic relationship from which a true psychoanalytic understanding can evolve (Weinshel 1988).

But the most frequent criticism came from everyday clinical experience. Many psychoanalysts and psychoanalytically oriented psychotherapists thought that most borderline patients could not tolerate the techniques embedded in Kernberg's approach: strict limit setting, technical neutrality, and systematic analysis of the archaic, primarily negative transference and the defenses against envy. They maintained that instead of approaching these patients as possessing an archaic defensive structure designed to protect them from intrapsychic conflict, one could as well understand their current predicament and their past histories not as defenses, but as the outcome of developmental failures resulting from phase-specific vicissitudes in the experience of the mother–toddler relationship. According to these critics, the therapeutic relationship should have a more reparative role aimed at building, strengthening, and consolidating the missing structure.

Margaret Mahler made the most diligent effort to describe this structural defect by relating it to the separation-individuation process. She and her co-workers proposed that failure in the rapprochement subphase produces a relatively unassimilated bad introject around which the child's inner experience is organized. Specifically, it is the upsurge of aggression at this time of the separation-individuation process, maintained by a lack of optimal emotional availability on the part of the mother, that provides the conditions for the organization of the borderline intrapsychic economy. Early ambivalence is not overcome, object constancy is not achieved, and the individual depends throughout life on external objects to provide himself with a sense of cohesive self-experience.

The hypothesis of a link between a circumscribed developmental failure and a specific form of psychopathology is always enticing but undoubtedly simplistic. Such a position ignores the fact that psychological development is subject to many elaborations of a progressive or a regressive nature. For example, we know that perplexities over separation and individuation are critically reworked in adolescence and early adulthood. Mahler (1971) herself eventually came to believe that there was no direct connection between the findings of child observation and subsequent borderline pathology.

Mahler's emphasis on the centrality of the rapprochement crisis for the development of object constancy and whole self- and object-representations served as the basis for many variations. In one of these, Adler and Buie (1979) brought together Piaget's findings on the achievement of evocative memory in the toddler, Fraiberg's thoughts on mental representation, and Winnicott's concept of the holding environment. Around the age of a year and a half the child's mind gains the ability to evoke the memory of an object despite the absence of visual cues. From the inanimate object, he or she progresses to the memory of the human object, the mother. The ability of the child to evoke (remember) the image and the associated ministrations of the mother enables him or her to overcome the devastating sense of aloneness and panic that results from separations. The central deficit that leads to borderline pathology, then, is a deficit in positive soothing introjects stemming from the failure to achieve solid evocative memory, which in turn is a result of inadequate maternal holding experiences.

Adler and Buie's hypothesis rests on a primary inner representational deficit; this calls into question Kernberg's emphasis on splitting, since in their view there is no good object representation to begin with, one to be contrasted with the bad representation and actively kept apart from it through splitting. Their approach addresses itself to a subset of inner experiences and behaviors of the borderline centering on separation issues. It attempts to explain the craving that borderlines have for intense attachments and their tendency to react with fragmentation, terror of abandonment, and painful aloneness every time a disruption of an important relationship feels imminent. The goal of psychoanalytic psychotherapy, accordingly, is to provide a relationship of safety, security, and trust in order to enable the patient, through optimal disillusionment, to internalize the therapist as a positive introject and to develop the capacity for evocative memory, a developmental advance that will permit the patient to overcome the state of aloneness, panic, rage, and emptiness.

This general line of thought, which highlights the external world, puts the emphasis on the crucial role of the mother's availability and her attunement to the child's phase-appropriate needs. In its de-emphasis of instinctual aggression, unconscious fantasy, and primitive defenses, it came to be known as the theory of psychological deficit. It was supported and facilitated by the emerging presence on the American psychoanalytic scene of the psychology of the self, a new and controversial set of propositions regarding psychological development and its theorization.

Heinz Kohut originally developed his ideas in order to attend and respond to extremely sensitive patients suffering from serious problems of self-esteem regulation. He felt that these patients developed different types of transferences that demanded more empathy and less, if any, interpretation of defenses (Kohut 1971). As the psychology of the self gradually developed its own theoretical postulates and terminology and its own operational concepts, it expanded its theoretical and technical claims beyond the narcissistic characters to the realm of the borderline disorders and the neuroses (Kohut 1977).

The psychology of the self alters all previous psychoanalytic concepts: it drops the economic point of view and puts the emphasis on the structure of the self, including subjective conscious and preconscious experiences—continuing into adolescence and adult life—of selfhood and the self in relation to sustaining selfobjects. This self is not involved in instinctual expression but seeks relatedness. Drives, therefore, are seen as the breakdown products of an endangered or fragmenting self.

The psychology of the self recognizes the individual's need to organize his or her psyche into a cohesive configuration, the self, as the most fundamental essence of human psychology. It also recognizes the need for the establishment of relationships between the self and its surroundings, relationships that evoke, maintain, and strengthen the structural coherence and vitality of the self and the harmony among its components. The primary means of data collection becomes sustained, empathic introspective immersion in the patient's subjective world, as reflected in the transference: what Kohut calls listening from the patient's frame of reference. The individual's sense of compromise or failure is thought to stem from defects in the self brought about by unempathic responses, during childhood, on the part of selfobject figures.

To a certain extent the emergence of the psychology of the self and its distinctive role in American psychoanalysis can be understood in the context of the earlier intellectual monopoly of ego psychology. For almost thirty years object-relations theory—that spectrum of psychological explanations that are based on the premise that the self is composed of elements taken in from the outside, primarily aspects of the functioning of other persons— was not treated as an equal partner by the ego psychologists. No genuine cross-fertilization occurred. This was reflected in the teaching and the practice of psychoanalysis: defense interpretation and technical neutrality were put in the center of clinical inquiry, while the patient's subjectivity was assigned a peripheral role.

Since the thinking behind object-relations theory was not permitted to become gradually integrated with ego psychology, it was inevitable that it would "march in" in the form of a fully articulated theory aimed at reversing and replacing all previous concepts. It is my hypothesis that, had the writings of Fairbairn, Winnicott, Guntrip, and Balint been read at the time they were published with the same open-mindedness and commitment that greeted the writings of Hartmann, there would not have been a psychology of the self, at least not in the form we know today. (Parenthetically, a frequent criticism raised against Kohut is that he did not sufficiently acknowledge his indebtedness to Fairbairn and Winnicott.)

According to the psychology of the self, borderline states involve serious, permanent, or protracted enfeeblement of, and damage to, the self, but complex defenses cover this basic deficit and protect the individual from close relationships that might activate the underlying fragmentation. The damage to the self is caused by severe and ongoing failures in parental empathic response to the selfobject needs of the child. Because of the constant threat of loss of cohesion, the child cannot undertake attachments to selfobjects; he or she remains with a chronic and overwhelming sense of dread which contributes to problems in self-regulation, self-control, self-soothing, and maintenance of self-esteem. In later life he or she may resort to compensatory stimulating activities such as drug abuse, indiscriminate sexuality, eating disorders, and so forth.

Kohut at first thought that the borderline individual could not form stable selfobject transferences (the expression of the need for idealizing, mirroring, or twinship in the therapeutic relationship). He later moderated this position and stated his belief that some borderlines with an unusually empathic, dedicated, and facilitative analyst could come to understand both their selfobject needs for affirmation, admiration, and soothing and their parents' genetically pathogenic responses, and could be transformed into narcissistic personalities (Kohut 1984).

Kohut's cautious position was modified to the extreme by Stolorow and colleagues (1987), who argued that the borderline condition is totally iatrogenic, brought about by insensitive therapeutic techniques. They claimed that the borderline structure (or the borderline personality organization) does not exist; primitive defensive operations (splitting, projective identification, etc.) are nothing but indications of the failure of archaic selfobject relations.

Epilogue

From this brief survey of the development of the borderline concept in American psychoanalysis, it is clear that no theory generates a satisfactory account of all aspects of the condition. Each approach tends to describe and explain best one or another aspect of the syndrome while failing to account equally well for other aspects. Each one starts out from a different reference point within the spectrum of psychoanalytic models, and its explanatory power varies accordingly.

It is possible that what we call borderline pathology is untreatable by psychoanalysis. The pathology is rooted in the pre-verbal world and involves deficits in symbolically encoded ideation, whereas psychoanalysis is essentially a verbally mediated communicative effort presupposing at least a minimal development of symbolic thought. What is more certain is that, as far as pathogenesis is concerned, all the divergent theoretical approaches, no matter how elaborate they are, need to anchor themselves on one or the other side of the radical nature-nurture dichotomy. Thus Kernberg's construct assumes pregenital oral aggression; Kohut's focuses on the selfobject.

Addendum

There are several early French psychoanalytic contributions to the definition of the concept of the borderline.

In one of his late publications Charles Odier (1948), a pioneer of the Société Psychanalytique de Paris and the Swiss Psychoanalytic Society, described a central clinical characteristic of borderline pathology—fear of aloneness. The third chapter of his 1948 book *L'angoisse et la pensée magique* (*Anxiety and Magical Thinking*), is entitled "La névrose d'abandon" ("Abandonment Neurosis"). This was to become the title of a book by the Piaget-trained Swiss psychologist Germaine Guex (1950). In both publications, the extensive description and elaboration of the fear of abandonment is remarkable, considering that they predate by thirty years the work of Adler, Buie, and Kohut. As if to suggest a new nosological group, in the manner of hysterics or phobics, these patients are called *les abandonniques*; it is assumed that there is no evocative memory of the soothing introject, and technical recommendations stress the primacy of validation of the patient over insight.

In the work of that most creative French psychoanalyst, Maurice Bouvet (see especially his paper on "La relation d'objet" in Bouvet 1967), we encounter the description of the *neurosis of depersonalization* as contrasted with the depersonalization crises of neurotics, and the description of a pregenital object relationship distinct from those of the psychotic and the neurotic. Bouvet clearly anticipates later notions such as Kernberg's borderline personality organization.

Finally, the work of Jean Bergeret is characterized by typically French psychostructural thinking. For him, the borderline state is a disorder of narcissism in which the object relationship remains anaclitic. Bergeret recognizes the existence of two authentic developmental lines of psychic structure, that, once in motion, lead to either a neurotic structure or a psychotic one; each is independent of the other and there is no intercommunication. Between these domains lie the borderline states, less rigid, less definitive, less solid, and much more mobile.

According to Bergeret (1993), when the ego, after having surpassed early frustrations and prepsychotic fixations, is ready to be engaged in normal oedipal evolution, it undergoes a significant psychological traumatization. This traumatization is experienced as a precocious, massive, and brutal encounter with the givens of the oedipal situation. In order to maintain its narcissistic equilibrium, the ego seeks to integrate the experience along the lines of early frustrations and threats. The child can no longer rely on the love of the father in order to feel supported against the threat of its hostile feelings toward the mother, and vice versa. The ego becomes obliged to resort to other defensive maneuvers such as denial, projective identification, primitive idealization, and the like. As a result of this first psychic disorganizer, libidinal evolution stops, and the ego precociously enters a stage of compromised pseudolatency that lasts up to adulthood. This common origin of compromised pseudolatency (*tronc commun aménagé*) is not an authentic psychic structure, since the usual clinical criteria of fixity, stability, and specificity do not apply.

From then on, development varies enormously. If a second psychic disorganizer (postpartum depression, marriage, loss, social upheaval, accident) occurs in the life of the individual, then the provisional compromise falls apart and the borderline adopts the neurotic, the psychotic, or the psychosomatic solution. Without a second disorganizer there is a gradual evolution either towards perversion or towards chronic characterological disturbance. Some borderlines remain in the pseudolatency stage for all their lives, decompensating in old age or unexpectedly resorting to suicide.

For reasons of space I can only mention by name some of the more recent French contributions to the subject of borderline pathology: André Green (1977), Janine Chasseguet-Smirgel (1978), and Joyce McDougall (1979).

REFERENCES

Adler, G., and Buie, D. H.(1979). Aloneness and borderline psychopathology: developmental issues. *International Journal of Psycho-Analysis* 60:83–96.

Akhtar, S. (1992). *Broken Structures: Severe Personality Disorders and Their Treatment*. Northvale, NJ: Jason Aronson.

Bergeret, J. (1993). Les états limites et leurs aménagements. In *Psychologie Pathologique*, ed. J. Bergeret. Paris: Masson.

Bleuler, E. (1911). *Dementia Praecox or the Group of Schizophrenias*. New York: International Universities Press.

Bouvet, M. (1967). *Oeuvres Psychanalytiques*. Paris: Payot.

Chasseguet-Smirgel, J. (1978). Reflections on the connexions between perversion and sadism. *International Journal of Psycho-Analysis* 59: 27–35.

Deutsch, H. (1942). Some forms of emotional disturbance and their relationship to schizophrenia. *Psychoanalytic Quarterly* 11:301–321.

Diggins, J. P. (1993). *The Promise of Pragmatism*. Chicago: University of Chicago Press.

Erikson, E. H. (1950). *Childhood and Society*. New York: Norton.

Falret, J. (1890). *Etudes cliniques sur les maladies mentales*. Paris: Baillière.

Freud, S. (1919). On the teaching of psychoanalysis in universities. *Standard Edition* 17: 169–174.

Frosch, J. (1964). The psychotic character: clinical psychiatric considerations. *Psychoanalytic Quarterly* 38: 91–96.

Green, A. (1977). The borderline concept. In *Borderline Personality Disorders*, ed. P. Hartocollis, pp. 15–44. New York: International Universities Press.

Greenacre, P. (1941). The predisposition to anxiety. Part II. *Psychoanalytic Quarterly* 10:610–638.

Grinker, R., Werble, B., and Drye, R. (1968). *The Borderline Syndrome: A Behavioral Study of Ego Functions.* New York: Basic Books.

Guex, G. (1950). *La névrose d'abandon.* Paris: Presses Universitaires de France.

Gunderson, J. G., and Singer, M. (1975). Defining borderline patients. *American Journal of Psychiatry* 133:1–10.

Hoch, P., and Polatin, P.(1949). Pseudoneurotic forms of schizophrenia. *Psychoanalytic Quarterly* 23:248–276.

Jaspers, K. (1913/1923/1946). *General Psychopathology.* Manchester: University of Manchester Press, 1963.

Kernberg, O. (1967). Borderline personality organization. *Journal of the American Psychoanalytic Association* 15: 641–685.

———— (1975). *Borderline Conditions and Pathological Narcissism.* New York: Jason Aronson.

———— (1984) *Severe Personality Disorders.* New Haven, CT: Yale University Press.

Kety, S. (1975). Mental illness in biological and adoptive families of adopted schizophrenics. In *Genetic Research in Psychiatry,* ed. R. R. Fieve et al., pp. 147–165. Baltimore: Johns Hopkins University Press.

Knight, R. (1953). Borderline states. *Bulletin of the Menninger Clinic* 17: 1–12.

Kohut, H. (1971). *The Analysis of the Self.* New York: International Universities Press.

———— (1977). *The Restoration of the Self.* New York: International Universities Press.

———— (1984). *How Does Analysis Cure?* Chicago: University of Chicago Press.

Kraepelin, E. (1905). *Einführung in die psychiatrische Klinik,* 2nd. ed. Leipzig: Barth.

Kretschmer, E. (1925). *Physique and Character.* New York: Harcourt Brace.

Leichtman, M. (1989). Evolving concepts of borderline personality disorder. *Bulletin of the Menninger Clinic* 53:229–249.

Mahler, M. S. (1971). A study of the separation-individuation process and its possible application to borderline phenomena in the psychoanalytic situation. *Psychoanalytic Study of the Child* 26:402–424. New York: International Universities Press.

McDougall, J. (1979). Primitive communication in the use of countertransference. In *Countertransference,* ed. L. Epstein and A. Feiner, pp. 267–304. New York: Jason Aronson.

Meissner, W. W. (1984). *The Borderline Spectrum.* New York: Jason Aronson.

Odier, C. (1948). *L'angoisse et la pensée magique.* Neuchâtel: Delachaux & Niestle.

Perry, J. C., and Klerman, G. L. (1978). Clinical features of the borderline personality disorder. *American Journal of Psychiatry* 137: 165–173.

Pinel, P. (1801). *Abhandlung über Geistesverwirrungen oder Manie.* Vienna: Carl Schaumburg.

Pritchard, J. C. (1835). *Treatise on Insanity.* London: Sherwood, Gilbert and Piper.

Reich, W. (1925). *Der triebhafte Charakter.* Leipzig: Internationaler Psychoanalytischer Verlag.

Schmideberg, M. (1947). The treatment of psychopathic and borderline patients. *American Journal of Psychotherapy* 1:45–71.

Schneider, K. (1923). *Psychopathic Personalities.* Springfield, IL: Charles C Thomas, 1958.

Spitzer, R. L., and Gibbon, M. (1979). Crossing the border into borderline personality and borderline schizophrenia: the development of criteria. *Archives of General Psychiatry* 36:17–24.

Stern, A. (1938). Psychoanalytic investigation and therapy in the borderline group of neuroses. *Psychoanalytic Quarterly* 7:467–489.

Stolorow, R., Brandchaft, B., and Atwood, G. (1987). *Psychoanalytic Treatment. An Intersubjective Approach.* Hillsdale, NJ: Analytic Press.

Stone, M. H. (1986). *Essential Papers on Borderline Disorders.* New York: New York University Press.

Weinshel, E. M. (1988). Borders of the borderline: modesty in psychoanalytic diagnosis. *Psychoanalytic Inquiry* 8:333–354.

Zilboorg, G. (1941). Ambulatory schizophrenia. *Psychiatry* 4:149–155.

4

A Borderline State of Humanity and the Fragmented Ego of the Analyst

PROFESSEUR PIERRE FÉDIDA

Just like the young woman who came to see me for her "unbearable suffering at twilight," we may have to go as far as to conceptualize as an everyday condition a borderline state of humanity—without humane melancholy—that hints at the unavoidable *occurrence* of a form that is still unknown to us. This event is not part of the past, nor can it be imagined as something to come. Can we still call an "occurrence" what is experienced as a slow disintegration of time and the insidious advance, perceptible at every moment, of a deadline that has already begun? Is the "planetary man" the person who experiences psychically, in his life, the geological evolution of the earth and of species? *Mutation* is infinitesimal, and this is surely why it assumes the appearance of a spellbound passion— perhaps one that would take the form of a female Christ. This female Christ is a *mutant* who, through her/his "suffering," causes the inhuman to arise in humanity. This physically psychic suffering is her/his *flesh*. The incarnation is the work of disintegration of time that produces the reverse side of the face. That's what the incarnation of the inhuman is.

What this young woman, Cynthia, called a "borderline state of humanity" was certainly not without reference to her own family history; her paternal and maternal grandparents were victims of Nazi extermination, which her mother, born in a concentration camp, had miraculously escaped. But today, as far as she herself was concerned, it was as though the Holocaust were neither in the past nor in the future but were taking place in that unavoidable time that the everyday can no longer restrain. And nothing was holding together: the stitches were unraveling before her eyes. Can we speak of "the present" and "the everyday" when reality no longer has the slightest substance and nothing comes along but *decomposed time*? It was not the arrival of evening that Cynthia dreaded. Although she had no memory of childhood anxiety at twilight, and although now she had come to anticipate a "powerful catastrophe," she nonetheless knew that such a catastrophe would not occur in the world or in her life. The "borderline state of humanity" was, as it were, fixed *backwards* and yet without a past. Surely, then, being deprived of the anxiety of a catastrophe is a sort of proof of the inhuman, just like the inability to feel fear or dread, which are human feelings. And so the "suffering" that tormented her was like flayed skin that has to be rubbed all the time so that one can feel alive.

In holding on to her suffering in spite of herself—perhaps so that she would not disappear—she was taking the suffering for the sufferer! For Cynthia could not speak *of* her suffering, in the sense that she was unaware of its contents. But as it spoke, this suffering that "disfigured" her took on the compulsive aspect of rubbing the skin "in order to bleed," and it was this that made her "hold up" and "stand straight and keep moving." There could be no rest, according to her, for one who was on the lookout. And for this reason the suffering did not permit the carelessness of forgetting, in the same way that it granted her "lucidity" when she was unable to sleep: it made her "translucent" to others who wandered around like automata without gestures, without words, without faces, able to communicate with one another only through a dumb-show of long-lost feelings. These "automata" were horribly cruel, yet at the same time they slipped away from her on the street, in the subway, outside cafés.

A "borderline state of humanity" is therefore not a term one would apply to suffering that is inhuman because it is psychically unbearable. If human beings suffer psychically—suffer because there *is* a psyche—this uncontrollable suffering is that of the consciousness and the memory which we cannot do without as long as we are of human flesh. We cannot keep ourselves from seeing what is human come undone all around us. And indeed, this suffering is none other than what is endured in the passion of the living Christ on the cross. Is it a matter of saving an alliance between man and God, or, in so doing, of revealing the other face of the human—

the inhumanity of the human being? The "borderline state of humanity" is the fulcrum at which the grimaces, simulating affects, of anonymous normality tip over into the slow destruction of their appearances. It is also the exhaustion of the dream by the insomnia of cruelty. Could we say, then, that this fulcrum gives the woman the advantage of being more naked than men and of knowing, at the same time, the hope for an animality and the anorexia of death? If the suffering *of* the psyche was supposed to be, for the woman, the true flesh of her sex, then this "borderline state of humanity" can avail itself of the most intimate acquaintance with the suffering Christ, who is, in some way, the mirror of all the symptoms of the human— the ultimate misshapenness.

As I listened to Cynthia saying these things in her first sessions, it would certainly have been easy for me to recognize in her many of the distinctive features of what is commonly called the "borderline personality." But her own designation of her "suffering" as a "borderline state of humanity" kept me from making use of the diagnostic markers of a nosographic or transnosographic *category* and allowed me to grant her speech that time in which existence names itself in the experience of destruction by time. In what way, I thought, is the "borderline personality" the conventional clinical manifestation of this "borderline state of humanity" that could be seen in the suffering of Cynthia, whose intelligence enabled her to say so many things that other patients could not express?

Cynthia *knew* how she could be and what she could do in order to "trick her way out of" the suffering that, however, she asked me to *see* by coming to *see me*. As she said a long time after beginning her psychotherapy, the first time she left my office she had had the thought that in showing me her suffering she had also run the risk of "seeing you as being obscene like the others" or of "annihilating" me. Wouldn't it have been better to "be deceptive by passing myself off as someone else"? In her work (she was a graphic artist) she was not only well-adjusted and creative, but others sought her out socially. Popular with men, she knew how to dress in a provocative way without agreeing in the least to sexual acting out, which was reserved for the times when she would "freak out" and wanted to avoid being tempted by the hard drugs that would be "appropriate" given her "state."

Her "normality" was composed of rules and regulations that she observed scrupulously every day "to make it seem as if I'm alive": taking various pills upon awakening, exercising, dieting, jogging, relaxing in the course of the day. As a result of all this no one would notice anything, and she would look like a human being after all. She said: "You always have to walk quickly in the street, and ahead of other people, because as soon as you slow down and linger people look at you lecherously as a woman and there's no time to pull yourself together again." Walking at an energetic pace was the best way to make an impression on others and thereby not to let them become repulsive. "You have to be allergic to other people" and never let them in any way "rob you of the suffering that you're made of." But "making believe" in order to live was "exhausting": basically, there was nothing to feel or to experience, since "everything positive that comes to you from other people isolates you in a solitude." The human was this mystification of feelings.

We can certainly recognize in Cynthia's case defense mechanisms such as splitting that are characteristic of borderline personalities. The patient spoke of her intolerance of interpretations on the grounds that they dissociated her from herself ("they make you guilty of an unconscious desire"), and she was distrustful of getting attached to a person—the analyst—who could lure her into annihilation. Although Cynthia claimed that she was capable of remaining alone with her suffering, nothing was more threatening to her than absence, which would "plunge [her] into the void" and make it impossible for her to do anything. On the occasions when this happened she would stay in bed, taking sleeping pills and alcohol to "dissolve all thoughts." She manifested a predominance of archaic defense mechanisms (like denial) against devastating psychotic anxiety; likewise, shifting projective identifications seemed to make up for the impossibility of symbolization. States of derealization, as evidenced in her sexual acting out—which, for her, meant that she had to apply a real technique of depersonalization to her male partner, who was always unbearable—went along with a denaturation of the object's genitals in favor of behaviors, which she called "anti-hemorrhagic," designed to keep her alive.

The threats of annihilation, quite distinct from the disorganization caused by suffering (which, paradoxically, was supposed to safeguard her identity), were also associated with a disidealization of the object—or of a transference—and with depression, when the "figures" in her acting out no longer held together and the coherence of her part-objects could thus no longer be maintained. The suffering, which could be anesthetized for a time, would always return stronger than ever as idealization turned into devaluing. The ascetic regimen of suffering that she so readily undertook on a daily basis suggests obsessional thought processes such as we encounter in certain depressed anorexics; Cynthia, who presented this way when she came to "see" me, believed that this regimen enabled her to preserve an ego identity and a capacity to feel and think.

Cynthia began regular psychotherapy (two sessions a week), but after two months she asked to come three times a week and to use the couch. What happened is that she had quickly realized that her speech could not be the same now that she had "begun dreaming again," and the face-to-face position made it impossible for her to recall her dreams in the sessions. She said that it would be of little interest to her to tell me things that she had already thought, and she had the feeling that faces could get in the way of recollection. Even though she was afraid that lying down would give her the absolutely detestable feeling of being naked and immobile and would cast her into a lifeless depression—or, conversely, into a "wild craziness"—she preferred to take the risk instead of clinging to the vigilance of her insomniac thought. And it was out of the question for the sessions to make her put on her "best manners," that is, her techniques of normality. As for me, I had no objection to seeing her three times a week on the couch, but I was concerned that dissociative episodes might arise. Cynthia gave me ample opportunity to observe how well-informed she was about the speech that establishes an analytic situation, and it was for this reason, too, that dissociation in the course of the process could not be ruled out.

The abundant literature on the psychotherapeutic treatment of "borderline personalities" is far from ignoring the difficulties inherent in the countertransference of the analyst, which is, in such cases, elicited all the more because the transferences are often so mobile and volatile from one moment to the next that it can be hard for him to maintain a continuous perception of his identity. We might even wonder whether the theory of the "borderline personality" grew in the favorable soil of ego psychology in order to constitute, simultaneously, its critical challenge and its doctrinal confirmation. The descriptive and explanatory concepts of the metapsychology of borderline states have a yardstick in the form of a theory of the ego and of identifications that makes use of technical awareness of the mechanisms brought into play by the treatment. The recent work of the school of Otto Kernberg (Kernberg et al.,1989) demonstrates to perfection this tendency to view technical difficulties as justifying all sorts of precautions and arrangements to preserve the integrity of the therapeutic identity of the analyst's ego. Some years ago I investigated this approach to the metapsychology and the treatment of borderline cases (Fédida, 1979), and I attempted to show how the borderline patient had, for a number of analysts, become the clinical projection of ego psychology right down to the details of this paradigm of a negative normality participating in a functional analogy with an ego ideal. These considerations led me to wonder whether "borderline personalities" are not fundamentally captives of the ideological crisis of analytic practice and the crisis affecting the theory of the regression of the ego.

In his seminar on *The Ego in Freud's Theory and in the Technique of Psychoanalysis*, Lacan (1954–1955) devotes several pages to the Dream of Irma's Injection. His reading of this dream—the "specimen dream" in that it inaugurates a theory of the ego and of the subject of the unconscious—occurs at the point where he is reinterpreting the concept of regression introduced by Freud in Chapter 4 of *The Interpretation of Dreams*. Among other things, the Dream of Irma's Injection reveals the "fragmentation of the ego" that may be said to be the condition *in the analyst* for a regression that makes possible the regression in the patient's transference:

> What happens when we see the subject substituted for by the polycephalic subject?—that crowd I was speaking about last time, a crowd in the Freudian sense, the one discussed in *Group Psychology and the Analysis of the Ego*, made up of the imaginary plurality of the subject, the spreading, the blossoming out of the different identifications of the *ego*. At first this seems to us like an abolition, a destruction of the subject as such. The subject transformed in this polycephalic image seems to be somewhat acephalic. If there is an image that could represent for us Freud's notion of the unconscious, it is certainly that of an acephalic subject, a subject who no longer has an *ego*, who is at the farthest edge, decentered, with regard to the *ego*, who doesn't belong to the *ego*. And yet he is the subject who is speaking, since he's the one who gives all the characters in the dream their nonsensical lines—whose nonsensical nature is precisely the source of their meaning. [p. 167, translation modified][1]

And a little further on:

> . . . it is just when the world of the dreamer is plunged into the greatest imaginary chaos that discourse enters into play, discourse as such, inde-

---

1. *Translator's note*: The French term for "the ego" is *le moi*, "the me," corresponding in its experience-near simplicity to Freud's *das Ich*, "the I." In the passage just cited, the word *ego* is used, italicized, in the original. Elsewhere, although I have followed convention in translating *le moi* as "the ego," it should be kept in mind that the French understand this to be "the me."

pendently of its meaning, since it is a senseless discourse. It then seems
that the subject decomposes and disappears. [p. 170]

And finally, in connection with the Wolf Man's dream of the primal scene:

> As in the dream of Irma's injection, the subject decomposes, fades away,
> dissociates into its various "me's." Likewise, after the Wolf Man's dream,
> we witness the real start of the analysis, which makes possible the disso-
> ciation inside the subject of a personality so singularly composite that it
> marks the originality of the style of the case. As you know, the problems
> left unresolved by this analysis were to be so serious that in the aftermath
> it would degenerate into psychosis. [p. 176, translation modified]

The transferential crowd of identifications could be what is called the
"borderline personality." And precisely if the "borderline personality" is in
some way the clinical projection of a representation of the crowd-ego obey-
ing structural criteria (poor frustration tolerance, psychopathic impulsivity, predominance of splitting mechanisms and defenses such as idealization, omnipotent denial, etc.), these criteria derived from the analysis of
the ego and its Freudian metapsychology are compartmentalized here and
hence directly observable *from the viewpoint of an ego psychology.* In other
words, Kernberg (among other authors) is inclined to characterize the *borderline ego* structurally with reference to a metapsychological entity, the
ego, defined (especially in the analyst) as ensuring a stable and economi-
cally integrated unity of the images of the self, and object relations determined by a mobile libido. We could sum up as follows: *the borderline personality is a psychopathological entity that reveals symptomatically an immature
and fragmented structure of an ideally normal ego.*

Here is where Lacan's critique of ego psychology is so illuminating.
As we have seen in the light of the passages cited above, the fragmentation
of the ego by anxiety in dreams expresses, in a sense, these decenterings
that give rise to the borderline ego: Isn't the analyst, as he dreams, in effect
the locus (or loci) of borderline identifications or even of borderline processes of ego disorganization? We might even dare to conjecture that nothing is closer to the analyst's dream than the borderline personality! But here
is precisely where what is at issue in the debate comes down to the place
granted to this dream (the "kettle with a hole in it"[2]) in the definition of

---

2. *Translator's note*: The reference is to a passage from Freud's *Interpretation of Dreams*
discussed by Lacan, 1954–1955, p. 151.

regressive states of the analyst's listening capacity ("the dream" beyond this dream) and of the status reserved for Freudian metapsychology.

Let us briefly return to the case of Cynthia. The traits that identify this patient as a borderline personality are based on the psychological observation of the behaviors called for by primary processes. It is true that such observation compares the representations of object and sexual pathology with the analyst's image of his ego identity and with subjective countertransferential strategies. But to stop at this point would be to ignore a consideration as important as the one this patient communicated in connection with the insomniac suffering of her awareness, of which she later said, associating to a dream of a concentration camp, that she was perhaps a kind of psychic cadaverization paradoxically trying to resurrect and revive her maternal grandmother next to her mother as a baby. And if it is as important for her suffering to *be seen* by *me* as it is for her *to see* if she can *destroy me*, it is from the time I became her analyst—that is, from the time that her speech made me able *to dream a fragmented ego*—that her own dreams can shelter the chaos and return fragmentarily to memory in the speech of her sessions.

In the case of Cynthia, as with other borderline patients, as I have often had occasion to note, everything the patient describes under the heading of behavior in the world of external reality in fact belongs to the undreamed remains of the night inserted into waking life. And one of the most difficult tasks in the establishment of the analytic situation with these patients is without a doubt the creation of transferential conditions that will enable the dream to return to nighttime sleep. These transferential conditions are those of a regression, in this case always with hallucinatory intensity; they are also those that I have called, for the analyst, "the site of the stranger": the demand for the neuter and the breaking into pieces of the ego (see Fédida 1995).

One day Cynthia arrived for her session in a very agitated state. It was July, a little more than two years since the beginning of the treatment, and the day was very warm. When I opened the door I noticed that she was wearing a short, very elegant, but quite revealing summer dress. She rushed into my office, weeping, and lay down immediately on the couch, covering her legs with a blanket. She then stopped crying and told me about her dream of the previous night, in which she had come for a session only to find the place totally devastated, "as if a bomb had blown up the inside." Nothing was the way it had been before, but while she expected to see charred walls and "all the inside objects destroyed," she noticed that the explosion had "stripped off the coverings" and by way of ruins showed "metal and stone structures, very simple." She asked me whether I planned to leave things that way. In the dream, she suggested that I "keep this emptiness" and above all that I "not replace the objects." "In my dream, you were there but I didn't see you, and I knew that you were talking to me but it was my own voice that I heard."

Immediately afterwards, she said, in the session, that men in the street were starting to come on to her "in a disgusting way, because they don't even know how to fuck a woman." This would always happen whenever she slowed her pace; "I have to walk like a metal blade," she said, and added that she would like to have child, as in a recent dream: "Why is it forbidden to have a child with one's father? It seems that fathers are so afraid of incest with their daughters. That's the only thing that's not acceptable." The relationship she had had for some time with a man of her own age suited her as a good incestuous relationship between brother and sister. Finally, speaking of her tearful outburst when she arrived for her hour, she said that when she saw me the thought that I was going to die had come into her mind. She was surprised to have had this sudden thought upon entering, whereas on the outside a similar thought could occur to her without emotion. And she wondered whether her feeling like crying was really connected to that thought or to her unconscious disappointment at always finding things unchanged here. "Maybe it's because of my dream." And before the session was over, she added: "Now you have to help me make you disappear, because I think your desire to cure me is getting in the way of the human things that I can experience."

REFERENCES

Fédida, P. (1979). Clinique psychopathologique des cas-limites et métapsychologie du fonctionnement-limite. *Psychanalyse à l'Université* 5(17):71–96.
———— (1995). *Le site de l'étranger—La situation psychanalytique.* Paris: P.U.F.
Kernberg, O., Selzer, F., Koenigsberg, M. A., et al. (1989). *Psychodynamic Psychotherapy of Borderline Patients.* New York: Basic Books.
Lacan, J. (1954–1955). *The Seminar of Jacques Lacan. Book II. The Ego in Freud's Theory and in the Technique of Psychoanalysis,* ed. J.-A. Miller, trans. S. Tomaselli. New York: Norton, 1991.

5

The Concept of Borderline in French Psychoanalysis

PROFESSEUR DANIEL WIDLÖCHER, M.D.

We rarely hear an exposition of the history of borderline states as complete and nuanced as Dr. Kouretas's paper on the subject of this pathology that has been singled out for special attention in the United States. As a brief introduction to the discussion, I'd just like to mention the context in which the term arrived in France.

In listening to Dr. Kouretas, I was reminded of a remark made by the late Serge Leclaire when I first met him, at St. Anne's Hospital, in the small group that at that time constituted the French Psychoanalytic Society. He said, "There's a lot of talk about the psychoanalysis of the psychoses, but we ought to get back to treating neuroses." The terms *psychosis* and *neurosis* give a good idea of the spirit in which psychoanalysts worked in those days. We essentially thought in terms of two structures, two frameworks, one in which psychoanalysis was at home—the neuroses—and another into which we ventured—psychosis.

But this structural duality became less and less adequate. When the term *prepsychosis* came on the scene (a term used from a very structural perspective and especially with reference to children), to be followed several years later by the term *borderline*, which we translated as *état-limite*,[1]

---

1. *Translator's note*: literally, "border-state." *Limite* also means "boundary" and "limit," and Dr. Widlöcher will go on to make use of this range of meanings.

we began to see a new possibility opening up, a path leading to two different orientations. The first was to try to revise our nosography. We could
outline a third domain whose boundaries would lie between neurosis and
psychosis, in effect creating a new nosographic entity. This would allow
us to describe a structure, a mode of organization, and a mode of development. Another approach, one to which I have always felt closer, was to
reject the nosographic viewpoint and instead to consider the borderline
state as a limit with respect to any reference, to the nosographic concept as
well as to the concept of psychosis.

But what was on the other side of this border? New boundaries of
thinking about anomalies that neither the paradigm of neurosis nor that of
psychosis had allowed us to see before. Dr. Kouretas' talk illustrated these
anomalies very well: identity diffusion, a concept defined by Erikson in
connection with adolescence and taken up again by Kernberg; projective
identification; the reference to narcissism; emptiness of thought; and so
forth. In the end, the borderline state opens up for us adventures in thought
that we have to explore and not a mental illness that we have to describe.
It is just such adventures that this colloquium will offer us.

Part II

Dialogues and Controversies

6

Empathy and the Therapeutic Dialogue: An Historical-Conceptual Overview of Self Psychology and a Brief Clinical Example

PAUL H. ORNSTEIN, M.D.

INTRODUCTION

In keeping with his view of psychoanalysis as an empirical science, Kohut's psychoanalytic psychology of the self is essentially based on his experience-near conceptualization of his clinical observations of patients he regarded as suffering from various forms of primary self disorder. Just as Freud's theories originated in his study and treatment of the neuroses and were subsequently extended by him over the entire spectrum of psychopathology, so did Kohut's theories originate in the study and treatment of the analyzable self disorders and were subsequently extended by him over the entire spectrum of psychopathology (including the secondary self disorders, i.e., the neuroses). At first he considered the borderline states, together with the psychoses, to be characterized by fragmented selves that never attained cohesiveness, and hence to be in principle unanalyzable. He later modified his stance, developed a more relativistic view, and allowed for the possibility that patients who appear borderline in one therapeutic setting may show a capacity for a cohesive transference in another.

Kohut's initial contribution in his by now classic monograph *The Analysis of the Self* (1971) was hailed as an extension of psychoanalysis because it analytically encompassed hitherto unanalyzable self disorders (originally called narcissistic personality and behavior disorders). Since he still used the language of classic metapsychology to express his ideas, however, few recognized in this first book an emerging new paradigm for psychoanalysis. By the time of his second monograph, *The Restoration of the Self* (1977), Kohut not only found a new language but also expanded his initial conceptions on narcissism into a comprehensive psychology of the self, intensifying the controversy that surrounded his work. With his posthumously published *How Does Analysis Cure?* (1984), Kohut further underscored the methodological importance of empathy, elaborated on the nature of resistance and defense, and advanced his understanding of the nature of psychoanalytic cure, thereby completing the broad outlines and many of the details of his new psychoanalytic paradigm.

It is my task to present a brief survey of the core ideas of self psychology; to define its basic concepts: the *selfobject* and the *selfobject transferences*; to elaborate on the centrality of the method of empathy (i.e., vicarious introspection); and to show how the theory of self psychology and its application in the analytic process depend on the systematic application of the empathic method of observation and on phrasing our interpretations from the perspective of the patient's subjective experience. A clinical vignette should serve as an illustration of the manifestations of a self disorder as well as of the usefulness of some of the core concepts of self psychology, and will provide a demonstration of the manner in which these concepts guide the analyst in his or her participation in the psychoanalytic treatment process.

METHOD AND CORE CONCEPTS OF SELF PSYCHOLOGY

Empathy. As you may already surmise from the preceding introductory comments, self psychology and its approach to the psychoanalytic treatment process cannot be fully appreciated without the recognition of the fundamental role assigned to empathy. Freud demonstrated through his self analysis that introspection and empathic entry into his patients' inner lives constituted the foundation of his psychoanalytic method. For a variety of complex reasons (not germane to this brief presentation) the methodological ground of psychoanalysis then shifted from the subjective world of the patient in Freud's own work (and in the work of many subsequent generations of psychoanalysts) to an external observer's view of the inner world, in the hope that this would make psychoanalysis more scientific. In part, this is what moved introspection and empathy out of their erstwhile central position in psychoanalysis.

In his seminal work on "Introspection, Empathy and Psychoanalysis: An Examination of the Relation Between Mode of Observation and Theory" (1959), Kohut reclaimed this central position for introspection and empathy (i.e., vicarious introspection) in the psychoanalytic enterprise, both in theory formation and in the treatment process. He later redefined the psychoanalytic method as the analyst's sustained empathic immersion in the inner life of patients (especially their transference experiences). In this context he viewed free association and defense analysis as auxiliary methods that made introspection and empathy more reliably available as tools of scientific data-gathering. Later on he also placed introspection and empathy in a central position in the interpretive process as the only avenue of "direct" access to the inner life of another. In Kohut's definition, then, empathy as vicarious introspection became the way in which one could feel oneself and think oneself into the inner life of another. Once we take up the empathic observational position we are led into the domain of clinical psychoanalysis: the patient's subjective experiences, those that are immediately available to awareness as well as those that become available as the analytic work progresses. Special note ought to be made of the fact that these subjective experiences naturally include the way the patient feels about the analyst; that is, these experiences inevitably include the patient's transferences.

The Selfobject Transferences. What distinguishes Kohut's contributions to psychoanalysis is the fact that he discovered new transference configurations, and these served as the basis for all his other discoveries and theoretical formulations; they are thus clinically based and experience-near. It is in his observation and conception of the selfobject transferences that we can most clearly see the linkage between method, findings, and theory. It follows from the method of empathic observation that the analyst will immediately be sensitive to several clusters of the patient's needs, which, under favorable circumstances in the analytic situation, coalesce into one or another of the cohesive, sustained, selfobject transferences. One cluster contains the need for echoing, approval, validation, affirmation, and admiration: the craving for the presence of the gleam in the mother-analyst's eyes, which Kohut subsumed under the broad umbrella of "mirroring"—

the mirror transference. Another cluster contains the need to have an idealizable analyst, in order to partake of his or her power, wisdom, omnipotence, and omniscience so as to acquire internalized values and ideals and the capacity for self soothing and self calming—the idealizing transference. Still another cluster involves the need for attachment to someone like oneself, an alter-ego or a twin, to feel a part of like-minded others, often peers, so as to allow one's innate skills and talents to unfold—the alter-ego or twinship transference.

In these transferences thwarted archaic needs are remobilized, nonjudgmentally accepted, understood, and explained, with the aim of achieving belated maturation and structure building: the acquisition of capacities thwarted by traumatic experiences in infancy and childhood.

The Concept of the Selfobject. It is from the observation and working through of the selfobject transferences that Kohut formulated his foundational construct, the developmental, clinical, and theoretical conception of the selfobject. What is a selfobject (or a "selfobject experience," as is nowadays preferred)? The term refers to certain specific functions provided by an other who is experienced as part of the self. During infancy and childhood such functions by caretakers are crucial to the attainment of a cohesive, well structured self. In an empathic climate of infancy or childhood the functions of the selfobjects will become transmutedly internalized into abiding psychic structures. *Transmuting internalization* (Kohut's term for the process of structure building in infancy and childhood as well as during psychoanalytic treatment) is the process in which, under felicitous circumstances, the archaic precursors of psychic functions in the self-selfobject matrix mature and become readily available later in life. Faulty or missing selfobject functions will be experienced as traumatic during infancy and childhood, leading to a derailed, arrested, or deficient development of the self.

It should now be evident that in self psychology the primacy of the drives has been replaced by the primacy of the selfobject functions or selfobject experiences. This is a drastic change for conceiving personality development in health and illness. And combined with the method of empathic immersion in the subjective experiences of the patient, this change amounts to a new psychoanalytic paradigm.

And now to the clinical vignette, which shows the impact of these methodological and theoretical changes on the conduct and process of analysis.

CLINICAL VIGNETTE[1]

A 25-year-old single industrial engineer came to analysis because he was unable to perform adequately on his new job; he was too preoccupied with himself and had no direction in his life. On the job he could not read or sit still long enough to finish any of his projects, and at home he could not do any work when alone. Only if one of his many girlfriends sat with him in the same room could he read a bit or do some work for brief periods. To exemplify his extreme restlessness and lack of enduring relationships, he related immediately that he had to move from one woman to the next almost nightly, obtaining no pleasure from any of these (often somewhat bizarre) sexual exploits. He added that these served the purpose of draining him of his tensions, and that the women were a better outlet than masturbation. It soon emerged that when he was bored he immediately had to search for some exciting, self-stimulating experience, and when he was overstimulated and could not calm down spontaneously he had to search for some calming experience: masturbation, sex, hot showers, cold showers, or running around the block, which served more or less either purpose.

During the initial phase of the analysis the patient continued to enact his various methods of self stimulation and self calming with undiminished intensity and frequency. At the same time he latched on to the analyst and the analysis with an addiction-like intensity and felt that being able to talk unhindered, with the analyst's attention fastened exclusively on him, made these sessions a tremendously helpful "outlet." He inundated the analyst with the most minute details of his daily activities, especially his sexual exploits, and expected to elicit the analyst's admiration for the "Don Juan" in him. But instead of responding to the content of these communications, the analyst remarked (in a Monday session) that the patient had seemed more frantic than usual during the preceding weekend; it sounded as though he had had to engage in a variety of sadistic exploits under some pressure, even though he did not want to do this, in order to manage his tension and restlessness. The analyst's aim was to recognize with the patient his states of over- or understimulation, along with his habitual modes of coping with them. This led to an interesting response on the patient's part, which heralded the developing idealizing transference. He was much calmer the next day and expressed the hope that he might be able just to stay home, put his feet up on a chair, and read. He then added: "You commented yesterday that perhaps I had been so keyed up for so long that I found it hard to slow down and relax. I must

---

1. This highly condensed vignette was first published in Ornstein 1982, and a more comprehensive presentation of the analysis as a whole was published in Ornstein 1978.

say, of all the comments anybody ever made to me yet, all have been what I have thought of myself, too, before, but this was different." He kept thinking about it and wondered whether he could give up these frantic activities, but he decided that he could not do so yet.

The patient, although at first disappointed that he could not be analyzed by the city's most prominent psychoanalyst, now began to feel not only that he was well understood, but that his analyst understood him in a unique way. The development of the idealizing transference was underway, which reduced the frequency and intensity of the patient's enactments. These were well contained as long as the analyst responded adequately and understood the patient's various communications. After the consolidation of the idealizing transference only its unempathic disruption resulted in the renewed outbreak of the patient's sadistic enactments. It was then possible to trace those intra-analytic experiences that had originally led to the disruption of the transference and to understand the dynamic (and also the genetic) reasons for the patient's repeated fragmentations. Such reconstructions would usually re-establish the continuity and cohesiveness of the transference until the next inevitable disruption.

I shall now illustrate the depth and intensity of the idealizing transference, its disruptions, and the working-through process it usually permitted. Along with this patient's idealization of the analyst, his own helplessness, powerlessness, and feelings of insignificance moved into the analytic experience. Once he asked thoughtfully, with some despair in his voice: "Why do I have to have *you* acknowledge that I feel good before *I know* I feel good?" His own further reflections were of considerable significance:

> [He felt that he was] a splat on the wall—when you throw hot rubber against the wall, it hardens and is like an octopus with suckers on it, clinging to the wall. Then nothing matters, only the clinging like a splat. It can't tolerate the rumbling of the wall. Any disconnection is a threat to the survival of the splat. That's how I am with T. [his girlfriend] and with you. I want you to be the wall—shut up and listen! If I would no longer have to be a splat on the wall, it would be a major accomplishment.

He could feel strong, powerful, and important only in his attachment to the idealized analyst. Whatever disrupted this attachment—weekend separations, vacations, or even slight unempathic rebuffs—all felt like the "rumbling of the wall," endangering "the splat."

The analysis of the disruptions of this idealizing attachment invariably brought back some relevant early memories. Disappointments in the idealized analyst led to renewed increase in masturbation and a preoccupation with what he called a "fetishistic drive to look at girls' legs that doesn't listen to reason. It's a hateful, mean, needful pursuit of women. I am chasing them because I feel unloved; I withdraw into myself; I masturbate because I am unloved, turning to myself as if I were my own mother."

The analyst's absences for scientific meetings, for example, and the emotional withdrawal that may have been occasioned by the advance preparation for them, provoked rage and revengeful death wishes—and then led to considerable insight. "I seem to care about you only as you affect me—because my life is dependent upon you. I need you without a blemish [i.e., as a better mother and father than he had had], but it's such selfish stuff not to give a damn about you."

Disruptions of the transference were now experienced as "big rips" or "big cracks in the wall," endangering the "splat." But the analytic "repair" of the rips and cracks in the wall slowly transformed the splat from "an octopus with suckers on it" to one with "legs and feet, with a chance for separate existence." The transformation was slow, with frequent regressions.

The details of the working-through process cannot be illustrated further in this brief presentation. It should only be added that this process ultimately led to a lessening of the analyst's importance as an idealized parent imago and a concomitant acquisition by the patient of an increasing capacity for self soothing and self calming via transmuting internalizations: the bit-by-bit acquisition of new capacities. The resulting greater ability to regulate inner tension was at first more apparent outside of the analytic situation. In the analysis, a further pathognomonic regression revived the grandiose-exhibitionistic self in the mirror transference. It was this secondary mirror transference, then, that carried the analysis to its resolution and termination.

A dream will illustrate this shift to the mirror transference, in which the grandiose-exhibitionistic self demanded admiration and affirmation:

> I was fishing in this pond or lake. There were lots of fish. I could see them. Cast the jitterbug and was bringing them in. Maybe my Dad was there; I don't know. Decided to go after something better, caught a big turtle. Got scared and ran ashore.

His associations included many memories of fishing trips when he would have wanted his father to be there, to witness and to admire his prowess.

He realized that the anxiety in the dream related to his current wish that the analyst admire him and praise him.

For most of the early phases of this mirror transference the patient experienced the analytic situation as a "stage" and his own intra-analytic "performance" as a "floor show," in which he had to have the center of the stage and the approving-admiring "clapping" of the analyst. Highly sensitive to the analyst's responses and to their absence, he was easily overstimulated and often felt intruded upon by the analyst's interventions. He finally said that he wished he could lie down in a room full of cotton, where he would be protected against overstimulation and its consequences of falling apart. The occasions for overstimulation became increasingly more manageable, and transient fragmentations, though still numerous, were of shorter duration, until finally they occurred only in dreams. It was around these experiences that the analytic work in this sector of the personality took place during the termination phase, consolidating the patient's ability to regulate his inner tension and the severe fluctuations of his self-esteem. A dream during the last week of the analysis illustrates an important aspect of what the patient has accomplished. This was "a great dream of success," he said:

> T. and I were out fishing and I saw a muskellunge. It came right up, took my bait, and I said to T., "You got to net this fish; you got to bring your line in, shut the motor, and bring your net in." She didn't listen. Some guy on the shore was yelling, 'Take a picture of it; hey, do this, hey do that!" In exasperation I reached over with one hand, got the net, and I got him—that's easy! Big fish. I was tickled to death; in my family that is a great thing. We went ashore, walked along a promenade lit up with bright colored lights at night, and we've got the muskie with us.

The work on this dream led us to what the patient called his "final landing." He was pleased with his dream and said that if he had not been able to catch a fish like that in the past, the next best thing was to dream about it. He felt lucky and wondered whether he was trying to fulfill his father's expectation of him in the dream, or the analyst's, or his own? Did he still want to show off the giant catch to the analyst-father for approval and admiration, the approval and admiration he never had from his father? He thought the analyst was ashore, yelling to him what to do but he said to himself, "Quit listening to him and net your own fish."

DISCUSSION

The preceding vignette illustrates various facets of the patient's self disorder as well as the sequential mobilization at first of the idealizing transference and then of the mirror transference. The most pervasive aspect of the disorder was the patient's profound inability to regulate inner tension and the many sexualized efforts to cope with it, all of which had an "addiction-like" quality and were compulsively pursued. It would have been easy for the analyst to be seduced by the content of the patient's free associations and attempt to analyze them. Instead, he focused on the patient's subjective experiences and repeatedly offered his tentative understanding of what the patient's various enactments were designed to accomplish regarding his tension regulation. These efforts paid off; the patient felt understood and the development of an idealizing transference was visibly in the offing. The patient's own imagery conveyed the depth and intensity of his idealizations. It was important to accept them rather than interpret them as defenses against some underlying hidden hostility. It was necessary and helpful to focus on moments of disruption, to explain why they were experienced as so painful and how the patient was attempting to cope with them. Here again it was not the pursuit of the psychic content of the state of fragmentation that furthered the analytic process, but reconstructing what happened—what had led to the momentary fragmentation—and showing the patient the function of his sexualizations and rages that emerged as a consequence of the disruption of the idealizing transference.

The clinical vignette further illustrates the shift in the nature of the transference, in the emergence of archaic grandiosity and a wish to show off, first in a dream and then more pervasively in the patient's intra-analytic enactments and free associations. The mirror transference established itself and became the target of the working-through process. Here too interventions had to be directed toward explaining the disruptions and their consequences, which invariably brought back some significant memories and expanded the analytic process in depth and in breadth.

REFERENCES

Kohut, H. (1959). Introspection, empathy and psychoanalysis: an examination of the relation between mode of observation and theory. *Journal of the American Psychoanalytic Association* 7:459–483.

————— (1971). *The Analysis of the Self.* New York: International Universities Press.

————— (1977). *The Restoration of the Self.* New York: International Universities Press.

————— (1984). *How Does Analysis Cure?* Chicago: University of Chicago Press.

Ornstein, P. H. (1978). The working through of a mirror transference. In *The Psychology of the Self: A Case Book*, ed. A. Goldberg, pp. 124–157. New York: International Universities Press.

————— (1982). On the psychoanalytic psychotherapy of primary self pathology. In *Annual Review of Psychiatry*, ed. L. Greenspoon, pp. 498–510. Washington, DC: American Psychiatric Press.

The Signifier at the Crossroads between Sexuality and Trauma: Response to the Paper of Paul H. Ornstein, M.D.

PROFESSEUR MONIQUE DAVID-MÉNARD

In his summary of Kohut's theory and in his case example Paul Ornstein offers an answer to the question: What, in a patient's psychic material, must be recognized by the analyst in order for an analytic process to take place?

A CONCEPTUALIZATION OF THE CLINICAL OBSERVATIONS

The patient's compulsive sexuality and the lack of direction in his life are repeated in the analysis through what the author calls the mirror transference, that is, the craving for a gleam of approval in the mother-analyst's eyes. Another transference involves the idealization of the analyst, in which the patient partakes of the omnipotence and omniscience that he attributes to the analyst and can thereby internalize a sense of values and a capacity for tension regulation. In the dynamics of the treatment this magic enables Dr. Ornstein's patient to tolerate, in a manner different from his sadistic sexual acting out, the alternation of omnipotence and severe depression that had previously governed his life outside of his awareness.

In a kind of dream evoked by the context of the treatment, the patient says that he feels like a splat on a wall, like hot rubber that sticks when thrown against a wall, like an octopus that clings to the wall with its suckers and fears the rumbling of the wall because it might not survive if it can no longer remain attached. As he brings into the transference the issues involved in his frenetic activities, the patient gives a shape to his anxieties and can therefore cope with them.

But this is to assume that the analyst understands these disintegration experiences in and of themselves, without measuring them against a presumed normative condition of instinctual drives. The novelty of his approach as compared with previous psychoanalytic reference points lies in its abandonment of the practice of interpreting images and dream reports as phases in drive integration. The analyst no longer has to interpret transferential aggression as a resistance connected to defenses against a genetic process of oedipal maturation. He accepts the patient's material in the register in which it is presented, and as a result the patient can bear the threat of disintegration that forms the counterpoint to his sadistic fantasies and to the erotic and transferential dependence that he was at first unable to tolerate. Repetition in the transference (which the patient no doubt feels able to risk because of the quality of the analyst's listening) gradually allows these threats, which had been enacted in the patient's extra-transferential erotic life, to become linked to transferential reveries and eventually to dreams. The compulsion to act out is thereby modified.

A COMPARATIVE THEORETICAL VIEW

As an analyst who was not trained in the analysis of defenses or in the formation of the ego, nor in the theory according to which drives have to find whole objects in a process of normative development ending in genitality, I find this clinical presentation easy to follow in one sense: it would seem that Kohut and Lacan, though taking different paths, both distanced themselves from an overly simple genetic concept of sexuality. But in contrast to the interpretative method Freud originally established, the inner world became objectivized in an attempt to make psychoanalytic theory scientific. The theories of drives, of the ego, and of defense mechanisms are part of this objectivization, and the analyst is transformed into an observer who stands outside the manifestations of his patient's intrapsychic life. Normativity of analytic listening in regard to drives is a further entailment of this objectivization, since analyzing a patient's defenses implies viewing his material as a refusal to attain the "adult" sexual ideal supposedly represented by the analyst himself.

In Kohut's (1979) "The Two Analyses of Mr. Z," the analyst asserts that in the first treatment he was unaware of what was really at stake in the clinical material precisely because he viewed Mr. Z's dreams and his dependency on his mother in terms of an unwillingness to confront his oedipal rivalry with his father. The analyst was considered to represent the adult sexuality towards which the healthy part of the patient's ego was striving, and Mr. Z's pregenital sexuality was a resistance to be overcome via the transference. In the second analysis, on the other hand, Kohut emphasizes the fact that his patient's identity was bound up in his mother's pathology and that his struggle centered around his inclusion in maternal fantasies. The analyst now supported the so-called archaic sexuality and no longer sought to bring it into a normative line. Mr. Z became able to reevaluate his relationship to his father not by means of access to genitality, nor by the working through of oedipal rivalry, but because he discovered that he had had a father after all. Now that the analytic situation facilitated such a discovery, he reinvested certain memories of his father that had lain dormant until then.

Kohut also emphasizes that this discovery was a kind of creation within the transference, that is, that the points of commonality that Mr. Z "discovered" between the father of his childhood and the analyst were like inventions of his, or at any rate were connected to the initiative of which he became capable at this point in the second treatment. This aspect of transferential invention, made possible by the way the analyst listens to so-called archaic material, is also very apparent in Dr. Ornstein's clinical example. And this work that takes place by virtue of the transference reminds me of Lacan's (1964/1981) observation in Seminar XI that the unconscious has to do not with the unreal or with the derealized, but with the *non-realized*,[1] a point also made by Freud (1895) in connection with the diphasic nature

---

1. "*Non-realized*" refers to what awaits realization in the child's sexual development, since sexuality is established in two phases: the infantile period and puberty, separated by the latency period. In the context of treatment the realization that remains in abeyance is the patient's ability to formulate his desire and the analyst's ability to recognize it. The unconscious is the inexhaustible storehouse of what remains pending—of dreams, for example. This is more important for Lacan than the common view that the unconscious is unreal (that is, imaginary) or derealized (delusional).

of sexuality, with the belated primary memories of which symptoms consist, and so forth.[2]

But then we must ask whether, in this case example, we are really dealing with pathology found in specific patients called *borderlines*, or whether what we call archaic material is not the material of every analysis.

As for Lacan, he did not attribute to Freud the genetic theory of drives that he wanted to distinguish from his own position. In Seminar XI he makes it clear that drives are the speaking being's modes of relating to otherness, orality corresponding to the demand addressed to the Other and anality to the Other's demand. Thus it no longer makes sense to refer pregenital sexuality to the archaic. In clinical practice, he says, the patient tends to lose himself in the idealization of the Other, as happens with falling in love. If this idealization, accepted by the analyst, is in one sense what allows the analysis to take place, in another sense it represents a hindrance that the analyst must mitigate by bringing the patient back to what, in the vicissitudes of his drives, makes his existence unique in a way that cannot be reduced to any totalization of an object.[3]

In contrast to Paul Ornstein and Kohut, Lacan does not throw the baby of drives out with the bath water of defense analysis. Nor does he use the term *empathy*; that is to say, he does not criticize Freud's objectivism by appealing to notions that seem to him to accord little importance to the asymmetrical setup of the treatment and to the way in which theory is able to account for it. Empathy, introspection, access to the other's inner life—all these terms seem to Lacan to be a legacy of nineteenth-century psychology. To go beyond Freud's objectivism it is not enough to return to a subjectivism that is its counterpart. We must, instead, conceptualize in a new way the division of the subject that is called for by psychoanalytic practice.

---

2. Freud is referring to the fact that the events triggering the formation of a symptom (especially phobic symptoms, as in the case of Emma) are not in themselves pathogenic. They become so only by virtue of an associative link to the memory of a traumatic childhood event that remained in abeyance for the subject until puberty.

3. See Lacan 1964/1981, pp. 167f., 181–184, 194. According to Lacan, the object of desire is not primarily the object that brings satisfaction but instead the object around which the drive turns. In the metaphor of the circuit of drives, the trajectory begins at a place on the erogenous body of the subject and goes towards an object on the body of the other. The way out and the way back on this trajectory are not the same and do not "capture" the object, which, consequently, does not fulfill the narcissistic need of the lover.

But this debate of Lacan's with terms inherited from pre-Freudian psychology must also be set in the context of postwar French philosophy. Lacan separates himself from phenomenological and existentialist concepts of intersubjectivity on the grounds that they are part of a philosophy of consciousness that Freud had shown to be unworkable.[4] This is why an analyst influenced by Lacan encounters some initial difficulty in situating self psychology, even if his own practice shares some of its elements.

The terminological differences that reveal both differing cultural contexts and, undoubtedly, divergent views on the theory of treatment have implications as far as technique is concerned. A Lacanian analyst finds it hard to accept the need to work with a mirror transference, since for Lacan the model of the mirror has an entirely different meaning. It refers to the fact that every identification entails a degree of illusion that, in the life of every desiring subject, perpetuates the original mirror situation. When the child recognizes his own mirror image at an age when he does not have motor autonomy and is still an *in-fant* (literally, unable to speak), this identification with his own image is in part a decoy, a lure. Although it gives him the reassuring illusion of autonomy and thus has a positive effect on his maturation, especially in the area of language, it also implies that any desire for wholeness necessarily involves a threat of disintegration.

To the extent that an analysis is more a locus of truth concerning the processes of desire than it is a locus of maturation understood in the genetic sense, an analysand—like the patient Dr. Ornstein describes—must confront self-representations in which he does not coincide with himself. The patient's reverie makes use of the analyst as a mirror reflecting back to him the part of his image that is unacceptable to him, that is separate from him and yet at the same time constitutes him in his relations with other people. The analyst is a good mirror not because he accurately reflects the patient's image as mirrors ordinarily do, but precisely because, in the sequence of oral, anal, and, as Lacan says, invocatory drives (for there are sonorities in this reverie),[5] he reveals what it is that cuts the patient off

---

4. Lacan worked and wrote at the same time as Sartre and Merleau-Ponty, but for him the division of the subject cannot be conceptualized in an approach that privileges consciousness and meaning; what is needed is a structural model of the unconscious and of consciousness.

5. For Lacan the invocatory drive invests the voice of the subject who is seeking to address another subject.

from himself. For a Lacanian, in short, it is also in the register of the partial drives themselves that the impossibility of wholeness, of the complete fulfillment of our sexual desires, must be analyzed. Neurosis is connected with an over-eager dream of completeness that spares the subject the experience of anxiety that inevitably emerges when the corner of the veil is lifted from the enticing illusion that is involved in our identifications. This is why it is so important, in Dr. Ornstein's case example, that images produced in the transference enable the patient to tolerate the threat of disintegration so that he no longer needs to spend his life averting it by means of acting out. Such images serve as a container for the patient's psyche.

To return to the details of the case in order to compare the terms in which Dr. Ornstein describes his work with the ones I myself would use, I would certainly not say that in his two related dreams about fishing the patient is seeking to arouse the analyst's admiration and respect in the context of a mirror transference. For, as the author himself makes clear, the analyst here is being summoned up not as a person but as a *persona* in the Latin sense of the word, a theatrical type containing within itself the relationship between various psychic figures: in these fishing dreams the patient, supported by his attribution of certain traits to the analyst, replays his relationship to his father.

What is really important here is not the person of the analyst, nor only the person of the father as it appears in the patient's memories, but rather this psychic figure that is woven in the relationship between analyst and patient. Since the actual father in the patient's history left his actual mark on his memories and on his formation as a subject of desire, this weaving together enables the patient not to invent a father for himself in the analysis, but to reopen the way to what had remained unrealized in his relationship to a psychic figure from whom he expected recognition. The patient's frantic search, at certain points in the treatment, for his analyst's agreement and approval can be understood as the beginnings of the search for what Lacan calls the symbolic, precisely because it does not coincide with any specific figures but is created in the space between patient and analyst by virtue of the transference. Because the analyst's desire[6] gives substance

---

6. The analyst's desire is his initiative, his taking responsibility, as he urges the patient's desire to express itself in words.

to this intervening space composed of the relation among several scenes, we would not say that he understands his patient. Understanding would prevent the patient from constituting this space as a space and would confine him in the relationship that Lacan, contrasting it with the symbolic, calls imaginary, a relationship in which the patient would have contact only with real people who, as they usually do, would block his access to his own anxiety.

But even if the Lacanian concepts of Symbolic, Imaginary, and Real invite us to use other terms in describing the transference, it is clear from Dr. Ornstein's account that he did not confuse himself with the imaginary figures that he agreed to represent temporarily in the transference.

THE QUESTION OF THE SELF

As far as the clinical material is concerned, the reader could wish for a fuller account of the connection between the patient's symptoms, the contents of his transferential fantasy (the octopus on the wall), and those of his dreams that have a reorganizing function. What was the signifying connection between the images that were evoked at the beginning (the octopus-suckers stuck onto the analytic screen) and the two dreams with similarly aquatic content? What is represented by the sea, fishing, and the sea creatures in the patient's family history? Isn't the signifying material the trace, the matrix of the interweaving of the traumatic and the erotic that constitutes the failures in the formation of a self?

A final question arises about the meaning of this "self" as contrasted with the Lacanian notion of the subject. If the drives can be conceptualized otherwise than in the context of a genetic theory and the analysis of defenses, why is it necessary to oppose the self and the drive? Dr. Ornstein tells us that the self must be allowed to become cohesive for the first time in the patient's life, but it is difficult to see what this cohesiveness would involve if not the capacity, acquired thanks to the analysis, for tolerating a certain incoherence that the patient must not reject but, instead, recognize within himself. Should we really separate from the drives this pole of identity that Ornstein calls the self? But then again, we might ask the Lacanians how they would connect the subject with the drives, in view of the fact that Lacan says that drives are acephalic. . . .

REFERENCES

Freud, S. (1895). Project for a scientific psychology. *Standard Edition* 1: 281–397.

Kohut, H. (1979). The two analyses of Mr. Z. *International Journal of Psycho-Analysis* 60:3–27.

Lacan, J. (1964/1981). *The Four Fundamental Concepts of Psycho-Analysis*, ed. J.-A. Miller, trans. A. Sheridan. New York: Norton.

Excerpts from the Discussion

Radmila Zygouris: In connection with the discussion of empathy, a very controversial term here in France, I'd like to note that Freud's concept of *Einfühlung* does not entail reciprocity. It involves the mother's ability to sense something about her child even before the child can speak. If there were no maternal *Einfühlung* she would not be able to interpret her child's crying and its different movements.

Juan-David Nasio: It's true that "empathy" is not part of our usual vocabulary, but it's interesting to consider whether what this word designates corresponds to anything in French clinical practice. According to Dr. Ornstein, empathy is vicarious introspection, feeling and thinking oneself into the inner life of the other. This corresponds to a state that I experience when I work with certain patients and that precedes the emergence of the interpretation. I wouldn't say "feeling and thinking myself," since these aren't terms we use. I want to use the term "fantasy." First the analyst perceives the fantasy in the analysand, then he identifies with one of the figures in it, and—this isn't always the case—he may be able to name or say what that figure would have said.

Janine Chasseguet-Smirgel: Even non-Lacanians get angry at the idea of considering the analytic situation to be a symmetrical one between patient and analyst. It is profoundly asymmetrical; the entire setting, the entire frame, is in effect a product of asymmetry. We try to plunge the patient into a kind of regression, and the invisible analyst, the recumbent analysand, the fixed sessions (not always the rule in Lacanian practice), all promote a regression on the part of the patient and not on the part of the analyst.

As far as the idealizing transference is concerned, I think self psychologists may emphasize something that seems to me—and to a French author like Bela Grunberger—to be entirely natural and indispensable to the very constituting of the analytic relationship and to taking the plunge into the analytic situation. And it is very close to the distinction Freud made between narcissistic neurosis (his original name for psychosis) and transference neurosis. When beginning treatment an analysand projects a hope onto the analyst, which leads to his projecting his narcissism, his ego ideal, onto him. This situation must of course not continue to the end of the analysis, but it is indispensable for getting the process underway.

Jacques Hassoun: Dr. Kouretas raised the issue of whether Kohut's theory isn't that shadow zone that is a kind of protest against the delimitation of two structures: neurosis and psychosis. But isn't Lacanian theory, which pays no special attention to borderlines, also able to open up such a gray area?

With regard to empathy, the question arises as to the place from which the analyst speaks, from which he intervenes, when he invokes the concept of empathy, since there has to be a third place in order for there to be an interpretation. If empathy means engulfing the other, then there is no analysis but instead a psychotization of the analytic setting. Although we come from different theoretical orientations we have all explored the issue of the third space, the space from which the analyst intervenes and that must be there in order for analysis to take place.

(French Analyst): I'd like to hear a bit more about the theory of psychic conflict, since this seems to be missing in what both sides are saying. For example, you have been emphasizing the value of empathy, but what do we do when we can't stand a patient, when we want to hurt him?

Paul Ornstein: Let me first say that I deeply appreciate Professor Monique David Ménard's immersion in the paper I presented and her having come up with a complex discussion, some of which I feel understood me and some of which passed me by. I'd first like to say something about how to listen to clinical presentations done from another perspective. I came to Paris determined to enter the field, absolutely unknown to me, of Lacanian analysis, which in the past I had unfortunately dismissed as something that didn't touch my analytic work.

Since I have been here, I really feel rewarded in having opened my-self to looking at it from the inside. Now, we can't completely enter an-other perspective; that is impossible. We bring our baggage with us, and that limits our capacity. It is the same with empathy: empathy is a univer-sal capacity in us, but given our personal experiences, training, and so on we have only a narrow band of capacity which needs to be broadened and widened—through further experiences with patients who are dissimilar to us, through encountering other cultures, or by coming to Paris and learn-ing about Lacan. And this is what allows us to enter more successfully into these other perspectives. Vicarious introspection, as I think both Dr. Nasio and Dr. Hassoun seem to understand, allows us to try to enter the inner world imaginatively. We can't penetrate; we can't be accurate. It is in the dialogue that our empathic capacity, or its limit, evolves. We cannot say, "Ah! I empathized; I understood!" Until the patient *feels* understood, what we may claim is of no great significance in the analytic process.

I was particularly appreciative of Dr. Janine Chasseguet-Smirgel's comment about idealization, because I had the feeling that there is a con-tact point which I knew about between us, and Bela Grunberger, and your work on idealization. Idealization is an absolute necessity, but, as you said, it needs to get transmuted and changed in the course of the analytic pro-cess so that it doesn't remain as archaic as at the beginning. As far as asym-metry is concerned, in the past we accepted a great deal of asymmetry— "analyst here/patient here." We have begun to feel, over the last decade or so, that the expert in the room about the patient's inner world is the patient. We have to make the effort to listen in such a way that we can understand, and communicate that understanding to the patient. Now, if we have a blueprint of the unconscious, or theories about conflicts or the stages of drives, we think we are the expert, but we are not. On what level do we feel that the patient has, in a sense, the last word about his or her own inner experience? That will determine how we conduct the analysis.

7

Primary Self Pathology and the Process of Healing: A Clinical Example

ANNA ORNSTEIN, M.D.

My patient, Dr. White, a research scientist, has been in treatment for nearly three years. He is a short, very slightly built man. His pale, heavily lined forehead and graying beard are in sharp contrast to his very lean body and extremities, which look as if they belonged to a 12-year-old boy rather than to a 45-year-old man. He has all the symptoms associated with a severe case of anorexia, except that of a distorted body image: he feels thin and is fully aware of the dangers involved in keeping his weight barely above acceptable limits. Like others with this disorder, Dr. White is preoccupied with food all the time. He weighs himself several times a day, engages in lengthy exercises every day, and is compelled to deprive himself of anything that could potentially give him pleasure. The patient sets his alarm for 2:30 A.M. but frequently gets up before that in order to complete a lengthy routine of weightlifting and running. With his near-starvation diet, strenuous exercises, and chronic sleep deprivation, he is always exhausted and has to take several short naps during the day.

The patient first came to see me because he feared that his marriage was on the brink: he feared that his wife would soon ask him to leave because he had not been able to be a father to his children, or a husband to her. His own parents had divorced before he was 3 and he had not seen his mother since then; he does not have any memory of her and does not know what she looked like. He only knows that his mother was alcoholic and that, after the divorce, his father did not permit her to visit him and his sister (who is two years younger). Only recently did he learn from his father that he was repeatedly hospitalized for broken bones, bruises all over his body, and burns on his hands and feet, injuries that his mother had inflicted on him. His father, also a scientist, had extremely high standards for the children's behavior and raised them with strict puritanical methods. Dr. White was always an "A" student, but he does not recall having ever felt satisfaction, nor that his father ever expressed satisfaction with him or with his accomplishments: he was always left with the feeling that he could have done better. In spite of the fact that he has been able to secure prestigious and good-sized grants over the years, he is constantly worried that he will be asked to leave his current job because he does not meet the high standards of the institution where he works.

Dr. White had been a chubby child, and his father, in order to teach him good eating habits and self restraint, did not allow him to enter the kitchen before going to school. Instead, he would bring the patient an orange for breakfast to his room. Father also stressed the importance of athletic activities, and the patient became a successful long-distance runner, earning several trophies.

Dr. White does not recall any time when he was able to ask for physical or emotional comfort freely and directly. As far as he can remember, he has been living with a wall firmly erected around his emotions. He no longer experiences the longing for close emotional contact in its original form; this is now mixed with shame, and it finds expression in a behavior pattern in which he presents himself in a pitiful, sorrowful way: he walks with his shoulders hunched, frequently emits a deep sigh, and whenever he has the opportunity he makes degrading remarks about himself or about his work. This is a behavior pattern in which the masochist's bid for affection expresses hidden sadism (Berliner 1958). Predictably, this sadomasochistic behavior (in which sadism is expressed indirectly by making "others," his current transference objects, responsible for his mental suffering) does not produce compassion in those who witness it. Instead, the opposite is true—friends and family turn away from him.

Because of this indirect communication of displaced rage, Dr. White suffered repeated rejections by the very people whose accepting and validating responses he needed and wanted most urgently. Eventually he realized that, even when others were responsive to his indirect appeals for emotional comfort, he could not reciprocate. For while he had an enormous need for affection he was unable to give any.

Since his wife became Dr. White's most important transference object, he was strongly motivated to display this behavior in her presence. In the course of treatment, he began to pay closer attention to this feel-sorry-for-me behavior and to recognize the importance of the context in which it was likely to emerge. For example, one day when he was particularly successful at work and was looking forward to going home in a reasonably good mood, he realized that as he was nearing his home he became increasingly more irritable and depressed. By the time he reached the house, he convinced himself that the good feelings of the day were nothing but an illusion. He realized then, he said to me, that "presenting myself as a failure is the best way for me to communicate my despair. I am afraid she [his wife] will see me feeling good."

The longing for a caring and accepting response became associated not only with shame, but also with jealousy and envy of those whom he experienced as receiving attention while he felt excluded or dismissed. In his jealous rages he would humiliate and verbally abuse his 4-year-old son, the recipient of his mother's affection. The patient was convinced that it was the birth of this child that "pushed [him] over the brink," and he dated his depression, his suicidality, and the anorexia to the birth of this child. Not long ago he told of an episode in which he literally tore the child away from his mother because he was touching her breast. Apparently the son touching the wife's breast had activated an intense need for physical comfort and intimacy. Once the need for the hug and the touch was activated, so was his sense of frustration that caused him either to strike out impulsively or to withdraw in hurt and anger. The angry and guilt-provoking retreat would say in essence: "You are depriving me; you are a bad, withholding mother, and even if you tried to give to me, I know it would not be enough—or not exactly what I need."

After a rageful outburst at his son for his ordinary 4-year-old behavior, Dr. White would experience intense shame and he would become acutely suicidal. In order to protect himself as well as his family from his outbursts and the shame and guilt that would follow them, he frequently remained at work until late at night and left the house before the children woke up in the morning. He rarely participated in family activities, and in fear that his fantasy of a "perfect holiday" would not be fulfilled, he would take on extra assignments and would stay at work during the holidays. At these times he would be filled with self pity and a renewed determination to kill himself before the next major holiday.

Beside their 4-year-old son, the couple has an 8-year-old daughter; his love for his daughter and feeling loved by her at first kept him from thinking about suicide. Following the birth of the son, however, he came to believe that the daughter, too, would be better off without him. He has kept a vial of a highly toxic substance in his drawer for the last four years. When he feels particularly desperate, he finds solace in knowing that he could put an end to his mental anguish anytime he wanted to. However, he complains of lacking courage to kill himself: "I'm tired of living, but too scared to die," he says frequently.

Because of the severity of his depression and the suicide risk, the patient was put on an anti-depressant that, after some time, began to relieve the symptoms of anorexia and gave him some relief from the depression. However, the medication did not alter the sadomasochistic behavior pattern and he continued to feel emotionally isolated.

COMMENTS ON THE NATURE OF THE PSYCHOPATHOLOGY: A SELF-PSYCHOLOGICAL PERSPECTIVE

How do we understand the self-degrading behavior, the suicidal depression, and the periodic outbursts of rage from a self-psychological perspective? Self psychology, like all other psychoanalytic theories, has to be able to explain the nature of the psychopathology in keeping with its theory of development. The development of this form of psychopathology (as with all other forms of personality disorder) reaches deep into childhood. In cases of self-degrading, suicidal behavior, we postulate two interrelated traumata: one is the absence or partial absence of phase-appropriate caretaker responsiveness to infantile grandiosity and exhibitionism, and the second is the possible coupling with physical and/or emotional abuse of caretaker indifference to the child's legitimate need for affirmation.

The developmental theory of self psychology asserts that it is the phase-appropriate validation of infantile grandiosity and exhibitionism by caretakers that makes possible the transformation of narcissistic structures into pride and pleasure in one's self and in one's activities. Self-esteem is gradually built by the caretakers' unambivalent responsiveness to the child's uniqueness and his/her accomplishments. When caretaker responsiveness is absent or faulty, infantile grandiosity persists in the adult psyche and patients will cling to a sense of absolute perfection with tenacity. Failure to develop adequate transformation of infantile grandiosity and exhibitionism is also responsible for a lack of vigor and aliveness, a form of characterological depression. The faulty consolidation of the nuclear self results in extreme vulnerability to slights and to any indication of nonacceptance or rejection, to which patients react with unforgiving rage or withdrawal. When physical abuse is added to this scenario, the result is that the child—and later the adult—experiences him/herself as evil and undeserving of love. The suicidal ideas that these patients express appear to be the consequence of self loathing and a feeling that what they are experiencing cannot be understood by others and cannot be shared. Since they feel emotionally isolated, death offers relief and suicide acquires a tremendous appeal.

In Dr. White's case, the neglect and physical abuse by one parent (the mother) was coupled with conditional acceptance by the other. When acceptance and appreciation are thus conditional, the child grows up with a nagging sense of self doubt, doubt about his intellectual and/or physical abilities and attractiveness. Though these are frequently bright and accomplished individuals, their achievements are not accompanied by a sense of satisfaction, pride, and contentment.

In childhood, the frustrations related to the developmentally needed responses and the suffering due to the physical abuse are endured silently, the reactive rage remaining unconscious in order to preserve an already precarious connection to the rejecting or abusive caretakers. The defensive psychological structures that protect the poorly developed, fragmentation-prone self from retraumatization are also the very ones that constitute the building blocks of the now evolving symptomatic behavior. Defensive psychological structures with unarticulated rage at their core are responsible for chronically embittered, paranoid attitudes, and for various degrees of depression, criminality and suicidality. In severe self disorders, all these personality features may be present with one or the other taking center stage.

COMMENTS ON THE TREATMENT PROCESS

While it is not possible to describe in a few observations a therapeutic process that sometimes takes years to evolve, I shall try to convey its essence by citing a brief segment from Dr. White's treatment.

> More often than not, the patient would arrive for our twice-weekly sessions profoundly depressed. He would enter the office with a sigh, lower himself into the chair as if that were too much of an effort, and express a sense of profound hopelessness. In this particular session, the patient told me about a poem that touched him deeply. He was particularly impressed by a line that went: "No one knows the depth of his fellow man's suffering." I said to him that he probably liked this line because it expressed his own feeling that nobody could possibly know what it is like to go through life feeling the way he does. The patient nodded in agreement, and I added that we understood from previous discussions that the pitiful, feel-sorry-for-me behavior that he cannot stop from repeating was intended to demonstrate his mental suffer-

ing so that those around him, especially his wife and myself, could have an idea of what he was experiencing. He was convinced, I said to him, that if others knew how he felt this would make him feel better, that sharing the pain was the only thing that could possibly relieve his mental anguish. "Yes," he said, "I don't know how others feel about it, but this is the most important thing to me: I want others to know what it's like for me. I also think Joan [his wife] is responsible for the way I feel. She never puts her arms around me. She is never affectionate." There was silence, since we both knew that even when his wife expressed affection he would fend her off because he would perceive a flaw in the way she expressed it; he experienced her as cold and withholding of affection, rather than as someone who could, potentially, compensate him for past deprivation.

After a brief silence, Dr. White asked, "Why can't I accept her efforts? Why do I constantly find fault with her and what she tries to do for me?" I said that the way I understood this was that his wife had become his mother in his mind. As a child he probably felt deserving of mistreatment, believing that if he were a "good boy" his mother would love him. Now, as an adult, he wanted to rid himself of the feeling that he was bad and wanted others, primarily his wife, to take the responsibility for his sense of deprivation and misery. I understood, I said, that it was difficult for him to consider that the way he felt today might have more to do with the past than with the present.

This was the first time that I had made a connection between his childhood experiences and his holding his wife responsible for his past deprivations and abuses. Dr. White greeted my comments with a sigh and another silence. He left saying that he would have a great deal to think about between then and our next meeting.

When he returned, he said that while my explanation of his behavior made sense to him, he now felt worse because he could see more clearly the childishness of his feelings and his behavior. In an effort to help him accept his "childish" feelings, I added that I could see how after the birth of his son the longings for unconditional acceptance, love, and attention from his wife had become more imperative. Dr. White then remembered that he had had similar problems after the birth of his daughter but was able to overcome them.

In my clarifying and interpretive comments I continued to emphasize that, for an adult, these feelings are very hard to accept and this was why he had adopted a feel-sorry-for-me mode of behavior: conveying his emotional misery in this manner, he hoped for a caring, compassionate response. Dr. White hung his head and made a barely audible comment about the unreasonableness of his behavior, saying that it was he, himself, who had the greatest difficulty accepting the childishness of his needs.

While the transferential nature of his relationship with his wife reactivated his infantile longings, a recent therapeutic conversation revealed the nature of the patient's transference expectations in relation to me. He began the hour by telling me that the day before he had felt good. He had gone home at a reasonable hour and had had dinner with his family, something he hadn't done for a long time. He had not run off to the basement to do his exercises as he usually does. But now he was already worried that this was not going to last, that tonight something might set him off, and once that happened he would not be able to stop himself from repeating his old pattern in which, once he feels hurt, he has to retaliate immediately or withdraw in fear of abusing his family.

The patient then told me two stories which he had heard on the radio. The first one was an account given by one of Nureyev's dance partners. The woman was describing Nureyev's magnetism, how at times she was so enthralled by him that she would miss her cue as she was waiting in the wings for her turn. The patient was struck by the fact that, though she was almost at the end of her dancing career, Nureyev's presence had started a new life for her. (I thought his telling me this story was likely to be related to a feeling on his part that our relationship has had a profound impact on him.)

Since I did not say anything, the patient went on to tell the second story. He had heard a man describing the sexual experiences of another person. At first he had thought that it was a gay man describing the sexual experience of another man, but then he realized that the man was talking about the sexual experiences of a woman. How could a man know anything about the sexual experience of a woman? Though I could not be sure, I said, I did have an idea why these stories came to his mind now and why he may have wanted to tell me about them. I thought these stories had to do with what we were discussing earlier: how important it was for him that others know how he felt. The story he had just related to me, about a man who knew what a woman experienced sexually, made me think that he must be wondering how I could know what he was feeling, since, after all, my life experiences had to be different from his. "Yes," he said, "I've often wondered about that. . . ." As a matter of fact, he added, he often worried that, should he doubt my understanding and appreciation of how much he was suffering emotionally, then in this relationship too he might feel compelled to resort to doing something drastic in order to convince me. For example, imagining that I would become upset and distraught upon hearing about his suicide, he would feel elated: Could he actually go that far to assure that I knew the extent of his mental anguish? He had thought about this the other day and had realized that, though I had never discussed his suicidal intent with him directly or tried to talk him out of it, he felt that my understanding the depth of his despair—my being able to put into words feelings that he himself could not articulate—made his inner world more accessible to him. His feelings had become less mysterious, and he now believed that they might be alterable. He went on to say that what was particularly useful to him was that I helped him understand the reasons why he tried to get attention from his wife with his feel-sorry-for-me behavior, and how it was this behavior that finally alienated her from him. He added: "You are my last hope that what I feel can be known. Otherwise, being miserable is my 'lifeline' to others."

SUMMARY

With the help of a clinical example, I described the developmental precursors of a severe form of self pathology in which the clinical picture was dominated by depression, anorexia, and suicidality. In presenting a few highlights of the treatment process, I underlined the healing potential of the feeling of being understood. I hope to have demonstrated that it is important not to address the manifest symptoms in isolation but to recognize and interpretively respond to the underlying vulnerability of the self. In the course of treatment the patient demonstrated, in small but significant ways, structural changes that enabled him to reflect on his emotions, so that he no longer became instantaneously enraged in such a way that he felt compelled to retaliate or withdraw, a behavior that was intended to make his environment feel responsible for the psychological pain that was inflicted on him. Dr. White no longer considers suicide to be an option for him—not because he thinks that he is too cowardly to undertake it, but because, with increasing frequency, he enjoys his work and spending time with his children. Since he has put on weight, he has become increasingly more resilient physically and emotionally.

REFERENCE

Berliner, B. (1958). The role of object relations in moral masochism. *Psychoanalytic Quarterly* 26:358–377.

The Scope and the Limits of the Theory of the Self in Psychoanalysis: Response to the Paper of Anna Ornstein, M.D.

MARCIANNE BLEVIS, M.D.

There is a widespread opinion that by now, over eighty years after the Freudian discovery, analysts speak such very different languages that they can hardly understand each other anymore. In inventing psychoanalysis, Freud, according to this view, somehow gave us our "natural language," and this original language then became differentiated into as many languages as there were theoretical advances, with the result that analysts, new inhabitants of a Babel of the unconscious, can no longer understand one another. From here it is just a short step to the belief that these foreign languages have given rise to psychoanalytic populations with totally different customs. I would not wish such a fate on our discipline, nor would I want us to have to leave it up to a linguist of the future to assess what we have in common.

Although we speak different languages they are nevertheless not foreign to each other, since we share the same method of deciphering the unconscious that was established by Freud, and we use this method to deal with the sufferings and the demands of our patients. But is it then the case that we are all talking about the same thing, only with different analytic languages? Certainly, when we study the various theories that have arisen in the analytic domain since Freud, we cannot fail to observe that on many points the very same theoretical issues appear under different names. We can only wonder at the tendency to make a great fuss about discarding certain concepts when we find that they continue to exist, under a different name and in a different guise, sometimes in the very same theoretical field. If we think of the fate of certain controversial notions such as the death instinct or penis envy, which some analysts have abandoned resolutely the better to bring them back under other names, we have before us an interesting project in analytic epistemology that we might well approach from a psychoanalytic point of view!

And yet it would be doing an injustice to the majority of great psychoanalytic thinkers to suggest that they have merely reiterated the Freudian discovery, appropriating it in their own words. To do so would also represent a denial of any theoretical progress in our discipline. For there are advances, and theories that attempt to give them shape, and analysts to put them to good use in their clinical work, and also, sometimes, associations of analysts that are formed to defend these advances. When we speak of theoretical advances in the analytic domain we must acknowledge that, just as in the domain of scientific discovery, certain concepts may be abandoned for good or bad reasons, leaving as our sole guide clinical results that it can be difficult to evaluate.

Is there any other way to think of the contributions that different theories have to offer? It seems to me that what would allow for a set of psychoanalytic concepts is not so much positing a unique, immutable "truth" about the human subject; it is offering analysts who use that set as their theoretical base a *field of decision*. Let me explain. The analyst's activity is one of intense decision making: whether he remains silent, intervenes, or interprets, he is at the intersection of unconscious, sometimes contradictory or paradoxical force fields to which he opens himself as he listens and as he receives into his own unconscious the material his patients address to him.

Deep inside this field of forces the analyst is anything but neutral, since he is the site of an intense effort of decision and hence of orientation. In contrast to the ordinary, well-intentioned listener, the analyst is sustained in his task by the body of theory to which he subscribes. We do not, perhaps, analyze in the same way if we are Kleinians, Kohutians, Lacanians, Winnicottians, and so forth, because the creation of certain analytic concepts marks out and delimits a certain field of decision, sometimes in a very narrowly prescriptive fashion (something for which the Kleinians, for example, have been criticized). What makes the task a bit harder is the fact that there are a number of analysts who profess loyalty to a given theoretical movement but who, when we look at their actual practice, turn out to adhere to an entirely different decision-making schema. And the issue becomes even more complex when we consider that the field of decision in which certain treatments are conducted can combine theoretical orientations, sometimes outside of our awareness.

And so we can only be very grateful to those who, like Anna Ornstein, describe their clinical practice in an effort to illustrate the field of decision in which they work. There can be no doubt that analyses proceed—and proceed successfully—with very different analysts representing very different conceptual configurations. Nevertheless, in emphasizing the field of decision as defined by each of these configurations, I want to stress the fact that a decision is judged by its consequences. In looking at the way an analysis proceeds, we can assess the consequences of the aspects of decision that governed the analyst's efforts: How far could the treatment advance within this field of decision; or, if we have reached an impasse, might another field of decision have been more effective? And so forth.

Defining the essential mechanism of the change that we can expect from treatment, and locating herself in the tradition of Kohut, Dr. Ornstein emphasizes the need for the patient to feel profoundly and nonjudgmentally understood. Now no one would deny that a patient has a need to feel understood by his analyst; the problem is that feeling understood can be something of a paradoxical process. It is quite difficult to know how a patient feels understood when we do not rely only on the manifest content of what he says, since the patient may wish to please his analyst to the point of asserting full agreement with him. Is this compliant submission or genuine agreement?

Without pushing the paradox too far, we must keep in mind that certain patients may also resort to a hostile transference in order to provoke the analyst into verbalizing a limit to the violence that courses through them without their recognizing its origin. Through this type of transference they call on the analyst to utter the words that they were too defenseless to muster in their childhood in the face of what they experienced as a destructive bond forced on them by a parent (Searles 1986). Occasionally such patients will wait until the end of their analysis (or even until long after that) before they can risk acknowledging that they were understood by the analyst. It can certainly be narcissistically trying for an analyst (especially before his colleagues) to put up with being a figure, or rather a place, to which nothing but criticism is directed. And yet. . . .

Now you may well reply that there are signs by which the analyst can be confirmed in his feeling that he is conducting the treatment properly, even though the patient claims the opposite, but then again how deeply worried an analyst can become if he is not covered with an armor of paranoiac convictions! Is it useful to consider that, if a given patient cannot part with this symptom made up of complaints and reproaches, he is not analyzable or analysis will not help?

There are in fact some patients—not typical, perhaps, at the border of analyzability, no doubt, but can we forget them in a conference on borderline conditions?—who are unable to live unless they surround themselves with a solid carapace of suffering that they cannot relinquish too quickly without danger. (Incidentally, we might do well to ask ourselves what "suffering" means in such cases.) A subject consults an analyst because he is suffering, surely, but note that his suffering allows him to say "I" in the phrase "I'm suffering," and therefore he is not the mere plaything of his unconscious determinants. With this "I" he breaks through the alienating discourse that traverses him. Other patients are unable to say what they are suffering from: they cannot represent their suffering. When a patient says "I'm suffering" from this or that, he is stating that he seeks to enter upon the path of representation of the cause of his suffering so that he will no longer have to be its passive instrument. This desire is the foundation of any treatment. Following Lacan, we use the term *jouissance* for what stands outside of representation—for example pain in its raw state that has not been able to become a suffering expressed by a complaint that "I" am suffering. This *jouissance*, referring to what is outside the system of representation, belongs to the category that Lacan calls the Real, which is distinct from the reality in which we live, the reality made up of words, images, narratives. At most we can say that *jouissance* refers to what has no form, since a form is a minimal organization.

The fact that we are endowed with the capacity for language, that our cerebral functioning increases through connections to other people, shows that we have a need, one that is as vital as breathing and eating, to superimpose onto this Real a grid of images and of words, the Imaginary and the Symbolic. For Lacan, the grid of the Imaginary and the Symbolic is tied to the Real in order to make livable the relation we maintain to our reality as sexually differentiated, separate, and mortal individuals. What is at stake in any treatment is reweaving the gaps in this symbolic grid. Lacan conceptualized the relationship of the Imaginary, the Symbolic, and the Real in terms of the Borromean knot, which consists of three rings interlaced in such a way that if one of them is broken the other two will come apart. He thereby tried to express, without *a priori* assumptions, the extraordinary diversity of the ways in which a subject reconnects with his foundational signifiers, and these distinctions are of essential interest to anyone concerned with the processes that are at play in a psychoanalytic treatment. If Lacan (1964) also said that the unconscious is structured like a language, this in no way implies that our everyday language is that of the unconscious, but rather that the unconscious is organized by signifying elements that the analyst can try to decipher.

Several authors, in particular Piera Aulagnier (1975), have attempted to set forth a theory of different stages of the elaboration of this unconscious language that organizes the tensions affecting the psyche, a process in which the Imaginary, the Symbolic, and the Real become linked. To envision this more concretely, consider the ordinary night terrors of a small child who sees, as if it were real, a man in his room who threatens him when the light is turned off. The child is so frightened that he fears impending death. That the man turns out to be his father has no bearing on the status of this apparition. Our interpretation should not focus on the oedipal imaginary without taking into account the fact that although, to be sure, the child hallucinated a "father," this was a "Real" father, part of whose import remained without symbolic meaning for the child but was brought to him by a hallucination in the imaginary register along with the affect of terror. Seeking out the elements pertaining to the Real enables us to separate it out, in our handling of the transference, from what is based on the Imaginary or the Symbolic. This is the only way to conceptualize the resolution of the trauma by trying not to replicate it and thereby to perpetuate its activity in the unconscious.

We can easily imagine how, in the huge task that awaits him at the beginning of his life, the human child meets up with obstacles that are a function of his parents' unconscious representations, representations that concern various elements essential for his individuation. A paradox of the human condition, the language the child hears from birth on, even before he can understand its meaning, conveys—in what is unsaid as well as in what is said—the best and the worst, the possibility of naming the world and the encounter with the unnamable, the possibility of a representation and its destruction. There can be no doubt that the way in which a child undertakes his task of individuation involves violence, since every child, in order to exist, must make his own what has been given to him, and he does not do so through some innate malice as Melanie Klein has suggested. If this necessary violence comes up against massive prohibitions, the child is then inhabited by the history of his family without being able to get hold of himself, see himself, represent himself in this torrent of meanings in which he is assigned a place that is sometimes impossible to live in. Isn't this the case with Dr. White? We can therefore better understand why it is that *representing oneself* as suffering can be a true breakthrough in what has stood outside of representation.

It can also happen sometimes that treating a patient compels the analyst to adopt a certain violence, the violence that must be exerted against Thanatos, the antilife forces that lurk inside each of us and that can become fixed within the unconscious representations of our parents' murderous desires. It is for the analyst to discover, in and through the transference, the multiple strata of the self. Dr. Ornstein speaks of early traumas and the failure of caretaker responsiveness. According to self psychology, the people around the child must maintain an empathic stance towards him, one that will differ according to his age and will therefore be more or less adequate and appropriate. Kohut's theory of the development of the self also has the clinical aim of restoring to the subject the means by which he can reconstitute a self that is more cohesive, more flexible, better able to face the rejections and disappointments encountered in everyday life. But doesn't this view place too little emphasis on what the child does with this environment that is or is not empathic and appropriate, is or is not good enough, the environment with which he will struggle with his resources, the signifiers and the ideals of those close to him (and those less close), which will give him the chance to take hold of life? Analysis, as Freud said, is not a therapy of love aimed at repairing the damage each of us has undergone in this area, but rather a treatment uniquely specific to the human subject who, because he speaks, has the opportunity throughout his entire life to try to symbolize the elements of the Real in his history that were unsymbolized at an earlier time.

Let us look at Dr. Ornstein's case to see how this theory allows for the exploration and the reconstruction of the self in the course of treatment, but with the question in mind of whether the scope of the theory is not limited by definition. Is it possible to separate the domain of narcissism from the rest of the formations of the unconscious without running into major theoretical and clinical difficulties? Is it right to think that there could exist in the human psyche nonconflictual areas that guide the practice of the transference? And, finally, doesn't the issue of the self refer in a restrictive manner to a fundamental, much larger issue that Freud (before he abandoned the term) called self preservation, and that Lacan left unexplored when he merely indicated the conditions for the linkage of the Real, the

Symbolic, and the Imaginary with no further commentary? This is an issue that haunts psychoanalysis. In short, doesn't self psychology lead the analyst to guide the treatment in such a way as to repair developmental damage by supplying the empathy the patient lacked, in so doing avoiding the necessary and sometimes risky confrontation with conflicts that can be unpleasant, disagreeable, or disturbing to each of the protagonists?

Dr. Ornstein shows in a very striking way how her patient, Dr. White, constructed a solid wall against his emotions; even his anorexia was a way of treating himself with the same indifferent harshness shown by his father, an unconscious accomplice to the mother's mistreatment of her son. It is remarkable to see how this patient exactly reproduced, in his anorexia, his father's behavior towards him (prohibition against going into the kitchen, maniacal attention to the amount of food ingested, the special value placed on excessive physical activity), so that we may wonder whether this anorexia comes under the heading of the type of sadomasochistic behavior that the analyst emphasizes in other contexts. The fact that the patient retained an undistorted body image, that he knew he was dangerously thin, would support this conjecture. In true anorexia the body image is most often completely unreal if not unrealistic; patients in the full throes of their anorexia do not perceive themselves as thin, but on the contrary they ceaselessly try to effect the real castration of their body that their image never satisfies.

In the history of patients presenting in adulthood with sadomasochistic behaviors, it has been observed (Enriquez 1984, Stoller 1975) that they had a parent who, because of an illness of the child's, was passionately attached to a part of the child's body. This strange investment of one part of the body at the expense of the rest of the child's identity, a part often associated with the idealization of a stoic heroism imposed on the child, had, in the case of Dr. White, the result of silencing every expression of the child's suffering. It led him to idealize, in imitation, the annulment of all his legitimate experiences of refusal, of rage, of revolt. From that time on he had no way of symbolizing his illness and his pain in a mode of suffering that could potentially be recognized by an other, even if it could not be shared in reality.

The consequences of denying the rage that such a child can rightfully feel extend to every affect that poses a danger to the narcissistic equilibrium constructed with such difficulty. Isn't this what is going on with Dr. White? He must have felt doubly abandoned: he lost his father as a witness against the abuse inflicted by the mother and he lost "a" father when the latter proved to be a torturer in his own right. He had no choice but to treat himself with the same—and even more—severity if he were to retain any sort of bond with "a" father who would protect him against the even greater threat of the loss of bodily boundaries. This is the paradoxical function of the symptom, what Freud called a compromise formation and Lacan the sole means of access to the Real. Dr. White's symptoms represent the Real of the father (his traumatic and senseless role) behind the imaginary, grotesque, and torturing father, so that in spite of everything, the patient could give himself a phallic limit in the face of a threat of disintegration that was even greater. When one part of the body attracts all the erotized attention of a parent while the rest of the child's expectations are left unheeded, the child experiences this as a deep contempt for his feelings and a complete absence of meaningful connection with others. If later on a masochistic perversion develops, it represents an attempt both to master and to reverse, through erotization, the suffering that has been denied. This scenario takes the place of the lost suffering (Khan 1979).

In what we are told of Dr. White, however, no distinction seems to have been formulated between sadomasochistic behavior and a corresponding fantasy. It makes an essential difference, both in understanding what the patient says and in handling the transference, whether we approach the problematics of a subject through fantasy or through what led him to adopt a given behavior. If we speak in terms of sadomasochistic behavior, we are in the register of an identification, indeed an imitation, which does not take into account the fact that the entire reality of these behaviors is motivated and determined by the elaboration of fantasies whose purpose is to protect the subject from madness, from non-sense, from the loss of bodily boundaries.

This difference in approach to the conduct of an analysis is fundamental enough to warrant our stopping to look at it more closely. The term "behavior" refers to a way of acting that, as we observe in the analysis of Dr. White, may be borrowed from the behavior of an other (his father or mother), reducing it to being merely a bit of inert matter into which the wishes of an other are stamped and which is then replicated in an entirely passive manner. The Freudian discovery has surely taught us that the human subject must surrender to the omnipotence of words, the words, spoken and unspoken, conscious and unconscious, of the others who receive us into the world, words that we apprehend before we understand them, in such a way that Lacan was able to say that we are spoken by these signifiers of desire that come to us from a place that seems external to us and is yet deeply ours. If the human subject were the pure reflection of the omnipotence of words, nothing would be his own; he would be merely a machine proceeding in a straight line, as Freud said, in the shortest path towards his death. Through his life instinct every subject resists this course, taking hold of the elements that program him and arranging them in the stable forms we know as fantasies. Isn't the narcissistic retreat behind a "wall" against emotions, which seemed to keep Dr. White safe, a rampart in the battle against affects that were too dangerous—a threat that also extended to his space for fantasies and language?

In speaking of a subject, when we locate ourselves in a theoretical context that takes fantasy elaboration into account (and in so doing we are following Freud as well as Lacan), we are setting out to explain the *activity* of every subject who must deal with trauma. No individual is exclusively a passive victim in the face of even the most major traumas. He is also an agent of his own survival, in that he makes use of a variety of fantasies that enable him to safeguard his subjective integrity and his integrity as someone of a given sex. Suffering is put into words in the language of these singular images that are fantasies. Actively constructing fantasies is one of the ways in which the human subject is able to articulate his traumas in language, traumas that are sometimes unspeakable, sometimes inevitable and inherent in the human condition that forces us to be monosexual, mortal, and abandoned to loneliness. It is a lengthy task to reveal, in the course of an analysis, the most archaic of these fantasies, since they are sometimes buried like a treasure in the wall of narcissistic defenses. Bringing them to light enables the patient to take up once again the path of fantasmatic elaborations that had gotten stuck around fragile archaic fantasies in which the subject was partially confused with an other and hence threatened in his identity, his uniqueness. But bringing them to light also involves interrogating the non-symbolized Real that produced them and to which they bear witness and give access.

Dr. Ornstein's interpretation of her patient's feel-sorry-for-me behavior enabled her to separate out, and hence to detach from the patient, a set of signifiers that was strictly determinative of his relations with others who could serve as transference objects. This behavior is common to many patients who state that they never succeed in communicating their suffering as well as they would wish to. These patients, always greedy and dissatisfied, demand that the analyst share their psychic life closely. For a long time, the time it takes for this type of transference to unfold, they are not aware that they have a need to show their suffering in a passive and accusatory way. It is interesting to see how the transition takes place, in the treatment of Dr. White, from the position in which the patient, confined in the reiteration of his utterances, can only show and hence merely demonstrate without genuine communication what he knows, to an entirely different position in which his suffering becomes his own. In isolating a feel-sorry-for-me complex, Dr. White's analyst made it possible for him to recognize himself in a kind of potential fantasy and thus to gather together the fragments of this fantasy that had been scattered in all his behaviors.

At the same time as he gave up his greedy and accusatory demands, Dr. White explored with his analyst the various configurations of the feel-sorry-for-me behavior, all the subjective positions concealed by this set of signifiers, until finally the poem about how no one is able to understand the depth of another person's suffering enabled him to represent for himself what he could now risk letting go of: the illusion of needing to be merged with someone else in order to be understood. Dr. White could allow himself to give up an illusion of completeness in order to achieve, on the symbolic level, another form of wholeness. What was at stake in his analysis was the possibility of representing himself as being understood by an other and of accepting the loss of the illusory register in which he wanted to be totally confused with an other in the hope of being totally understood. In such cases the analyst, too, runs the risk of getting lost in an imaginary (and omnipotent) transference in which he seeks to meet all of his patient's expectations.

What happens to the concept of the self when the processes at work in the patient are derived from splits or even from fragmentations of identity? For when it is said that, because of the indirect way in which he expressed his sadism, Dr. White was rejected by those whose accepting responses he most needed, aren't we dealing with the Kleinian concept of projective identification? The issue which then arises is knowing how the concept of the self does or does not allow us to take splitting into account (is the Kleinian concept brought in under the table?) and knowing how "the development of the self" does or does not presuppose the reduction of the splits in the guise of the concept of integration. These are not just academic distinctions. What is it that is split and fragmented? The fundamental problem in the treatment of these patients must then be knowing how these different parts speak and how to bring them together, to integrate them, since we are told that the treatment gives new impetus to movements towards the integration of the self. When Dr. White feared that his wife might see him "feeling good" because, as he put it, "presenting myself as a failure is the best way to communicate my despair," should we, with Dr. Ornstein, take this literally? Or would we instead do better to think that he feared leaving this theater of unhappiness in which he had taken refuge, and in which he continued to bring onstage the father who had abused him?

The very term *communication* used by Dr. Ornstein and her patient is perhaps problematic and subject to misunderstandings. This was the case when we found communication and projection assimilated to one another, and it is even more true when we are in the presence of actors on the psychic stage who are unaware of each other's existence. Can we really speak of direct communication, complete unto itself, when we hear in the utterances of certain patients a dialogue of identity fragments that are lost among several generations and that address one another? Let me explain. Searles (1986) describes how borderline patients evoke countertransferential feelings of rage or destructive envy in the analyst to the extent that they themselves did not feel entitled to experience these feelings in childhood, or perhaps because they were not even able to create a space within themselves in which to accommodate these affects that could undo their fragile narcissistic equilibrium. The analyst, then, must accommodate within *himself* the slow process of giving these excluded affects form in words and representations, and he must provoke, often by a kind of detour into angry countertransferential acting out, the patient's recognition of the intensity of his own inner life. These kinds of affects can sometimes originate with a parent who has no means of representing them, and who transmits to the child the burden of keeping the affect alive—to the child's detriment, of course, since the parent is transmitting only his *jouissance.*

To be sure, different modalities of transferential enactment may indicate intersections and differences among various theoretical fields of decision. Doesn't receiving into oneself affects and representations that are, as Winnicott would say, still formless amount to serving the patient as a transferential selfobject, which, according to Kohut (1984) involves essential communication between analyst and patient? Once again we encounter a problem with regard to the concept of the selfobject and what it entails. Whereas Searles, in a manner that seems to be unique to him, tries to conceptualize the way in which excluded or forbidden representations can emerge in the transference, the notion of the selfobject transference in its diverse manifestations (reflecting damaged ambitions, ideals, or skills) involves privileging the aspect of reparation in a way that restricts the scope of the transference. Although an analyst has no choice but to sustain the type of imaginary transference chosen by the patient, among which the mirror and idealizing transferences are just a few aspects among many, does this mean that he must believe that each area of imaginary transference completely sums up the patient's expectations? As Lacan and others have emphasized, the reparative aim is not absent from the analyst's intentions, but reparation does not occur only in the synchronic dimension of the here-and-now of the imaginary transference; it comes about chiefly through the process of discerning the ways in which the different registers of the Real, the Symbolic, and the Imaginary are connected.

One of the most fundamental problems separating different schools of psychoanalysis is the way in which the role of the generations is theorized. Conceptualizing it in the three registers of the Real, the Symbolic, and the Imaginary obliges us not to restrict ourselves to only one of these registers, which is something that always occurs in our theories when we ignore one of them and especially that of the Real. The Real, the site of traumatic chaos that escapes representation and meaning, bears witness to a defect in the symbolic transmission to which the so-called paternal function summons every man and every woman.

In what place was Dr. White put by his father? What unspoken question did he have to formulate for himself, in his father's place, towards what was addressed to him by another generation? I'm reminded of a patient, severely abused by her mother, who caught herself repeating inwardly "Forgive me! Forgive me!" We might think that she was addressing her mother, but the analysis uncovered a much more complex situation: the repeated "Forgive me!" was in fact directed to her maternal grandmother. The abuse my patient's mother inflicted on her was intended, in this woman's unconscious scenario, to prove to her own mother that there was a child who was worse than she was. In choosing her daughter to be this "bad" child, she exculpated herself in her mother's eyes. "Bad" by definition, my patient was always unsatisfactory; she had to devote her own life to relieving her mother of guilt, and in so doing she took upon herself all the evil in the world. Very early on, a child feels the need to relieve the caretaking parent of the unbearable part of that parent's psyche, and to his own very great disadvantage he dedicates himself to keeping that part active. The unconscious begging for forgiveness that her mother could not allow herself to formulate on her own behalf, lest she collapse, was uttered by my patient, who one day hallucinated the presence of her mother in my office. Thanks to the transference, an element of the Real of my patient's mother began to enter into a linguistic process and to take on meaning. We can see here how the model that each of us uses to conceptualize the relationship among the generations has a direct influence on the conduct of the treatment.

In his concern not to confine the patient to an exclusively oedipal mode of relationship, in which everything reflects defenses against incestuous wishes, Kohut nevertheless does not really manage to get outside of the exclusively dual mother–child or father–child relation, and this restriction leads him to privilege, in the transference, a mode of imaginary reparation the failure of which is necessarily linked to the analyst's lack of empathy. But to the extent that every subject is at the crossroads of a more archaic history, traversed by meanings and significations that he is not always able to conceptualize, the symbolic function is what each of us can reappropriate in order to put a stop to that which causes us to act without our knowledge. Dr. Ornstein has clearly shown how Dr. White was traversed by behaviors of whose meaning he was unaware, and how he sought in the work of analysis to construct a true identity in which he could experience his reality as a father, as a son, and as a man.

We may also wonder about the violence that Dr. White manifested towards his son. To be sure, he contrived a "theory" of the depressive state that had emerged in him when his son was born; he wanted to believe that his violence arose as an effect of the envy he felt of the intimacy that the baby, and later the child, could have with its mother. But must we believe him here, accepting as truth the theory he addressed to his analyst, who received it with much sympathy? He presented to his analyst a similarly imaginary elaboration of the reasons for the suffering that made him continue to blame his son. Note the intense shame that he experienced after giving in to his rage: Couldn't very condensed identifications with his abusive mother have been manifesting themselves on such occasions? The shame that Dr. White experienced after his outbursts can in fact alert us to the complexity of what was besetting him. If this had been merely an expression of envy of the intimacy his son was enjoying with the mother, while the patient himself was deprived of such a relationship, there would be no reason for him to feel shame; he would be more likely to feel guilt. If there was shame, as distinct from guilt, this is a sign of the way in which he participated libidinally in what he lacked the most, in what he was suffering from. Like terror or fear, shame is a particular affect pointing to elements of an unsymbolized Real transmitted by previous generations. Like any child, Dr. Ornstein's patient had interpreted his mother's pathological behavior as though it were an enigmatic demand addressed to him, a demand he had to satisfy if he did not want to risk losing the loving bond that kept him alive better than any food. A child has no choice but to respond to the neurotic, psychotic, or perverse impasses of his caretakers and those around him, and he responds with the means at his disposal, sacrificing the boundaries of his body, of his thoughts, of his difference. The hate that can come over a child put in this position of sacrifice must, understandably, remain disavowed, banished, turned against the self and erotized as in masochism, but, as Enriquez (1984) has observed, this hate is also necessary in order to maintain and validate the suffering.

It is interesting to observe that suicidal thoughts erupted at these times. What did Dr. White want to kill in himself? Here we are at the heart of a very complex problem having to do with the narcissistic constitution of subjects like these. For Joyce McDougall (1985), while certain narcissistic pathologies lead to the formation of adored or hated selfobjects, others are characterized by the type of retreat we find in Dr. White, a retreat in the face of archaic libidinal demands that are too dangerous or unacceptable. In these cases the pathology is associated with the persistence of objects that are partial, primitive, overlapping, sometimes confused with the subject himself. In his fits of rage against a son, Dr. Ornstein's patient may have been trying to confront, in a displaced manner, his inability to elaborate part-objects with which he would not be merged. His son seemed to arouse an insoluble conflict in this patient, while his daughter enabled him to get in touch with a more feminine, peaceful part of himself and thence to reconstruct a relationship with himself that was more tolerable, as a father and as a son.

In discussing Dr. Ornstein's case I must once again emphasize the value of the real concern underlying the work of Kohut and his followers, namely that they do not confine the patient and his utterances to an interpretative system dominated by a forced "oedipalization," and they do not hear everything the patient says as the expression of a system of defenses that the omniscient analyst can decipher, as it were, without letting himself be guided by the transference. In his discussion of the case of Mr. Z, Kohut (1979) clearly shows the impasses that analyst and patient can arrive at if watchwords govern the analyst's listening. But can we therefore conclude that there is a development of the self separate from that of the remaining formations of the unconscious, without running into even greater theoretical and clinical difficulties?

The notion of fantasy seems to be absent from the theory of the development of the self, and this has its effect on the conduct of the treatment. Even if we acknowledge the real concern of analysts following this theoretical model to remain as close as possible to their patients, we must still point out a fundamental difference in the very conception of what a fantasy is. Fantasy is not only a defensive system whose interpretation is open to challenge; it is also a crucible of images, memories, condensed experiences, and communicable verbalizations that serve to confront the traumas encountered in our past. Fantasy is a way of expressing in language the interpretation the child was able to put on his relationship with his caretakers. For, right from the start, a child enters into contact—for the pleasure of the exchanges between himself and adults and for all the other modes of exchange to which he is exposed—with the unconscious representations of his parents. He weaves his partial drives in this field of representations, and he elaborates fantasies to articulate his relation to this field that is so alien and at the same time so intimate because it predates the baby's even having a body of his own. Can't we understand the unfolding of the treatment around the need to help the self to evolve and to become integrated as also entailing an attempt to remobilize the more advanced elaboration of what had been fixed primitive fantasies?

Similarly, it is clear that Dr. White's narcissistic mortifications had very touching origins. When Lacan (1964) emphasized that we must think of the process of becoming a subject in conjunction with a new conception of otherness, he was trying to give a radical meaning to the fact that a child at first has to deal with an other from whom he receives everything and expects everything, and through whom he interprets everything, even before he is able to think of himself as separate from this other. The child responds, in effect, to what he believes to be the demands of the other, first with his body—his earliest language—and then with the elaboration of a differentiated system of objects, representations, and fantasies. He can be induced to sacrifice this system more or less completely, leaving himself vulnerable to losing his "I" because he has no barrier against the alienating discourse of those around him.

In other words, perhaps there is more to be gained from trying to theorize the way in which the development of the self is bound up with other formations of the unconscious that lead to conflicts than there is from setting these two approaches against one another as though they were entirely divergent analytic undertakings. Likewise, there is more to be gained from trying to understand as thoroughly as possible the ways in which our unconscious determinants are expressed, the ways in which they are inscribed as they pass through us, and the psychic space in which this inscription occurs[1] than it is to consider that the problem of the transmission of our determinants and our actions has been solved.

---

1. Freud (1923) envisaged the existence of a third unconscious in order to account for the presence of elements not repressed within the ego

REFERENCES

Aulagnier, P. (1975). *La violence de l'interprétation*. Paris: PUF.

Enriquez, M. (1984). *Aux carrefours de la haine*. Paris: E.P.I.

Freud, S. (1923). The ego and the id. *Standard Edition* 19: 3–59.

Khan, M. (1979). *Alienation in Perversion*. London: Hogarth.

Kohut, H. (1979). The two analyses of Mr. Z. *International Journal of Psycho-Analysis* 60:3–27.

———— (1984). *How Does Analysis Cure?*, ed. A. Goldberg. Chicago: University of Chicago Press.

Lacan, J. (1964). *The Four Fundamental Concepts of Psycho-Analysis*, ed. J.-A. Miller, trans. A. Sheridan. New York: Norton, 1981.

McDougall, J. (1985). *Theaters of the Mind*. New York: Basic Books.

Searles, H. (1986). *My Work with Borderline Patients*. Northvale, NJ: Jason Aronson.

Stoller, R. (1975). *Perversion: The Erotic Form of Hatred*. New York: Pantheon.

Excerpts from the Discussion

Juan-David Nasio: Dr. Ornstein, what is the position of the psychoanalyst, his role, his place in the transference, in your clinical practice? And in this context I'd like to try to make a distinction between the way we conceptualize the role of the analyst and the way you do. I'd like to know if you would agree with me that the selfobject in reality corresponds to the position of the analyst as the other—the "other" with a small "o," that is, an imaginary other who makes it possible for me, through his reflections and through what he gives back to me, to consolidate my being, or rather my ego, my self.

In my practice there are moments, with a patient, in which I have to do the same sort of thing you did with Dr. White, for example to send back to him a series of images. In other words, I place myself in the imaginary schema, so that I can share his psychic pain. But what you don't say is that this position of the analyst as the imaginary other is possible only if he can also be present as the *objet a* that isn't imaginary.[1] That is to say, the structural formation of the transference is essential for us. I can't share Mr.

---

1. *Editor's note: Objet a* is the ultimate object of desire, but one that eventually turns out not to exist.

White's psychic pain even if I try to understand, even if I'm empathic, except on condition that my role, my place—even if I don't necessarily have to occupy that place—on condition that in the transferential relationship there is a place for an object that serves as motor for the fact that the patient is there, that I am there, and that the transference exists. As you see, these are two different schemas. The first is the structure of the unconscious, where we recognize the place of the object as the motor behind the treatment, and the other schema, which the first one makes possible, is the one where I can function, at certain moments (carefully chosen, of course) as the imaginary other. If I understand you correctly, it's there, as imaginary other, that you locate the selfobject in the transference.

Anna Ornstein: One way to answer some of the questions would be to tell you how I understand your concept of the unconscious, and how we think about the unconscious. Once we have settled that, maybe it will be easier for us to talk about the issue that Dr. Nasio just mentioned: What is the place of the analyst? How does the analyst experience the patient's transferences? You understood the selfobject concept very well. That's what transference is, and was for Freud: The patient creates the transference, so the position we take is wherever the patient happens to put us. However, since there are many roles, many identities that the analyst assumes, obviously it is very difficult to know at any one time where the patient has put us. We bring to the patient's transferences our own ideas of the way the mind works. We bring our theories about the model of the mind, about personality development, about psychopathology, and with all that we develop a theory of cure.

So what is our notion of the unconscious? The longer I listen to my Lacanian colleagues, the more it seems to me that the way you think about the unconscious is the way Freud formulated it in the topographic model—as a system, "the" unconscious. Now in my own training, and whatever I've learned since then in American psychoanalytic theory, this is not the way that we think of the unconscious—as a structure, and now, with the Lacanians, as structured according to the rule of language. This is totally new and foreign to us. We think of *unconsciousness*, which is a quality of the psyche. In other words, what we are experiencing at one time can indeed be unconscious, but it has the potential of becoming conscious, which was, in the topographic model, only accorded to the preconscious. So we see a line coming from deep unconsciousness, if you wish, to—depending on the context, the situation—a time when things indeed can become more conscious, which is very different from your views.

Because of the way I see a difference between a *system* unconscious and a *quality* unconscious, I might as well stay on the subject of fantasy, a very important psychic phenomenon. I found here in France a very big difference in the way the concept is used. Some of the most important work on unconscious fantasies was done in the States by Jacob Arlow. He links them to the vicissitudes of the drives. In other words, the unconscious fantasy is the product of the conflicts and difficulties that arise in relation to the various developmental phases that a child cannot master for whatever reason. It is a deeply endopsychic notion. In self psychology, once Kohut no longer considered drive vicissitudes as being the motor behind development and symptom formation, many other things in our psychoanalytic terminology had to be reconceptualized. When Marcianne Blevis gives fantasy an organizing and essentially curative role, that is the way that I would like to consider it. So for self psychologists unconscious fantasy is associated with drive vicissitudes, while fantasy, the way that patients report about it and we all experience it, does not have to be considered as a defense, as in traditional psychoanalysis, but indeed as a way in which the patient is trying to get well.

What also comes into our dialogue is the difference in the way we view symptoms, which I now begin to compare to the way you view language. We view symptoms—the way, for example, that my patient had suffered from deep melancholia that contained the cruelty, and from anorexia—as a kind of language, a communication. This was the final common pathway that this man had found, over his lifetime, to deal with the various anxieties, including rage experiences, that he could not master any other way. So while you deconstruct language, in order to find your way to "the" unconscious, we deconstruct symptoms to find meaning.

Dr. Blevis raises the issue of what Dr. White really wanted to do with the symptom; did he want to deny the presence of rage, or did he want to communicate to the people around him how he was suffering? Now if you think of a symptom—complex, anxiety, defense, anxiety, defense—then you get a conglomerate in which the patient found a place for the sadism, for the longing, for reaching out, for withdrawing. This is the work of the psyche, like dreams, but now we have the symptom, which can be conceptualized in much the same way. So when the patient presents with a symptom, and the process of therapy or analysis begins, and the symptom becomes deconstructed, in a way, and more of the elements become obvious, then maybe I am no longer thinking in terms of "where is my space as an analyst?" I have been asked why I place such importance on the patient's feeling understood, since (it is argued) that should be just the ambiance, the context, in which a lot of other work is done. But our empathic capacity lays the groundwork for what the interpretive work has to accomplish.

This is our therapeutic stance, and you may say this is not an analytic stance, because a Lacanian analyst will want to get into the death instinct and you want to name everything that is in the unconscious. But what we are trying to do is have the patient feel that I make an effort to understand. And I will not fully understand; we never understand each other fully. But if they experience me as making an effort to understand, this is when one of the selfobject transferences will be established, as Dr. Nasio said. Where is the analyst in this? In the place in which the patient can now begin to experience himself. Because when my patient, Dr. White, has this experience with the mother and the child, it is not what he sees that is important to us, not the perception, because that's an external observer's perspective. What is important to us is what the patient felt. The patient felt envy and jealousy. And that is what was articulated by him and was recognized by us as a very important motive for his withdrawal and for his rage reaction. So understanding, or making an effort to understand, has the function of providing the patient with an experience of relative self cohesion in this very safe environment that is now offered by the analyst. It is under these circumstances that the patient can begin to look at himself and ask those different questions: "Where is my rage coming from? Why am I so angry?" and so forth.

8

Toward a Separate Line of Female Development: On Adolescence

JOAN J. ZILBACH, M.D.
AND MALKAH T. NOTMAN, M.D.

> No doubt this is the moment Alice ought to seize. Now is the time for her to come on stage herself.
>
> Irigaray, *This Sex Which Is Not One*

INTRODUCTION

How often, when we start with the subject of woman, do we slip easily and almost imperceptibly into considering the differences between men and women? Then our focus, which lighted briefly on one—woman—is on differences, between two rather than on one. The subject or focus has become man and woman. This paper is on one—woman—and her separate line of female development. We are so accustomed to masculine theory and images that this becomes a difficult enterprise. Even in one of his last papers, Freud (1938), after revising many aspects of theory, remained steadfast in his view of the first three years of life as "masculine" for both sexes:

> The female genitals long remain unknown. . . . With the phallic phase and in the course of it the sexuality of early childhood reaches its disso-

lution. Thereafter boys and girls have different histories. . . . *[B]oth start off from the premise of the universal presence of the penis.* But now the paths of the sexes diverge. [p. 154; emphasis added]

In pursuit of a steady focus on woman, I will start this presentation not in the beginning or the early years, but with female adolescence.

I look at my face in the glass and see a halfborn woman. [Rich 1978, p. 41]

[A] girl in the years of puberty becomes quiet within and begins to think about the wonders that are happening to her body. I experience that, too. . . . I think that what is happening to me is so wonderful, not only what can be seen on my body, but all that is taking place inside. . . . Each time I have a period—and that has only been three times—I have the feeling that in spite of all the pain, unpleasantness, and nastiness, I have a *sweet secret*, and that is why, although it is nothing but a nuisance to me in a way, I always long for the time that I shall feel that secret within me again. [Anne Frank, at age 14 years 6 months, quoted in Dalsimer 1986, pp. 117f; emphasis added]

What does the young "halfborn" adolescent girl see in the glass? She "sees" in adolescence, as she does throughout her life, with her increasingly feminine mind and half womanly, rapidly changing body, which provides particularly rich opportunities for observations on female development.

The adolescent girl is "halfborn" at puberty, since adolescence occurs between her early childhood years and womanhood, on the way but not yet having arrived. Puberty ushers in early adolescence and, as late adolescence wanes, adulthood begins. Work, both outside and inside the home, job, and career, and (potentially) pregnancy and maternity loom ahead. In the second quotation Anne Frank, at age fourteen and a half, poignantly expresses her early adolescent experience: " . . . what is happening to me is so wonderful, and not only what can be seen on my body, but all that is taking place inside." This paper has a particular focus on the "wonderful . . . inside" happenings of feminine development in adolescence.

Turbulence, discontent, rebellion, and the problematic tortuous paths of adolescent identity formation have dominated discussions in the psychoanalytic literature on adolescence. One classic and oft-repeated descriptive statement was made by Anna Freud (1958), who characterized adolescence as a period of craziness. Later psychoanalytic formulations emphasize redoing earlier separation-individuation processes and the *second chance* or *second individuation process* (Blos 1980) that is said to occur in adolescence. These concepts, based on classical psychoanalytic theory though changed and modified, contain explicit and implicit conceptions of female development which have remained essentially unchanged for many decades. In contrast to an emphasis on troublesome difficulties, separation-individuation problems, and other forms of female deficiencies, recent formulations of feminine development emphasize interdependence, mutuality, affiliation, connection, and a female "relational" self (Gilligan 1982, Gilligan et al. 1990, Miller 1984, among others). These theoretical formulations of feminine development are based on the concept of a separate line of development with unique female developmental characteristics. Other authors emphasize concepts of primary femininity, early pregenital identity development, and the ongoing influence of the mother-daughter relationship (Chodorow 1978, Notman et al. 1986, 1991, Stoller 1976, Zilbach 1987, 1990, 1993).

The widening psychosocial world of adolescents and their families has been characterized as filled with "separations" or "breaking away" from family instead of emphasizing loosening, expansion, and differentiation of the goals of the adolescent in her family. The oft-stated identity question: "What will I become?" is understood as a sign of impending rupture with the family, as opposed to heralding an expansion of differences from and within the family. Even future motherhood has been considered as imposing restrictions and limitations on the adolescent girl and on the adult female (Deutsch 1944).

With the ongoing psychological development of femininity in the center of our formulations, continuity, expansion, and loosening of ties in adolescence will be emphasized, not separation, autonomy, and independence. This requires a major shift in our thinking. For example, in this paper the ongoing vicissitudes of the mother–daughter relationship are considered to be as significant, in adolescence, as the daughter's increasing erotic attraction to and relationship with her father. This requires an inclusion and integration of continuity and change, rather than the "breaking" of ties, as a major factor in development within a multifaceted, always changing, ongoing adolescent daughter–mother relationship.

My focus will remain on central processes of feminine development in adolescence, and the term *adolescent female* will be used throughout this paper instead of *girl* or *young woman*. No intermediate term is available, and so *adolescent female* seems the best choice at present. *Female* is a term used by many authors, specifically for the biological aspects of women. As used by this author, however, *adolescent female* is a term which is meant to go beyond biology towards a broader biopsychosocial approach. For a discussion of adolescence, groundwork must be laid with definitions of some basic concepts—primary femininity and reciprocal identification— and a brief summary of early female development. I will then return to female adolescent development and discuss sexuality, identity formation, and the psychological importance of the development of a new female organ, the breasts, and a unique event, menarche, as well as the processes of menstruation.

PRIMARY FEMININITY AND ACTIVE ENGULFMENT

The term *primary femininity* denotes an early unconflicted sense of being female, consisting of several component elements: primitive female body awareness, early imitation and identification with mother, and a cognitive component of "knowing what goes with being a girl." This is a definition originally used by Stoller (1976) to fill in a missing gap, the empty space in female development in the early months and years before the occurrence of the so-called Oedipus complex. Observations of infants and toddlers make abundantly clear that a sense of being female exists well before the young child's observation of anatomical differences at age 3 and beyond. This paper presupposes the ongoing presence and evolution of primary femininity as relevant to all phases of female development. Primitive psychological manifestations of primary femininity appear in the earliest postnatal moments, if not before, and continue throughout a woman's life, undergoing many changes, with expansions and diminutions alongside continuity.

The concept of primary femininity defines a central aspect of femininity and the feminine self. However, the term primary femininity as a descriptor (or signifier) is rather bland, perhaps empty, and certainly colorless. The term *active engulfment* has been used by this author to characterize primary or core femininity or female life energy (possibly libido). Active engulfment describes a biopsychological center of early female psychological activity which continues throughout life. Active engulfment is a force of pro-creativity which will take many forms in the course of being tamed and civilized over the female life cycle (Zilbach 1987, 1990). The earliest biological form is the engulfing of the sperm by the egg at the moment of fertilization. At the important moment, the sperm does not penetrate; rather, the ovum surrounds the sperm (Johnson 1985).

One component of primary femininity, or female selfhood, is based on early internal female body awareness. Though the female infant's internal experience is largely unknown, we can speculate about the internal effect of external influences, particularly with her mother. Touching, holding, smiling, vocalizing, eye-to-eye contact, and attunement are of critical importance in the early bonding and attachment processes of mother and infant. The attunement of the mother to her female infant is to an other who is fundamentally like her. Thus the beginning and continuing growth of primary femininity is stimulated within the infant as an inner psychobiological resonance within her body.

By the middle of the second year, female body awareness in primitive body representations have become distinct. Masturbation is observed with frequency well within the second year of life (Clower 1979). Awareness of vaginal secretions and some primitive form of sensing the uterus as a container may contribute to an internal sense of the female body (Kestenberg 1968). As one expression of this, the wish for a baby becomes evident and has been carefully studied (Kleeman 1976, Parens et al. 1977, Roiphe and Galenson 1981). Infant researchers report their direct observations with general agreement that between 18 months and 3 years the little girl consolidates an irreversible sense of being female and thus has a primitive sense of a female self (Kestenberg 1968, Parens et al. 1977, Roiphe and Galenson 1981, Stoller 1976, 1980, Tyson and Tyson 1990).

A second component element of primary femininity develops from early imitation and identification with mother. From the beginning the mother–female infant relationship is characterized by an interactive process of reciprocal identification. The range of attunement responses of the mother to her female infant is based on mother's identifications with her own mother and with her infant daughter. The female infant receives the behavioral expressions of these identifications and develops responses as her part of the reciprocal identification process. Primitive reciprocal identificatory interactions are central to the development of primary femininity as active engulfment grows within the female infant. Maternal identifications are evident in the behavior of 2-year-old girls as they preen and practice baby care in doll play just like their mothers. The importance of the reciprocal identification processes is not limited to the early years of female development; rather, it is ongoing throughout a woman's life and will be emphasized in our discussion of adolescence.

The next periods of development contain much that is of interest, though only very selected aspects will be discussed.

EARLY CHILDHOOD/THE GENITAL OR "OEDIPAL" PHASE

The common use of the term *oedipal* is a serious misnomer for this period of female development. The story of Oedipus is a classic male myth about the boy's inevitable love for his mother and rivalry with his father. In this phase of female development, the young girl increases her expressions of interest in her father and develops a desire to have her father's baby. This desire combines with an already existing desire to have a baby, like mother, which was well established in the preceding period of development. Prior formulations have focused on the girl's interest in or turning toward father and away from mother, but her ongoing identification with mother is as important as her interest in father.

The turning toward father is assisted by the processes of reciprocal identification, receptivity of the mother, and the little girl's increasing identification with her mother. The varied and myriad manifestations of identification, being like mother, include mother's relationship with father. It is noteworthy that the wish for a baby is not a substitute for a wish for a penis, but develops at first from the little girl's ongoing identification with mother. Envy and turning away from mother may occur during this period, assisted by encouragement and love from both parents as well as acceptance of the young girl's angry and aggressive wishes, which usually are directed towards the mother.

After the initial establishment and early development of primary femininity, in this developmental phase there is a surge of genital interest and other manifestations of childhood sexuality. In little girls there is an increasing frequency of masturbation and vaginal exploration (Clower 1975, Kestenberg 1968). During this period the discovery of the anatomical differences between the sexes also occurs.

The little girl becomes more exhibitionistic and practices her expanding conception of femininity. Elaboration of a feminine ego ideal is an important aspect of psychic development in this period. The developing female ego ideal includes many aspects of identifications with mother, not only mother's breasts which she may envy, but also her intelligence, activity, and general sexuality (Blum 1976, 1977).

The complexity and outcome of this phase will be influenced by many forces, including temperament, cognitive development, and the environmental circumstances of the child's life. Mother continues to be more than the little girl's rival for father: there is also a similarity and a coincidence of interest between them. The oft-noted female characteristics of affiliation, connection, and cooperation will be present in a nascent form in this developmental period, observed in the growing and continuing reciprocal identificatory processes in the mother–daughter relationship (Gilligan 1982, Gilligan et al. 1990, Miller 1984, Notman et al. 1991).

LATENCY/MIDDLE CHILDHOOD

The "latency" or middle-childhood girl develops a further array of feminine roles which she carries into adolescence and adulthood. Female friendships flower during this period, and relationships with other important adults, both male and female, will expand and elaborate the structure and content of the feminine ego ideal.

Sexuality continues throughout this period, with masturbation and other genital sensations present though often disguised or hidden (Clower 1975, 1979). The importance of the clitoris as a female organ of pleasure becomes more evident (Kulish 1991). Active and exciting games such as riding horseback on father's knee will produce clitoral sexual stimulation. In this period, more independent games such as jumprope and other girls' games may provide stimulation of the clitoris, at times to orgastic proportions. At the same time, the development of the superego disguises, forbids, or obscures the sexual meaning of these activities (Tyson and Tyson 1990). Significant elaboration of the internal structures of femininity occur in late latency. Of particular importance are the body image and female body awareness, which contribute significantly to the developments in adolescence that we will discuss in the next section.

CLASSICAL FREUDIAN THEORY OF EARLY DEVELOPMENT

Early female development as conceptualized in the preceding sections is significantly different from the classical Freudian view of female development (Freud 1905, 1925, 1931, 1933). Since this is well known and can be found in many publications, only a brief summary will be presented here.

Freud postulated that the first three years of psychic life are the same, that is, masculine, for both sexes.

> The third phase is that known as the phallic one, which is, as it were, a forerunner of the final form taken by sexual life and already much resembles it. It is to be noted that it is not the genitals of both sexes that play a part at this stage, but only the male one (the phallus). The female genitals long remain unknown. . . . [1938, p. 154]

Divergence in the development of girls and boys occurs only with and after the discovery of anatomical differences. At that point the little girl discovers her lack of a penis, and this discovery becomes a central organizer of subsequent female development. Her deficiency, lack, or inferiority is the "bedrock" of classical female psychosexual development. As the above quotation from the last version of "An Outline of Psycho-Analysis" indicates, this conviction remained unchanged for Freud. In contrast, the early psychic existence and importance of the female genitals as part of primary femininity and reciprocal identification have been discussed in this paper as essential aspects of female development. These concepts, and not classical Freudian theory, are the foundation for our discussion of adolescent female development.

FEMALE ADOLESCENT DEVELOPMENT

Major changes in identify formation, the adolescent development of primary femininity/active engulfment, and modifications of the mother–daughter relationship are all part of the evident growing sexuality of female adolescents. Underlying female adolescent sexual activity is her desire to take-in in an adolescent version of primary femininity/active engulfment. Thus her sexually focused desire to actively surround, contain, and take in is in distinct contrast to the adolescent male's phallic desires expressed by thrusting and penetration. The adolescent female is not merely a passive partner for the sexual scoring of the adolescent male. Her desire to take in and surround describes active adolescent female sexuality, not her being passively penetrated. Painful and wounding aspects of the experience of adolescent female sexuality are often emphasized, but the positive feminine trait, the expression of adolescent active engulfment, is not adequately characterized by an emphasis on pain or on being penetrated. Being penetrated is only a part of the female experience of intercourse, and such a description has a strong, primarily phallic tone. This is in contrast to describing the female experience as taking in and containing, or actively engulfing, the penis. The entire genital apparatus and the entire female body (including the breasts), and not only the vagina, are part of and participate actively in female adolescent sexuality.

Breasts

> Sometimes, when I lie in bed at night, I have a terrible desire to feel my breasts and to listen to the quiet, rhythmic beat of my heart. I already had these kinds of feelings subconsciously before I came here, because I remember that once when I slept with a girlfriend, I had a strong desire to kiss her, and that I did so. I could not help being terribly inquisitive over her body, for she always kept it hidden from me. I asked whether, as proof of our friendship, we should feel one anothers' breasts, but she refused. I go into ecstasies when I see the naked figure of a woman, such as Venus, for example. It strikes me as so wonderful and exquisite, that I have difficulty in stopping the tears rolling down my cheeks. . . . [Anne Frank, quoted in Dalsimer 1986, pp. 116f.]

The exquisite wonder of the changes in the young girl's body as she develops breasts is a striking and neglected aspect of her feminine adolescent development. In early adolescence, primed by earlier pubertal changes, female sexual stirrings are stimulated by the early budding of breast development. These buds are new, and girls eagerly await the full flowering of their breasts as they very carefully scrutinize each other's chests. In some subcultures the existence of these new female body parts is marked by the acquisition of the first brassiere. The girl whose development lags behind in her peer group anxiously desires to join them. Comparisons are frequently made by the young adolescent girl of her breasts with the breasts of mother, her friends, female teachers, and other women. As her breasts grow larger, they become part of the girl's overall estimate of her own attractiveness. The female development of breasts is quite different from the pubertal male penile and testicular changes. These male organs have been present from birth, throughout the earliest years, and of course adolescent enlargement and changes in size and shape are important to the boy. The girl, in her earlier development, has seen and experienced her mother's breasts but has had none of her own. As mentioned earlier, the acquisition of her first brassiere is an important *rite de passage* to be noted as a unique event, marking the recognition of breasts in female development.

One of the classical psychoanalytic concepts of adolescence that is frequently considered explanatory is the "second chance" or second individuation process (Blos 1980). Though perhaps relevant to other aspects of development, this concept is noted here in order to emphasize the unique aspects of feminine adolescence. Breast development, menarche, and subsequent menstruation are not second chances—these are firsts! Moreover, adolescents, both male and female, are interested in and intrigued by the physical attributes of the same and the other sex. As stated by one author, "Adolescent girls visually undress boys routinely, just as the reverse happens, but girls keep this a secret among themselves" (Sugar 1990, p. 3).

Menarche and Menses

Menarche, or the first menstrual period, is another unique female event that does not have any previous versions in female development; it, too, is a significant first. The onset of menses marks and contributes to the ongoing development of primary femininity. The beautiful description by Anne Frank bears repetition:

> [W]hat is happening to me is so wonderful, and not only what can be seen on my body, but all that is taking place inside. I never discuss myself with anybody: that is why I have to talk to myself about this.
>
> Each time I have a period—and that has only been three times— I have the feeling that in spite of all the pain, unpleasantness, and nastiness, I have a sweet secret, and that is why, although it is nothing but a nuisance to me, I always long for the time that I shall feel that secret within me again. [age 14 years 6 months in Dalsimer 1986, p. 117]

Anne Frank, in this passage, refers to her "sweet secret . . . within," menstruation, in conjunction with what can be seen on her body. She has experienced earlier body changes, including newly curved hips, the emergence of breasts, and newly grown pubic hair. For many years the popular expressions used to denote menstruation, such as "the curse" and "monthly sickness," reflected a negative view of menstruation. Anne Frank's "sweet secret within," in the form of the term "I have my friend," has been added to the vocabulary of young girls as cultural attitudes have changed.

The female center of procreativity was defined above as primary femininity fueled by active engulfment. Menstruation as a biopsychosocial process adds significantly to the adolescent development of primary femininity. Though the little girl has had some early intimations of the presence of female internal organs, the menses focus and enhance the adolescent's positive awareness of her uterus and other associated reproductive organs.

In addition, menarche and the menstrual process create new possibilities in the girl's enlarging identifications with her mother. In many instances mother's instructions about menarche have induced the attitudes with which this event is received by the girl. However, it is not only the information but the underlying reflections of mother's feminine self image that are important in the mother–daughter interaction around menstruation.

Menstruation also marks the establishment of reproduction as a biological possibility for girls. There are changes in the feminine body image and feminine expansion of the ego ideal that now include her reproductive potential. This is further enlarged, particularly in late adolescence and in adulthood, if motherhood is accomplished.

Other Aspects of Adolescence

Adolescence is a developmental period of expansion of relationships outside the family and into the broader arenas of society. These have been characterized as separation or "breaking away" from the family, particularly from mother and from significant other adults. The terms *loosening* and *expansion* are more relevant descriptive terms for female adolescents. Though rebellion and turbulence may characterize this period, recent studies do indicate that there are other available pathways for adolescents. These include a rather steady and relatively calm progression through these years (Offer 1969).

The obvious and sometimes abrasive differences in the values and customs of teenagers from those of their parents are evident for both males and females. However, they may be seen as a difference as opposed to a total rejection of parental values. Though differing from and battling with adults is certainly important, a feeling of overall acceptance for the girl, particularly by her mother, continues to be most important. The differentiations and comparisons that female adolescents make contain an implicit ongoing identification with the mother. For example, adolescent girls will borrow their mothers' jewelry, makeup, and other items at the same time as they apparently express verbal rejection of their mothers' appearance.

As adolescence proceeds into late adolescence, the manifold expressions will include more obvious acknowledgment of the values and behaviors of mother and other family figures. These may be accompanied by verbal rejection, but if we look below the surface we see gender-identity development in late adolescence as containing many aspects of the young woman's family, and particularly of her mother.

CLINICAL EXAMPLE

A clinical example will illustrate some difficulties in the development of primary femininity and the mother–daughter relationship, especially in adolescence:

> Ms. A., an attractive professional woman in her mid-twenties, had symptoms of depression with crying jags, decreased appetite, and some weight loss. These symptoms and feelings were perplexing to her, as she generally regarded herself as well adjusted and having had, in her words, "a relatively normal and happy childhood." As Ms. A. told her story in her psychoanalysis, she soon developed a positive transference to her male analyst and explored the complexities of her relationship with her father and with the analyst. She was her father's acknowledged favorite child. He had taken care of her physical, emotional, and other needs, including academic ones. He was solicitous and loving, rubbing her foot nightly when, as a school-aged child, she had developed a recurrent, severe, undiagnosable "neuralgia." In addition, he did her homework with her every night, "not giving me the answers but asking me many questions so I learned to think." When doing this nightly work they sat together on a couch in which she was held tightly between the couch arm and her father. Several years of analysis seemed to suffice for a resolution of her "oedipal" ties to her father.
>
> Her life progressed, and yet she was unable to marry or have children. She returned to psychoanalysis, saying, "I could not really see myself walking down the aisle without crying and feeling miserable," and she began to cry, muttering "my father. . . ."
>
> A first dream heralded the work to be done: "I'm sitting at a table and a woman is pouring tea for me. Through a window I can see lush, fertile greenery. Inside we are sitting and the tea is being poured from beautiful pots into

lovely cups and saucers." She talked about fertility, pregnancy, and children in her associations to the greenery, and pleasure in having tea with this older woman. Her story this time revealed distress in what had heretofore seemed an entirely positive relationship with her father during adolescence. He had continued his interest in her studies but was not interested in growing aspects of her adolescent femininity such as her dates or the beauty of her prom dress. She felt disappointed and asked, "Where was my mother?" She complained about her mother: "When I started high school she was so strict, she did not let me wear nylons or lipstick. All my girlfriends were wearing makeup and even dating. She was not interested in what my girlfriends were doing. She had so many rules."

These are familiar complaints of adolescent females which seem to be filled with desire to rebel against mother and her rules. This is one aspect of these complaints, but as analysis proceeded, other aspects began to emerge. She repeated, "Where was my mother? She was not around, she was only in the kitchen, she was not with me." As the patient reviewed and explored her adolescent world that extended well beyond home, she became aware of the absence of her mother's influence. She discovered that she had missed her mother, saying her mother had delivered "rules but not recipes." She realized that emotional distance had developed and increased during adolescence, particularly between herself and her mother. She eventually said, "She [mother] didn't teach me how to be a teenager or a woman." In the psychoanalytic amplification of her material, her lack of connection with her mother indicated impediments to her identifications with mother in adolescence and earlier, which had interfered especially with the development of her femininity in late adolescence and early womanhood.

Her mother was a powerful negative force in adolescence, setting rigid rules about female behavior including dress, makeup, and dating. As indicated in Ms. A.'s statement, "She gave me rules but not recipes," her mother did not adequately nurture her adolescent feminine wishes and desires. Likewise, in childhood, mother had not assisted Ms. A.'s growing interest in her father. And it is likely that other aspects of primary femininity were not sufficiently supported. Particularly in the complexities of reciprocal identificatory processes, the relationship between mother and daughter was narrow, stilted, and impoverished.

In this example we note by its absence the importance of an ongoing and continuing enlargement of the full range of feminine identifications with mother that is necessary for female adolescent development. Ms. A. experienced increasing distance and nonexpansion of maternal identifications. Early development of primary femininity, though not seriously impaired, was characterized by impoverishment or weakness instead of full strength.

An example of this in early adolescence occurred at menarche, when the patient received "clean supplies—sanitary napkins but no talk" from her mother. Scientific information was then provided by her father, but this was not sufficient for Ms. A. to develop a full understanding or to receive affective support with regard to this important feminine event.

DISCUSSION

Borderline, narcissistic, and other serious psychic disturbances have received increasing attention, and most authors agree on the importance of pregenital pathology or disturbances of early development. Kernberg is an example of a current psychoanalytic writer who emphasizes this position in his classic volume *Borderline Conditions and Pathological Narcissism* (1975):

> Many of the authors referred to above [Fairbairn, Klein, Jacobson, Greenson, and Khan, among others] also consider the genetic-dynamic aspects of borderline personality organization, and all of them stress the importance of pregenital, especially oral conflicts in these patients, and the unusual intensity of their pregenital aggression. They also stress the peculiar combination of pregenital drive derivatives and genital ones. . . . [pp. 7–8]

Such statements often remain non-gendered, but Kernberg becomes more specific about the girl:

> Severe oral pathology of the kind mentioned tends to develop the positive Oedipal strivings prematurely in the girl. Genital strivings for father are used as a substitute gratification of oral-dependent needs that have been frustrated by the dangerous mother. This effort tends to be undermined by the contamination of the father image with pregenital aggression deflected from mother and projected onto him, and also because oral rage and especially oral envy powerfully reinforce penis envy in women. [p. 42]

Our discussion of the early genital period has emphasized the importance of assistance by the mother of the girl's feelings for the father and vice versa. Kernberg, like others in their non-gendered descriptions, seems to maintain the position of Freud in regard to early development, that is, there is no difference at best, or gender is masculine for both sexes in the first three years of life. When Kernberg describes the girl he resorts to explanations of premature oedipal strivings and penis envy. These are not only insufficient for the understanding of female development and pathology, but, as I have noted earlier, they are also inaccurate with regard to female development as far as the Oedipus complex is concerned. These formulations require an understanding of a separate line of development in order to be applied to women.

CONCLUSION

In this paper female adolescent development was characterized in terms of an expansion of primary femininity and female identity formation. The implications of breast development and menarche were discussed as new events occurring in early female adolescence, in distinction to what has traditionally been the primary explanatory concept of adolescence, namely a reworking in a "second chance" individuation process.

A separate line of female psychological development was presented, starting at birth or before, with emphasis placed on primary femininity/active engulfment, female identity development and the ongoing development of a mother–daughter relationship in reciprocal identificatory processes. Both differentiation and simultaneous interdependence were described as important aspects of the female adolescent's relationship with her mother in particular, as well as with others.

As far as the case presentation is concerned, without such a theoretical orientation in regard to development the difficulties of Ms. A. when she returned to analysis might have continued to remain outside the therapeutic arena.

In the first dream of the analysis, the mother/analyst is very much present in the wished-for tea party. In this dream the vessels, cups, and saucers, are beautiful and admired by both women. As in the dream, our analytic cups containing an understanding of, and theoretical formulations about, female psychology have been rather empty. In particular, female psychoanalytic theory has been, at best, minimal. Though our cups do not run over, we are beginning to pour tea, in a sense, as we focus on and formulate a separate line of female development.

REFERENCES

Blos, P. (1980). Modifications in the traditional psychoanalytic theory of female adolescent development. In *Adolescent Psychiatry, VIII*, ed. S. Feinstein. Chicago: University of Chicago Press.

Blum, H. (1976). Masochism, the ego ideal and the physiology of women. *Journal of the American Psychoanalytic Association* 24(5):157–191.

——— (1977). *Female Sexuality: Contemporary Psychoanalytic Views*. New York: International Universities Press.

Chodorow, N. (1978). *The Reproduction of Mothering*. Berkeley, CA: University of California Press.

Clower, V. (1975). Significance of masturbation in female sexual development and function. In *Masturbation: From Infancy to Senescence*, ed. I. Marcus and J. Francis, pp. 107–143. New York: International Universities Press.

——— (1979). Theoretical implications in current views of masturbation in latency girls. In *Female Psychology*, ed. H. Blum, pp. 109–125. New York: International Universities Press.

Dalsimer, K. (1986). *Female Adolescence: Psychoanalytic Reflections on Literature*. New Haven, CT: Yale University Press.

Deutsch, H. (1944). *The Psychology of Women, vols. 1 and 2*. New York: Grune and Stratton.

Freud, A. (1958). Adolescence. *Psychoanalytic Study of the Child* 16:255–278. New York: International Universities Press.

Freud, S. (1905). Three essays on the theory of sexuality. *Standard Edition* 7:135–243.

——— (1925). Some psychical consequences of the anatomical distinction between the sexes. *Standard Edition* 19:243–258.

——— (1931). Female sexuality. *Standard Edition* 21:225–243.

——— (1933). On femininity. *Standard Edition* 22:112–135.

——— (1938). An outline of psycho-analysis. *Standard Edition* 23:141–208.

Gilligan, C. (1982). *In a Different Voice: Psychological Theory and Women's Development*. Cambridge, MA: Harvard University Press.

Gilligan, C., Lyons, N. P., and Hanner, J. J. (1990). *Making Connections: The Relational Worlds of Adolescent Girls at Emma Willard School*. Cambridge, MA: Harvard University Press.

Johnson, L. (1985). Personal communication.

Kernberg, O. (1975). *Borderline Conditions and Pathological Narcissism*. New York: Jason Aronson.

Kestenberg, J. (1968). Outside and inside, male and female. *Journal of the American Psychoanalytic Association* 6:457–520.

Kleeman, J. (1976). Freud's views on early female sexuality in the light of direct child observation. *Journal of the American Psychoanalytic Association* 24:3–27.

Kulish, N. M. (1991). The mental representation of the clitoris: the fear of female sexuality. *Psychological Inquiry* 11(4):511–536.

Miller, J. B. (1984). The development of women's sense of self (Work in Progress No. 12). Wellesley, MA: Stone Center Working Papers Series.

Notman, M., Klein, R., Jordan, J., and Zilbach, J. J. (1991). Women's unique developmental issues across the life cycle. In *Review of Psychiatry, vol. 10*, ed. A. Tasman and S. Goldfinger, pp. 558–577. Washington, DC: American Psychiatric Press.

Notman, M., Zilbach, J. J., Miller, J. B., and Nadelson, C. (1986). Themes in psychoanalytic understanding of women: some reconsiderations of autonomy and affiliation. *Journal of the American Academy of Psychoanalysis* 14(2):241–253.

Offer, D. (1969). *The Psychological World of the Teen-Ager*. New York: Basic Books.

Parens, H., Pollock, L., Stern, J., et al. (1977). On the girl's entry into the Oedipus complex. In *Female Psychology*, ed. H. Blum, pp. 79–107. New York: International Universities Press.

Rich, A. (1978). *The Dream of a Common Language: Poems 1974–1977*. New York: Norton.

Roiphe, H., and Galenson, E. (1981). *Infantile Origins of Sexual Identity*. New York: International Universities Press.

Stoller, R. J. (1976). Primary femininity. *Journal of the American Psychoanalytic Association* 24:59–79.

——— (1980). Femininity. In *Women's Sexual Development: Exploration of Innerspace*, ed. M. Kirkpatrick. New York: Plenum.

Sugar, M. (1990). The atypical adolescent and sexuality: an overview. In *Atypical Adolescence and Sexuality*. New York: Norton.

Tyson, P., and Tyson, T. (1990). *The Psychoanalytic Theory of Development: An Integration*. New Haven, CT: Yale University Press.

Zilbach, J. J. (1987). *In the "I" of the beholder: toward a separate path of development of women*. Slavson Lecture, American Group Psychotherapy Association, New Orleans, February.

——— (1990). Adam's Rib: Early Development of Women. Psychoanalytic Forum: Boston College, Boston, MA, November.

——— (1993). Female adolescence: toward a separate line of female development. In *Female Adolescent Development, second edition*, ed. M. Sugar, pp. 45–61. New York: Brunner/Mazel.

In the Beginning Was Sexual Difference: Response to the Paper of Joan J. Zilbach, M.D., and Malkah T. Notman, M.D.

JACQUES HASSOUN, M.D.

Joan Zilbach's paper is remarkable in more ways than one. It forces us to clarify our theory of the femininity of the girl-child, and it introduces us to a *psychology* of femininity based on biogenetic considerations that we have had little occasion to inscribe in the field of our thinking in France, at least among those of us who are in the tradition of Freud and Lacan. We must nevertheless not lose sight of the fact that these issues seem to be crucial for a number of North American psychoanalysts who make reference to the imaginary of the anatomical body in the context of "political correctness" when they speak of femininity. So I want to examine some of the major points of Dr. Zilbach's contribution and to try, for my part, to set forth my own theoretical investigations concerning what is shaping up to be an especially fruitful difference of opinion.

It is indeed likely that the little girl receives, from different parts of her body and hence also from her clitoris and her vagina, proprio- and enteroceptive sensations. (The registration of proprioceptive sensations from the uterus seems to me to be much more problematical.) Now these sensations, in and of themselves, cannot convey any information about the nature of these organs. Since they are concealed from view, nonfunctional, and generally not erotized by the mother's speech or handling, such sensations remain perfectly enigmatic for the little girl, whereas for the little boy "making peepee" is immediately visible, immediately caught up in the discursive network. This dissymmetry when it comes to the immediacy of visual and discursive perception will turn out to have substantial effects on the history of the little girl and the little boy.

Having said that, I want to return to Dr. Zilbach's hypothesis. We have to ask ourselves how, in this situation, an infant, a baby, can have a thought about difference?[1] Isn't it only later that the child can identify and give erotic substance to this zone? Is there really a recognition that this zone comes under the heading of what will *secondarily* be called the genital? Isn't it speech, a discourse, that establishes this designation in the mind of the child? And isn't it this process of naming that, *retroactively*, confers meaning on these initial sensations? Only this retroactivity of designation, since it is an effect of discourse, is truly inaugural.

It is in this context, therefore, that we can speak of the coming into play of different forms of identification. With reference to "direct observation"[2] and to Lacan's theory of the mirror stage,[3] it is clear that identification first takes place through difference, through separation. Thus it is only to the extent that the child recognizes the Other before recognizing herself or himself—*through deduction*—that she or he accedes to the first forms of identification. From imaginary identification to the kind we call symbolic, there is a journey that establishes the subjectivity of the child (here, of the little girl) and enables her not to be the clone of her mother. In this respect the mother's discourse, distracted from her daughter by an *other*, an *elsewhere*, establishes a structural difference that allows the girl to separate from her and introduces her to the concept of difference. This is why it is difficult for the girl to identify herself as a woman before she identifies with her *mother*.[4] Identify-

---

1. *Editor's note*: Difference cannot be reduced to sexual difference, even though it is sexual difference that gives meaning, retroactively, to the whole gamut of differences that first the child, then the subject, needs to symbolize.

2. I would like to mention to Dr. Zilbach that I founded the first group of psychoanalysts to be involved in French nursery schools (in 1966). From 1968 on, I was the first psychoanalyst formally attached to the main office overseeing maternal and child protective services in La Seine-Saint-Denis, under the directorship of Mme. de Chambrun.

3. To be sure, Wallon had already described this stage, but Lacan takes it up in other terms and extends it theoretically in a way that goes far beyond Wallon's observations. *Translator's note*: For Lacan's theory of the mirror stage, see Preface, above, and Lacan 1949.

4. *Editor's note*: The imaginary identification has its roots in the mirror stage: the self is first constituted by the image of an other. The symbolic, or secondary, identification links the child to the signifiers of the desire of the other.

ing with the *mother* at an early period and then detaching herself from this image, that is, constituting the mother as a woman at a later period in order to be able to identify herself with a *woman*, is the path the little girl takes. It is a journey that leads her to follow a trajectory, from the imaginary to the symbolic, that establishes her as a woman.

This tension of identificatory processes will recur in the so-called oedipal phase, which places the little girl and the little boy in structurally asymmetric positions. Hate/love for the father, hate/love for the mother in the little girl and little boy alike make for a play of rupture and continuity that allows the child to identify via difference and, at the same time, allows the little girl to establish her femininity.

I like to say[5] that it is at this moment that the little girl can ask herself a crucial question about her father: "What does he find in her [the mother] that he doesn't have?" This questioning with regard to *having* raises the issue of the father's castration, an issue to which the boy—fixated on "what he is afflicted with," the penis that he naively, stupidly confuses with the phallus—gains access only with the greatest difficulty.[6]

Indeed, if we consider that what introduces the child to her or his status as subject is represented by the first loss, the resulting detachment will make itself heard in the discourse of the desiring subject throughout her or his entire life. *It is in the time when a body is distinguished from the image of the maternal other that difference and limit are established.* This is not a datable moment, since it is caught up in the very time of the genealogy of the parental signifiers. It is represented by the event that I designate as child death, the psychic trace of the death of "His Majesty the Baby" with respect to the mother's desire.[7]

It is in this light that the child will have to be confronted, later on, with an organic differentiation that some try—in vain—to isolate from the rest, as if a brief glance at the body of someone who is different could have, as its source of light, an "elsewhere," radically foreign to the initial loss. Or, to bring up a question asked by Moustafa Safouan, "Does the eye," looking at the body of the other, at that moment "take a rest from

---

5. See Hassoun 1979a.

6. *Editor's note:* In Lacanian theory castration implies the recognition by both sexes that no one can be or have the phallus. Penis envy is a metaphor which stands for the girl's desire to be the phallus—the exclusive object of the other's desire—or to have it so as to be able to offer it to her mother.

7. This involves the first introduction of the signifier "mourning." Cf. Hassoun 1979b, 1987, 1995.

the gaze?"[8] Safouan was referring to a gaze directed at a picture, but at this moment that occurs as fixed in a unique temporality, doesn't the other's body, presenting itself as so astonishing, form a picture? Here I want to remind you that no gaze can ever take in the entirety of a body. There is always a part that remains absent, in the shade, and hence can be represented only by an effort of reconstruction.[9]

But the child, at this instant of discovery, tries to situate loss, and the geographical configuration of the female body to which he is directing his attention is there to remind him that there is always absence. Thus what is exchanged at this moment is a gaze. Gazes cross at a virtual point, a point of ascertainment of a *dis-equipping* that creates all the importance, the violence and the charm, always renewed, of the encounter. It should be emphasized that the ascertained absence and non-absence tend to demonstrate the radical dissymmetry of the masculine and feminine positions with respect to castration.

This leads us to interrogate that extreme surrender of the boy to frantic idealizations, a surrender that allows us to postulate that men who believe only their eyes (which makes them blind idiots) are those whose gaze returns onto their own bodies, remains fixed there, and thus no longer questions the body from the virtual viewpoint of the encounter. This astonished male will never complain about anything. Obviously.

Who isn't fooled in this story? And who is? Women who want to believe that there are some people for whom all is not lost? Perhaps. . . . Although, whatever the nature of the discourse—ideological or flowery—that is recounted to them, they always know in the end that there is a body, the mother's, in which absence is as important as it is for themselves, and that this is why it is the object of invocation and love.

As a repetition of the first loss, doesn't this moment of *ascertainment of difference* refer back to the moment when the girl asks the only person who cannot hear her, the father, the question about castration? Does the father becomes a sexual object for her because, since she herself could not be the object of her mother's desire, she identifies with the desire that

---

8. In Lacan 1964, p. 103 (translation modified).

9. And at this point, too, we may wonder—this is a question that was surely asked frequently in the past, but it (re)arises here very appositely—whether Picasso, when he fragmented the body on canvas by *seeming* to show the entire body, wasn't actually revealing the nature of this illusion of a gaze able to take in the body in its entirety.

motivates the mother? Does he stop being this sexual object because he has no answer to the girl's question about the castration in which, sooner or later, she finds him caught up just as she herself is? Or does the father's message, intervening as a prohibitive third party in this second phase, take on for the girl (more clearly than for the boy) the function of a metaphoric substitution for the mother's desire? Introduced by the maternal discourse, the message he brings is perceived and, eventually, understood, in the wake of the *secondary identification* of the girl's body with the body of *this woman who is the mother*, as that which establishes her as a subject. Isn't this recognition the basis of debt, the axis around which the existence of the speaking subject revolves?

In this passage from being to having[10] that the child (the little girl or boy) traverses, there are played out the different acts of a drama in which what is lost is symbolized as "before, it isn't there; afterwards it's no longer there." For, once it is symbolized, what is is no longer anything but *a language act caught in a snapshot whose function is to keep on slipping away.*

That cannot be represented, and this is what causes both of these elements to delineate the contours of an ever-renewed absence: "The eye takes a rest from the gaze," as Safouan says, and, as Lacan has it, what the painter shows "is never what I want to see," since the painter who puts on canvas colors and forms, and—why not?—even depictions of human beings, places there only what moves and stirs him, what is stamped by the seal of lack.[11]

The problem can be posed in a different way. Let us begin with the mythic body of the wondrous child of primary narcissism. The intervention of the third term at the time of primary identification with the father causes a split, and what is lost is represented by a twist like the one formed by the Möbius band. For the girl, identification with the mother's body and the attempt to draw closer to the father (as I have described it above) cause the band to twist a second time, so that now it does not return to its point of departure but, on the contrary, gets further away from it. It is located on another longitudinal plane but on the same meridian and thus signals the recognition that there is something different in the geographi-

---

10. *Translator's note:* The reference is to being the phallus or having it.

11. And to join, eleven years later, the debate between Wahl and Lacan (Lacan 1964, p. 118) on the "evil eye," I would say that there is only a *discriminative* evil eye: it represents the gaze in its *differentiating* qualities.

cal configuration of the body—even/especially when there is something similar to it—in such a way that "all the same, the same is transformed."[12]

Is it because the boy stays in, or around, the one original twist that he remains more subject than the girl to frantic idealizations?[13] That remains to be seen. . . .

Finally, if we consider that there are no stages (oral, anal, etc.) but instead phases that bear witness to the demand of the Other, doesn't the speaking subject's first structuring and founding loss appear at each of these phases and lend them its weight? In these circumstances, couldn't we assert that the loss, far from being spoken in two different registers, is outlined and re-marked only in the locus of the Other's listening? It is perhaps here that the reference to the geographic configuration of the body takes on its full weight so as to shuffle the cards all the better and leave the loss in a shadow zone.

In short, what seems to disturb the young adolescent male is the unexpected appearance of a silent beauty that, for him, has the status of "woman" more than of "a woman." The latter then acts out the complaint, because she seems incapable of uttering it. She acts out the complaint because she is "feminine in the beyond," in-human, un-livable.[14]

Perhaps this is what, from another perspective, accounts for the agitation that the father feels with respect to the little girl at the moment of

---

12. *Editor's note*: The daughter's encounter with her mother's desire (lack) is only secondarily connected to sexual difference. Moreover, unlike the boy, the girl has a second chance, so to speak, in the sense that she can seek in her father what may fulfill her desire (lack). Her primary "imaginary" identification with her mother will undergo a twist as she turns to her father and searches, through his signifiers, for a lead that will give her access to her femininity. As she follows the signifying path of his desire she will return to her primary locus of identification (the mother), but not the same as she was when she left her in the first place, that is, during the early stage of the oedipal complex. In other words, the girl's feminity is not identical to her mother's in that it has been informed by the signifiers of her father's desire.

13. *Editor's note*: The boy is more prone to denial about the true meaning of castration. Sexual difference as the realization of lack-of-being is confused with a sexual difference that attributes "lack" only to the other sex.

14. *Editor's note*: The woman's complaint consists in her not being recognized as a human being whose desire has been stamped by a lack that she fully acknowledges. She experiences herself as excluded from the realm of words, as if her femaleness served only as warrant for men's own denied fear of castration.

ascertainment, the moment when *she* ascertains, when she becomes the one who asks questions with no possible answer, since the man to whom she asks the questions is caught up in loss just as much as she is, especially if he wants to remain ignorant of it.

This question can be broken down into a twofold interrogation. The first, addressed to the mother, could be formulated as: "What are you looking for, in him, that you don't have and that I can't give you?" The second, addressed to the father, amounts to: "What do you find in her . . . that you don't have?"

Isn't feminine sexuality what allows us, nowadays, to draw up the critical catalog of the beliefs and convictions that enable us to posit the mother as mortal and the subject as traversed by a fundamental death? As a question, therefore, feminine sexuality can also be a means of approaching what is central in the desiring subject: the process of loss. But in order to get there, we have to leave behind the comfort of received ideas and go back to tracing the sad remains of the first truths that hinder and overwhelm us.

And, finally, if we consider that, as Safouan has said, the field of analytic experience is one in which thought slips between perception and awareness, if we consider, too, that only the madman doesn't know that there is always difference, we can then understand that the geographical configuration of the body, of the female body in part' 'lar, is always secondary—in all the senses of the term. Nevertheless, hasn't what manifests itself as absent, geographically absent, allowed us to suspend the question posed by loss at the point of understanding this absence as the source of an aberration that assigns women the one role, that of complaint? Is it this complaint that language indexes with the term *maternal*?

In any case, it seems to me that for the patient Dr. Zilbach calls Ms. A the dialectic of having was not an issue in her first analysis, and that later on, when she worked with Dr. Zilbach, she had to pass through the strata of this dialectic of having/not having that gave her access to symbolic castration.

These several considerations bring up epistemological questions about the passage from neurobiological categories to those of the unconscious, even if the unconscious cannot, of course, be understood except insofar as it is inscribed in the *erotic body* of the subject. The same remark is called for in connection with the expression "active engulfment" that runs through the amorous, passionate encounter in which the sexual culmination is only one of the parameters. . . . Is it useful to recall that if the boy "penetrates," he also does so in order to "be surrounded"? It is strange to consider that women usually fail to recognize this aspect of things.

However, it is obvious that feminine *jouissance* has its own characteristics, that it—partially—eludes phallic *jouissance*.[15] But what would be a *jouissance* that was not based on putting difference into play? What would be a *jouissance* that did not put into play the dialectic of same and other in accordance with what Lacan ascribes to the non-visualizable phallus? The cancellation of this hypothesis would reduce *jouissance* to the mere putting into play of the pleasure principle, which would not suffice to define or characterize the desiring subject.[16]

As for the issue of adolescence: it is remarkable to consider that this state, merely a virtual one until the end of the nineteenth century, appears nowadays as an actual fact. Although in primitive societies, as it happens, it is the little boy who, shut out from the language of mothers, from the society of mothers, undergoes a radical break at the time of initiation, the little girl, for her part, seems less subject to this separating violence. It is clear that contemporary western societies greatly prolong the time in which the adolescent continues to be a girl or a boy without the question of becoming a mother or a father arising immediately. In this regard, adolescence is a new development that has established itself in actual time, whereas before it was only a virtual time. *Thus it is the question of difference, and also of nonreciprocity, that from now on must be on the agenda.* It is the identification through difference (which implies the same and the other) that will predominate for the girl who, endowed with breasts, menstrual periods, and attributes of *maternity*,[17] will for a longer or shorter time have to deal with them as attributes of *femininity* before including them in a process that will inscribe her as a mother.

---

15. It should be kept in mind that the phallus is *not the penis*. The phallus that cannot be visualized is always written with a minus sign: -Φ. *Editor's note*: Phallic *jouissance* refers to the sexual pleasure that is produced by the acceptance of sexual difference. Yet Lacan suggests that, since women are less subject to the laws of castration than are men, they have access to an additional type of sexual pleasure, as in the mystical rapture of St. Teresa of Avila.

16. I recall that in 1973 I said to a young lesbian analysand in the course of a session: "Even in the case of a homosexual couple composed of two identical twin women, there's difference!" Needless to say, this intervention had a remarkable structuring effect on the patient.

17. Don't these secondary sexual characteristics in fact depend on the maternal, on that maternal part that intersects feminine sexuality?

All these questions lead me to conclude that Dr. Zilbach's contribution opens a crucial debate on the problems of imaginary and symbolic identification and on what underlies difference: a dialectization of continuity and discontinuity, without which identification would never be anything but an attempt to establish sameness, if not cloning, from one generation to the next—a mere *reproduction*.

Our theoretical differences have led me to state what is at the heart of Freud's (and Lacan's) system: the primacy of difference *on the basis of* what presents itself, and can only present itself, as defined by its quality of being non-visualizable. Such an actualization of difference (between the two of us as well) seems to me to promise a fruitful exchange, since this tension is maintained. In this regard the tension allows for the desirous circulation that is the very basis of what we call a "working transference."

So: to be continued. . . .

REFERENCES

Hassoun, J. (1979a). *La plainte*. Lecture presented in 1976 in the seminar of Moustafa Safouan. First edition, Paris: Payot, 1979; second edition, revised and enlarged, Paris: Point Hors Ligne, 1993.

———— (1979b). *Fragments de la langue maternelle*. Paris: Payot.

———— (1987). *Les Indes Occidentales*. Paris: L'Éclat.

———— (1995). *La cruauté mélancholique*. Paris: Audier.

Lacan, J. (1949). The mirror stage as formative of the function of the I. In *Ecrits: A Selection*, trans. A. Sheridan. New York: Norton, 1977.

———— (1964). Seminar XI, published as *The Four Fundamental Concepts of Psychoanalysis*, ed. J.-A. Miller, trans. A. Sheridan. New York: Norton, 1981.

Excerpts from the Discussion

Anna Ornstein: I'm wondering about what I heard concerning a kind of fusion between gender or gender identification, and sexuality. I think there is a heuristic value in separating these two, because with what we have now learned about gender identification and how early indeed that occurs, we do not have to resort to physical sensation as an explanation for whether a girl is able to experience herself as a girl. And here I found myself in agreement with Dr. Hassoun (though I don't know whether he meant to say this) that it will be in the mother's and father's gaze, in the very way in which they interact with their baby, that the little girl will experience herself as a girl-child, and the boy as a boy-child. This early gender identification is not, I believe, the same as what you described as the sexuality of the child as we witness it during adolescence. That sexuality is a hormonal, physical appearance, and it has to dovetail with what comes from the environment in terms of affirmation and validation.

Where I found myself in great disagreement with you is in connection with the mother–daughter relationship, and this comes from my analytic work and not direct observation. As she now moves into her sexual experiences, if her gender identity was firmly enough established earlier in her life the girl-child will absolutely need the mother's affirming and

validating response to the value of her sexuality. So I suggest that we recognize that the early gender experiences may be less dependent on physical sensation and more on environmental responses, and that in adolescence we have a very powerful addition from the hormonal and physical
part of ourselves and our identity. This dovetailing is what we need to watch
in the closer examination of our analytic work, because it does come out
in the transference.

Paul Ornstein: I found Joan Zilbach's exposition to be a tremendous im-
provement over the prior conceptualization in classical analysis. The notion
of primary femininity is appealing, but the paper seemed to me to fall short
precisely on the issue of the role of the father's and mother's response in
affirming the girl's femininity.

   The self psychologist views development, when it proceeds reasonably normally, as an affirmation of what is already innate or given, or available in the child as a tendency, or as something that is partly endowment,
partly in the parents' imagination of what this child's femininity, or this
child's masculinity, will be. Instead of seeing identification as a mode of
achieving psychological structure formation, we view it as occurring in
response to the availability of the affirmation on the one hand, and the
possibility of the idealization of the parental imagoes on the other. It is
this internalization that leads to structure formation—and I believe, therefore, also to the formation of femininity or masculinity.

Michel Feher: If you will permit a question from a nonanalyst: Dr. Zilbach
contrasted the traditional Freudian theory of feminine adolescence, one in
which female adolescence and feminine identity are constituted as secondary with regard to masculinity, with a theory of a more endogenous constitution of feminine identity. So we may well wonder why this was never
recognized before in history, and I would imagine, since you said that this
was a traditional feminist presentation, that the reason is that there is clear
evidence of patriarchal interests at work in classical Freudian theory.

   But there are two other historical determinants to be considered. When
you call yourself a traditional feminist, what tradition do you have in mind?
In American feminism, even recent American feminism—that is, from the
'60s and '70s—there are at least two traditions. A radical feminism was the
first to emerge; it remains quite Freudian, insofar as in the work of Kate
Millett or Shulamith Firestone, for example, male power over women is
seen in a problematic social context against which women have to rebel.

There is a strong emphasis on the rebellious aspect of adolescence. In the more recent movement of what is called cultural feminism, on the other hand, the emphasis is on the cultural, indeed natural, identity of women, and thus a feminine community needs to be reconstituted. Here what is important is not the adolescent girl's rebellion against her parents as guardians of the social and symbolic order, but instead the rediscovery of the traces of a buried feminine culture, in which venture the mother is the privileged ally.

As you describe it, the adolescent girl's emerging sexuality seems quite narcissistic; that is, the other is encountered at the endpoint of the development of the self. First there is the play of internal sensations, then on to the breast, and finally the other is somehow found. Is this something that was always there but was hidden by theory, or are you suggesting that there has been a sociological evolution with regard to the accession of girls to adolescence, perhaps in the lowering of the age of the onset of sexual activity, and hence a new subjective formation?

Lora Heims Tessman: I would conjecture that the inner organization of libidinal wishes is part of what determines the identity and character of the adult and is extraordinarily important from the beginning. I want to comment first on the infant girl, then the toddler's response to mother and to the sexuality between the parents, and then I'll skip briefly to adolescence.

We now have some data that weren't previously available about infant behavior. It turns out that infant girls, beginning at 66 hours—2½ days—respond to the cry of another newborn child more than infant boys do. Infant girls hold the gaze of the mother, in contrast to the greater tendency of infant boys to use gaze aversion to deal with stimulation. Infant girls, though generally less aggressive, are more fussy at one particular time, and that is if the mother interrupts the gazing dialogue for five minutes and then returns. I don't think of these aspects as meaning that the girl is more dependent on the mother and less differentiated (though much of feminist theory believes this), but rather that there is a libidinal organization having to do with connections to others that begin very early in life and are continued in the girl's inner fantasies in regard to later sexual sensations as well.

During toddlerhood—ages 2 to 3—girls are much more reactive to the frown of the mother than boys are, and mothers are apt to frown at them when the girl gets aggressive, more than at the boy. At the same age we find in girls but not in boys a correlation between doing something aggressive and a reparative, caretaking act. I'm not interested in comparing boys and girls at the moment, but in describing how these features of experiencing connections libidinally go with the girl's early female sexual sensations, which have an interiority, a circular motion—which "leak," as women in analysis will describe it, from one orifice to another and imply certain wishes to control that. Little girls of 3 or 4 in play therapy will describe accurately the exciting sexual connection between father and mother, not around the genitals, but around the ways of cherishing and fighting. And what was brought up here—what the father does not have, that he turns to the woman for, and what the woman does not have that she turns to the man for—the girl makes identifications, at that age, around those issues as well.

Women in analysis often reveal detailed surmising about their mothers' sensual, affective, sexual fantasies. They usually seek from the woman analyst that she be more sensual, less forbidding, less anxious about the experiencing of a libidinal overflow than their mothers were. This is something they often put to the analyst as a question.

Janine Chasseguet-Smirgel: Since a member of the audience has said that he is not an analyst, and there may be others, I just want to recall that today, November 5, 1994, is not the first time femininity has been characterized as primary. The existence of primary femininity, in contrast to Freud's belief that femininity is secondary to penis envy, has existed since the '20s, for example in objections made by Abraham in the course of his correspondence with Freud, and in the work of Josine Müller and Karen Horney, and, last but not least, with Melanie Klein, who never declared herself a feminist but who based her entire theory on the primary nature of femininity, which has major consequences for women as well as for men. All this nearly caused a schism within psychoanalysis at that time, so this is by no means a recent issue.

Lewis Kirschner: Dr. Zilbach, I wonder whether your discussion doesn't in a way deal with the idea that the girl assumes the femininity that the culture has prepared for her, as opposed to the idea that the femininity that the girl will find is somehow unique to her, has an unconscious meaning, which is what the psychoanalyst is most interested in. There's a risk of falling into a normative concept of what a girl should be. I'm not sure how you avoid that, with the way you use the concept of primary femininity.

Jacques Hassoun: One of these days we really are going to have to make up our minds to distinguish between the phallus and the penis. Because if the phallus is the penis, then long live SCUM, the Society for Cutting Up Men. This is an extremely complex matter, but why not make things as complex as possible? Dr. Zilbach has raised a number of questions that perhaps assume the role of a shibboleth between American analysis and French analysis. I find that women in France will occasionally say that they are terrified by the possibility of an imaginary identification with their mothers, and it really surprises me to learn that such an identification is apparently not so intolerable elsewhere.

Joan Zilbach: As Dr. Chasseguet-Smirgel pointed out, the question of primary femininity obviously did not arise in November 1994, nor even in 1920, 1935, or 1937, nor even when Freud asked Lou Andréas-Salomé: "What does a woman want?" He was not the first to ask that question, and the answers, of course, have been coming in for many years, and I hope they will continue to come in.

Dr. Anna Ornstein's comments about the differences between gender identity and sex are ones that I'm very clear about, though because of the brevity of the paper I may have left the impression that I didn't distinguish between them. In a fuller exposition of the development of gender identity, you would hear exactly the position Dr. Ornstein took. One brief comment about my use of the term "feminist." I said "classical feminist psychoanalyst," not "classical psychoanalytic feminist." This has to do with the process of naming. I was naming myself, and what I meant was the use of the term "feminism" to concentrate on a woman's experience. Another omission, certainly a valid point, is the aspect of the identification and the relationship with the father. With regard to Dr. Tessman's comments about infant development, I think that the research in this area buttresses some of what I was saying today, but that would need to be gone into in some detail.

Dr. Hassoun spoke of the mirror stage and identification, and of the idea that development proceeds (as I understood what he was saying) by differentiation and separation as recognized in the gaze. That is a very important difference between us, since I talk about the recognition of sameness and the fact that differentiation comes later. The importance of the psychobiological resonance, and the sameness, is an essential aspect of very early development. Dr. Hassoun spoke of cloning as the opposite of difference. It is this cloning, this dependence, that has led to a lot of confusion over the years. Identification and sameness with mother—such terms are always an oversimplification—is not the same as cloning, is not the same as dependence, in the negative sense, and is an essential aspect of my paper.

I want to make only one comment about the relationships and the intricacies of the so-called oedipal period, though here again we could discuss them in great detail. Dr. Hassoun seems to be saying that the castration effect is symmetrical, is found on both sides in the relationship. It is certainly true in clinical material that we, as psychoanalysts, hear aspects of castration. I don't deny that. But, again, a central argument of this paper is that lacks or deficiencies (of which castration is a symbol) are only one aspect, and that what has been empty is the other aspect. What has been empty has been the positive element, in whichever phase of development—feminine development in particular—one wants to speak of.

Dr. Hassoun then went on to talk about adolescence, about how in primitive societies little boys are torn away from their mothers. I'm sure many people in the audience are familiar with the fact that little girls in many societies experience clitoridectomies in one form or another, and that is a rather brutal aspect of a relationship to femininity that, either fortunately or unfortunately, came to my mind when Dr. Hassoun mentioned the brutal ripping of the little boy from the mother. This takes us to an entirely different realm, and I bring it up only as an aspect of what happens in our associations as we move through this rather difficult material.

I want to end by using a phrase of Dr. Hassoun's: the dialectic of continuity and discontinuity. I think an essential aspect of my paper is that, in the dialectic of continuity and discontinuity, continuity in relation to femininity has had short shrift. And that is what my paper was about.

9

Aggression in Women: A Re-Examination[1]

MALKAH T. NOTMAN, M.D.

I would like to say a few words about the origin of this paper. It represents the thinking of several of us who met together over a period of months some years ago to develop ideas on major questions concerning the psychoanalytic psychology of women. These ideas have been both shared among us and individually developed, for example in Dr. Zilbach's presentation and in the work of Dr. Jean Baker-Miller, at the Stone Center, that has gone in a somewhat different direction.

We were concerned with some clinical phenomena that are familiar to all of us, but that we felt were inadequately explained by current psychoanalytic theory, namely problems of self-esteem and of depression in women. We were, and are, also interested in integrating psychoanalytic theory with findings from research and clinical observation. This does not mean reductionist empiricism; it is an attempt to represent and understand the realities of female experience. I have been impressed with the fact that much emphasis has been placed on the symbolic meaning of experiences and events, for example, the meaning of pregnancy, but not so much on

1. An earlier form of this paper was coauthored with Joan J. Zilbach, M.D., Jean Baker-Miller, M. D., and Carol Nadelson, M.D.

real events in a developing girl's and woman's life, events such as menarche, breast development, and pregnancy. The first studies of normal pregnancy took place in the 1960s in the United States.

We are now discovering new information and developing new ideas. For example, in the relatively new field of women's health it turns out that tests of cardiac function are different for women and men, the metabolism of alcohol and the function of certain of the enzymes involved in that metabolism are different for women, and so forth. However, many characteristics that were thought to be fundamental male–female differences, such as patterns of expectations and behavior, turn out to be socially constructed. In this paper we examine some aspects of aggression in women: the interrelationship between self-esteem and aggression, and particularly the negative effect that women's recognition of their own aggression has on their self-esteem. We clarify these concepts in light of the recent changes in understanding of early childhood development and of the impact of parental and societal attitudes, expectations, and definitions on psychological functioning. We recognize also that the generalizations we make do not consider cultural variations or individual differences, but they do reflect clinical and research observations within a particular cultural framework.

Every psychoanalyst reflects his or her own culture, and the culture in which early pychoanalytic hypotheses about femininity and feminine development arose was a phallocentric one. This imposed a particular bias on the interpretation of data and on the understanding of female development and intrapyschic processes. Most theoretical constructs of human development and behavior tacitly assumed the male as the model. This was true also in clinical formulations, despite the preponderance of female patients. Until recently, experimental data have come largely from male subjects. The female has been seen as a variant or deviant, or data about women have been excluded. Conceptualizations of feminine development and experience are currently undergoing reexamination in many quarters.

A full exploration of the relationship between aggression and self-esteem in women would require a careful consideration of instinct theory and its derivatives and a review of the theoretical concepts of narcissism and masochism. That ambitious task is beyond the scope of this paper, but some theoretical constructs are referred to here in the process of exploring the main theme: that self-esteem in women is diminished by women's recognition in themselves of aggression or of its derivatives, that is, of assertion, achievement, competence, and success. This loss of self-esteem is manifested as a sense of worthlessness, failure, and wrongdoing. The same is true to some extent for men, but the pathways of aggression are different for women.

The view of aggression as a destructive force concurs in general with Freud's concept (1905, 1920, 1923). Other psychoanalysts have taken a different view. Thompson, for example, stated that

> [a]ggression is not necessarily destructive at all. It springs from an innate tendency to grow and master life which seems to be characteristic of all living matter. Only when this life force is obstructed in its development do ingredients of anger, rage or hate become connected with it. [1973, p. 6]

Greenacre (1971) believed that aggression can be considered the expression of the life force of growth and is thus instinctual. Rochlin (1973) focused on the defensive components of aggression, stating that when narcissisism is threatened we are humiliated, self-esteem is injured, and aggression appears. Aggression thus stems from frustration. Clearly, in both the psychological and the psychoanalytic disciplines, there is no general agreement on the definition of aggression.

We define aggression in this paper as those actions and impulses toward action and assertion that give expression to the individual's own aims and/or have an effect on others. Thus aggression may be instinctual or defensive, innate or reactive, or thought to be constructive or destructive, depending on its form and direction. Individual striving toward autonomous action and self-assertion is included in this definition. This is a central concept.

Traditional psychoanalytic theory stated that women's aggression is converted into masochism and an accompanying passivity. Freud (1925), Deutsch (1930), and others believed that the efforts to effect this conversion form the key steps in the development of femininity. There was an implicit assumption that women and men begin life with the same quantity of aggression. Women's lifelong task, then, was to divest themselves of their direct aggression in order to achieve femininity. Furthermore, Freud and Deutsch believed that masochism was actually an innate characteristic in women, so that when women achieved this conversion of direct aggression they were reaching their (possibly) biologically appropriate condition.

Although it met with some objections, the combination of narcissism, passivity, and masochism as the "feminine triad" was accepted until recently as the cornerstone of the normative development of femininity. But though these traits may be linked in some women, they are not uniquely feminine and may have different developmental origins. Many have found these characteristics present, perhaps in different forms, in both men and women and believe masochism to be potentially pathological in both. Blum (1976), for example, pointed out that a woman cannot carry out the function of "good enough mothering" if she has arrived at a predominantly masochistic resolution of her aggression. The implication of this statement has been that women do possess and express aggression and activity, which are acceptable as long as they are expressed in the "feminine" mode of service to others, as in mothering. However, passivity comes about in many women as a result of the struggle to transform aggression as well as through socialization to certain gender roles. It may go beyond acceptable character style and lead to symptom development. Women who attempt, in psychoanalysis, to change their passive, masochistic adaptation often encounter serious internal conflict.

Many observations suggest that women also channel their impulses into making and preserving relationships rather than into direct or self-interested activity. In any event, they do preserve relationships. In itself this is adaptive and constructive. Problems arise, however, when relationships substitute for activity and action and thus serve a secondary goal. They can become the means by which a woman can feel some power or effectiveness, and thus the major source of her self-esteem. To cite just one of many examples, the loss of a relationship is one of the important factors in the development of depression, and depression is more frequent in women (Weissman and Klerman 1977). The relationship is not only a loss in itself but may have served a secondary defensive purpose.

In the male, "aggression" or direct action is deemed valuable and acceptable. If a man can succeed in directing his energies, he has the promise of obtaining relationships (and love). That is, others will approve of and love him for his use of his powers and his success. Thus "aggression" both is rewarded in itself and leads to relationships. For women, "aggression" is first denied and then, secondarily, can be channeled into making relationships.

Early in life women incorporate the belief that not only destructive aggression but their own direct, self-generated, self-directed, and self-interested aggression is unacceptable. This perception is further elaborated with each succeeding stage of development. As the ego ideal develops for most women, it contains the image of someone who is not overtly "aggressive" but more oriented to service and sacrifice. Therefore, to acknowledge one's aggression is threatening to this ego ideal; in such cases the woman sees herself as a failure, inadequate and inferior, and her already low self-esteem is diminished further. Bibring (1953) believed that depression reflects a loss of self-esteem arising from the discrepancy between ego ideals and awareness of real or imaginary defect and helplessness. One significant set of goals is the wish to be loving as opposed to aggressive. He also spoke of the narcissistic shock accompanying the sudden discovery of one's own destructive impulses.

As you know, depression is more common in women. Evidence that aggression in women is diverted or modified depressively comes from many sources, which I cannot review here. Whether aggression as activity and assertion can be separated from aggression as action aimed at destruction is a difficult and unsettled question. For women, however, there seem to be special problems. Aggression as action and assertion is also experienced as a destructive force, inevitably carrying the implication of the intent to hurt or destroy another. Thus, when women begin to become aware of the extent of their own aggression in a context where it has not been clear to them before, it is most likely to be experienced as incongruent and inappropriate, and therefore as disorganizing and overwhelming, potentially adding to fear and self-condemnation. This may be changing in the domain of sports.

The following clinical example illustrates a woman's difficulty in recognizing and effectively utilizing aggression as "self-serving" assertion.

CS was the oldest of nine children. Her father was irresponsible and all of the activity of supplying the material and psychological needs of the family had been undertaken by her typically long-suffering mother. CS early assumed the role of her mother's main helper and sympathizer. She was bright at school and had been encouraged by her teachers, but (as was commonly the case with girls) never to aspire to a very high level. After high school CS began work in a professional job. She gradually moved to a psychiatrically oriented setting and became increasingly admired for her gifts as a member of a therapeutic team. She was perceived as warm, giving, intelligent, and insightful and was very highly regarded and praised by both superiors and colleagues.

Shortly after high school she married a young man, T, who appeared charming and appealing. CS perceived him as being more intelligent and attractive than she was, and their general plan was that he would pursue college and a career while she supported him in these efforts.

Within a short time, it became apparent that T's charm hid profound problems. He failed repeatedly at school and at work and became increasingly alcoholic. He became involved with numerous other women. His actions toward CS progressed from inattention to extreme derogation and abusiveness. After tolerating his behavior for an inordinate length of time, CS began the first of several attempts at separation. On each of these occasions, T would switch to pleading for her return, and she would rejoin him. CS entered treatment during this period, acquiring some understanding of her difficulties but remaining unable to carry through the separation from T. By this time, she had reached her late twenties.

It became apparent that a major component of her inability to leave T was her perception that leaving him was a clear act of aggression toward him that she could not allow herself. It would also be a step in her own interest that would lead to possible satisfaction and enhance her effectiveness. CS's conflict about this took several forms, short of considering the unconscious meaning of the relationship. One form of conflict particularly related to self-esteem emerged around her often repeated statement that she "could not imagine [herself] as a person who could do such a thing." The phrase was more than a mere colloquial expression. She literally could not form an image of herself as someone who used her powers in her own interest. The attempt to form such an image led her initially to a blank: there was no way to see herself at all in that light. Later it yielded an image of "something" very evil. Still later, the attempt to create such an image led instead to repeated fantasies of being viciously condemned. Each time that CS came to this point, she could see the reality that no one would actually condemn her. She would then cry uncontrollably and insist that she must suffer. At times she would invoke a quasi-religious world view that "life is meant to be suffering."

CS was psychologically minded and had a good sense of reality, so she was able to observe the unreality of what she was experiencing. She knew she would not be condemned but would be supported by friends and colleagues. She also knew that her condemnation fantasies contained a projection of the anger she felt toward T. This anger had been recognized, but it did not seem to be the critical stumbling block.

A related aspect was her fantasy that T would be destroyed if she left. CS recognized the invalidity of this theme on several grounds. She knew that T served some "sick" purpose for her and she for him. She knew and had dealt with the fantasy that T stood for her two suffering parents whom she felt she had abandoned and thereby hurt by virtue of growing up and becoming an effective and well-functioning person. The theme persisted that taking this action in her own clear interest must be destructive. It signified that her aggression was bad and powerful.

A different but related feature was the idea that T, for all his defects, did love her "for some odd reason" and that no one else could ever love her because she was so inadequate and deficient. What she first labeled as inadequacy, she eventually referred to as her "badness"; she was so bad that no one else could or would ever love her. This badness had several components. One of them seemed to derive from her anger at each of her parents for the deprivation she had felt from them. Anger directed toward her suffering, "good" mother was particularly difficult. Her badness also meant she had been active and now stood as successful and competent, good for all the world to see. T had served as constant shield, distraction, penance, and punishment for this "badness"; he also served as the constant guarantee that some-one would love her even though she had been so "bad and aggressive." In this case example "aggression" was her sense of activity and self-interest. She equated this aggression with evil—that is, taking direct action in her own self-interest was equivalent to conceiving of herself as evil, and therefore she saw herself as dangerous and worthless. After considerable work, however, she definitively ended the relationship.

It is interesting to note that all of CS's protestations of an inadequacy that was contradicted by reality seemed to serve the purpose of obscuring her recognition of her strength. This strength had to be obscured because it, too, was equated with the "evil" of aggression. This point is particularly important because perception of and even insistence on inadequacy is common in women. In many instances these defenses conceal a similar amount of power.

Another clinical vignette involves a 45–year-old woman who was exploring problems in her marriage to a manipulative, passive-aggressive man. She, as the more active and expressive of the two, took the initiative in seeking help and urging her husband into treatment for longstanding patterns of defen-sive avoidance and withdrawal. During an unsuccessful attempt at intercourse, in which he lost his erection, he had told her that this was her fault and that his troubles were due to his fear of her. She knew that the problem was not entirely hers but became guilty at being the active one and the initiator, and therefore the one who "stirred things up" and thus caused him to be afraid of her.

According to classical psychoanalytic theory, a child becomes able to accept her or his realistic limitations, to give up grandiose fantasies, and to restrict the expression of instinctual impulses. These impulses are replaced by ego-syntonic goals and by pleasure in those functions and activities that gain approval and support from parents. This process enhances the sense of both effectiveness and "goodness," which is part of the development of self-esteem.

Self-esteem is gradually modified by experiences with peers and others and by the mastery of physical processes and control of the environment, but the basic link to the parents is critical. The child needs and depends on parental love, help, and approval and, by and large, desires to live up to parental expectations and values, which are gradually internalized. The state of the parents' self-esteem and self-image is also critical in the development of self-esteem in the child. While self-esteem is as a rule constantly modulated in response to ongoing realistic experiences, with unconscious conflicts self-esteem is altered. The mastery of unconscious conflicts also leads to a basic sense of self-esteem. Thus, as the child moves further in her or his own development, she or he acquires some of the attributes of the parents and identifies with the elements of parental self-esteem, as well as parental values and attitudes, although always in a unique combination.

The importance of the maternal ego ideal in the development of the young girl's sense of femininity has become increasingly evident. This maternal ego ideal does not usually contain a component of aggression that is perceived as clearly available and is understood as potentially creative.

Another source of self-esteem derives from bodily experiences, sensations, and gratifications. A growing literature sees those experiences that are uniquely female in terms of the female body as the starting point and does not use concepts such as *castration* or *the phallus*. The classical view of the developmental origins of femininity and the need to give up active for passive aims must be considered here in relation to self-esteem. In the classical view, the girl turns away from her early positive tie to her mother because of, among other issues, her disappointment that she does not have a penis. She holds her mother responsible for this "lack." An overly concrete view of "penis envy" ignores the highly significant symbolic implications that may be central, but the development of femininity is seen in the context of disappointment.

For a woman whose mother does feel devalued, the struggle for positive self-esteem means some degree of psychic separation from the mother, or even rejection of her. Conflict emerges between the attachment to the mother and the need to be loved by her on the one hand, and the aggression toward her in the struggle for individuation on the other. This does not involve disppointment at not having been given a penis. Managing aggression in the context of attachment is a dilemma and a challenge for the girl.

Feminine psychology can be conceptualized in another light, with the focus on feminine development instead of on deficits. This involves understanding the development of femininity in terms of uniquely female experiences, not in terms of substitutes for absent male elements. Identification is a powerful force. The concept of primary femininity involves a separate feminine developmental phase with a positive self-evaluation in conflict-free spheres. This concept has been criticized as essentialist, but it is not meant that way.

We have referred to fear of aggression, the lack of integration, and the constriction of aggressive expression. In the psychoanalysis or psychotherapy of women, the need for a positive mobilization of aggression has often been ignored or missed. Such neglect can be seen as syntonic with the societal stereotypes present in both patient and therapist. Therefore we can see how women often experience their aggressive wishes and strivings as evidence of their defectiveness or lack of worth, rather than as a basis for positive self-esteem.

The implications of a model of development emphasizing the significance of early communication between parents and children have been expanded by a number of investigators. The evidence that parents have different expectations of male and female infants and, in fact, behave differently toward them is quite convincing. Rubin and colleagues (1974) found that there were consistent differences in the reports of parents about the characteristics of their infants, depending on the baby's gender. For example, 1-day-old female infants were seen as significantly softer, finer featured, smaller, and more inattentive than male infants, differences that were not objectively present. Gender role stereotypes exist from birth, and parents behave differently in subtle ways.

Evidence has accumulated to indicate that gender identity is generally established by 18 months of age (Money and Ehrhardt 1972). In contrast to Freud's original view that it is first formed in the later phallic stage with the child's perception of genital differences between boys and girls, recent data make it clear that this awareness occurs earlier. Among the many influences during this early period of life, bodily sensations, including those in the genitals, are believed to contribute to the development of gender identity but not to be its only basis. These aspects of development take place in the context of a child's earliest interactions with his or her parents and other significant people, who approach the child with deep-seated feelings, fears, and signals that vary with the infant's gender. Thus components of the self-concept of children include:

1. The primary and/or innate differences existing between boys and girls,
2. The way in which a child is actually treated by adults and peers,
3. Identification with parents.

There is evidence that biological differences exist between girls and boys in the development of the nervous system and in hormonal balance. However, the relevance of these differences has been difficult to establish because the influence of culture and the wide range of individual variation are so critical. Further, the factors find expression so early that it is difficult to draw conclusions about which characteristics and behaviors are, in fact, innate and immutable.

We have discussed some of the evidence suggesting that the interdiction of feminine aggression occurs early in life. We see that aggression is subject to different influences in girls and in boys. Its direct expression is restricted and more readily suppressed in girls; most often it is transformed into action that is in the service of others. The force of the self-destructive and self-blaming manifestations in masochism suggests the power of the aggression that is present. We also see that women are more likely to find themselves victims, for example, of rape, and that this is accompanied by self-blame.

Female aggression has been shrouded in horror and dread. The terrifying destructive violence exhibited by Medea stands as a male culture's perception of the dangerous and primitive nature of women's aggression, and also of its notions about her vulnerability to narcissistic injury. The fear of the powerful life-giving and potentially life-destroying woman reaches deep into psychic roots. It seems likely that this cultural interdiction affects the female as an infant. She is influenced away from active expression as a more straightforward path to growth and development. Her physical activity is also diverted and inhibited, and this too forms the basis for more complex inhibitions.

We suggest that these inhibitions are compounded at each developmental stage and form the basis of complex inner psychological barriers that have both limited women's development and created the groundwork for psychological distress.

REFERENCES

Bibring, E. (1953). The mechanism of depression. In *Affective Disorders*, ed. P. Greenacre. New York: International Universities Press.

Blum, H. (1976). Female psychology: masochism and the ego ideal. *Journal of the American Psychoanalytic Association* 24: 305–351.

Deutsch, H. (1930). The significance of masochism in the mental life of women. *International Journal of Psycho-Analysis* 11: 48–60.

Freud, S. (1905). Three essays on the theory of sexuality. *Standard Edition* 7:135–243.

―――― (1920). Beyond the pleasure principle. *Standard Edition* 18:7–64.

―――― (1923). The ego and the id. *Standard Edition* 19: 12–59.

―――― (1925). Some psychical consequences of the anatomical distinction between the sexes. *Standard Edition* 19: 248–258.

Greenacre, P. (1971). *Emotional Growth*, vol. 1. New York: International Universities Press.

Money, J., and Ehrhardt, A. (1972). *Man and Woman, Boy and Girl*. Baltimore: Johns Hopkins University Press.

Rochlin, G. (1973). *Man's Aggression: The Defense of the Self*. Boston: Gambit.

Rubin, J., Provenzano, F., and Luria, Z. (1974). The eye of the beholder: parents' views on the sex of newborns. *American Journal of Orthopsychiatry* 44: 512–519.

Thompson, C. (1973). On women: some effects of the derogatory attitude towards female sexuality. In *On Psychoanalysis and Women*, ed. J. Miller, pp. 52–69. New York: Brunner/Mazel.

Weissman, M., and Klerman, G. (1977). Sex differences in the epidemiology of depression. *Archives of General Psychiatry* 34:98–111.

Woman: Access to Male Aggression or to Desire?: Response to the Paper on Aggression in Women by Malkah T. Notman, M.D.

PROFESSEUR MICHEL TORT

The aim of Dr. Notman's paper is to reexamine the issue of female aggression. The text clearly forms part of an enterprise of scrutinizing traditional Freudian and post-Freudian ideas of feminine development that are seen as being dominated by masculine constructions. More specifically, the author takes pains to show that forms of feminine aggression are generally described in terms of their conversion into the passivity, masochism, and caretaking that are seen as the proper goal of womanhood. This position, which is the dominant one, has had the effect of making women themselves experience as "bad" any form of aggression that would enable them to assert their individuality as women, as opposed to enabling them to serve others. The main argument of the paper is, therefore, that social stereotypes, which tend to channel feminine aggression toward serving others, have a major symptomatic effect, namely to diminish women's self-esteem.

Two clinical examples are presented to illustrate the difficulty women have in not considering as bad any steps they take in their own interests (especially separation from their partners). The author emphasizes the role played by a maternal ego ideal, itself undermined by the mother's self-devaluation, in the formation of what is so often the woman's feeling of incompetence and inadequacy, and in the fragility of her self-esteem. Parental responses, which differ according to the parent's sex, therefore play a decisive role in the construction of an ego ideal that devalues the girl's active efforts when these are made solely on her own behalf.

The ideas presented in this paper raise a number of questions in a very stimulating way. These questions will be sketched briefly here and will be developed further in the discussion.

On one particular issue, an extremely important one—the woman's feeling of inadequacy and incompetence, with its depressive forms—I would like to propose a different reading of the genesis of this symptomatic conflict. Dr. Notman basically says that the dominant cultural models of feminine roles have given rise, in classical psychoanalytic theory, to an ad hoc model of feminine development. This model is characterized by a channeling of aggression into masochism, passivity, motherhood, unobtrusive service to others, and, finally, the stigmatization of aggression as such.

Dr. Notman goes on to say that the transformation of social roles that has increasingly mobilized practical aggression in the area of women's social proficiency has led to a growing discrepancy between their social activity and the function of an ego ideal modeled on parental ideals.

I would like to say right away that it is really very hard to disagree with this picture, this general description. We certainly find these ingredients in many of the classic psychoanalytic contributions to the theory of what is supposed to be femininity. But I would hasten to add that these are not the only ingredients, since from at least 1920 on, these questions have been, continuously, the subject of urgent and remarkably acute critical discussion by women analysts and by men as well. So I am presupposing agreement on the general description, and I would like to focus directly on the central point of the paper—aggression—and on the way Dr. Notman establishes a relationship between psychoanalytic theory and empirical findings concerning the evolution of the status of women (findings that I likewise see as uncontroversial).

A first point in the discussion of this schema obviously concerns the very nature of aggression. Dr. Notman attempts to set a high value, contrary to the established view, on a "constructive aggression," and, in fact, to undertake a reexamination of aggression in general in psychoanalytic theory. I would tend to go along with her here. This general reconsideration of aggression aims to resolve one of the implicit paradoxes of the dominant view, which comes down to an aspect of the double standard, of what, in the dominant discourse, is concealed under a pseudo-universality. For it is certainly true that aggression is perceived, at one and the same time, as globally negative in both sexes yet as positive in men and stigmatized in women. In other words, the double standard is more forgiving towards masculine aggression (both natural and cultural) than towards feminine aggression (as being unnatural?). What would be natural in the case of women is the masochistic turning of aggression against the self! This is spelled out in Freud.

I would therefore propose for consideration the following hypothesis. Perhaps we may conjecture that if aggression is, officially, solely destructive, this is in order to exorcise the ghost of aggression coming from women, aggression which would originally be a reaction to domination itself. "It is bad" means "it is bad in the Other (feminine sex), because it can challenge the position from which I (patriarchal system) declare it to be bad." But we have to see where this leads, and here I would distance myself from Dr. Notman's concept of a sort of "good feminine aggression" in a functional sense. It is not really enough to redefine an act of aggression as nondestructive and to enable women to benefit from it as do men, who have traditionally kept aggression for themselves. Because isn't it true that, were we to do so, we might fail to recognize a fundamental fact—namely that, of the forms of aggression being considered, the aggression that sets men and women against each other is definitely not the least? In other words, instead of defining a generally neutral aggression, or one that from now on will be shared by both sexes, it would probably be more critical to look at the generality of the aggression *between* men and women. That is more unpleasant, to be sure, but all the same it is the basic question.

This kind of aggression is admittedly difficult to define clearly. And yet it is represented on a large scale by the proven forms of misogyny, the hatred of women, the modalities of which are as numerous and variable as their bases are constant. Curiously enough, it seems to be more difficult to admit the intensity and the importance of feminine aggression aimed at men, aggression that attacks their virility in all the forms—and they are innumerable—in which it is vulnerable to castration. What is astonishing is the circumspection surrounding a phenomenon as widespread as feminine antiphallic violence. Perhaps it is as though the silence—including the silence of men themselves—were part of an effort to ward off danger.

To look at this issue from another vantage point, isn't it clear that so-called love relationships between men and women, far from being idyllic romances, are the site of a permanent struggle—and are so to the point where we may wonder whether it isn't this mutual aggression that constitutes the bond? But it is the case that Freudian and post-Freudian psychoanalytic theories have never taken the least interest in what is, nevertheless, in the foreground of daily life. This is so not because the unconscious stakes are more profound than the everyday scene, but because up to now the psychoanalytic theory of the relations between the sexes has juxtaposed the descriptions of two autistic sexed positions without paying attention to their interactive strategies. And yet these just happen to be what is most important for men and women!

Moreover, the clinical examples Dr. Notman provides illustrate this point, since it is not the aggression linked to social competence/competition that creates the symptom, but precisely the aggression that has to do with the relationship to a man. For this very reason, the question of so-called feminine aggression cannot be separated from the aggressive behavior of men themselves.

Let us approach the same problem in a different way, examining it more directly from the point of view of psychic conflict as such. What about the metapsychological reference points that come into play in a conflict where aggression is involved? Dr. Notman describes the nastiness of the patient, tracing it back to anger at disappointing partners, and, beyond them, to disappointing parents. The dearth of satisfaction she gets from her partner serves as punishment for her feeling of having abandoned or having been mean to her mother. This is the nub of the psychic conflict of daughter and mother. From then on, it seems that Dr. Notman discards the classical theory of the daughter's oedipal struggle with her mother, the main point of which is that the mother has not given her the penis, in favor of another view of the conflict. As Dr. Notman sees it, this latter conflict has to do with the opposition between the girl's attachment to the preoedipal mother and the struggle for separation and individuation. Such a conflict is exacerbated when the mother experiences herself as devalued.

This is certainly true, but the whole question here is to know what meaning to give to a critique of the classical Freudian concept of penis envy. I see no reason why we should not question the total explanatory power of the theory of penis envy in the analysis of psychic conflict in the girl. This critique has been carried out successfully by many authors. But can we, if we view this as a negative theory of femininity, replace it with a positive one? We are aware that this new positive version, based on self-esteem and separation-individuation with regard to the mother, is itself just as totalizing. In other words, even if the reference to penis envy needs to be reinterpreted—and I would grant this—it nevertheless has the value of an attempt at formulating those major aspects of psychic conflict that involve sex, sexual difference (*différence*).

To be sure, in order to get beyond a situation in which views like Dr. Notman's are set in an imaginary opposition to the most extreme phallocratic theories of penis envy, another problem arises. Classical views have neglected this direction, what I would call sexual dispute (*différend*), that is, the complex strategic relations between sexuated beings as sexuated. I mentioned an aspect of these relations in connection with misogyny and feminine hatred of men (which can eventually become the full-time activity of so many women in our societies). But I want to be careful to separate the two aspects of the question, and perhaps to accord more importance to the second point, although they are both connected.

An initial line of questioning would be as follows: Can we agree that the very question of the daughter's separation from her mother is bound up with the fact that the mother cannot be entirely reduced to her maternal function—that the mother represents an object of desire for a man and perceives herself as a desiring subject (and one who desires a man)? This is, after all, what we find in Dr. Notman's case example. The point is that the difficulty in breaking away from a man is not the simple repetition of the difficulty of becoming autonomous from the mother. As she subtly notes, one of the paradoxical ties of the patient to the man is that he loves her "for some strange reason." Now this "strange reason" (which is the man's) cannot be reduced just to the punishment/reparation function for which the patient uses it. It points discreetly to the complexity of the relationships of desire between a woman and a man—all the more so because the issue goes back to the previous generation for the mother, who must surely have maintained a relationship of desire with the patient's father. I would like to hear some more about this.

This point brings up a general topic for discussion. What are the implications and the consequences, as far as analytic treatment is concerned, of focusing exclusively on the supposed preoedipal relationships while setting aside the structural relations of desire? In other words, isn't the fundamental question for a woman—as for a man—to know under what conditions she will accede to the possibility of desire, and in particular, among other relations, to a relation of desire with someone of the opposite sex? The conditions for this access are defined by the manner in which she traverses the field of desire in which she is at the same time object and subject of parental desires before she herself can desire a man and accept being the object of his desire.

There is no doubt that manifestations of feminine incompetence, passivity, and devaluation are connected to the cultural stereotypes that muzzle aggression in women. But the whole question is precisely to know whether these symptomatic manifestations can be described and analyzed outside of any reference to relations of desire. Dr. Notman shows very well how a woman whose mother feels devalued will experience some difficulty in not rejecting her in order to separate from her—and will feel aggressive, bad. But as I see it, this formulation of psychic conflict leaves in abeyance the following question: What is the role of the mother's self-devaluation in relation to the patient's experience of herself as a desiring subject (and not only in terms of social competence whether valued or, especially, devalued)? In other words, the main issue for the mother may be her inability to think of herself as desiring a man. Here we have the essence of her self-devaluation. The mother's lack, that is, the daughter's perception of her mother's devalued position, may be a structural necessity for the girl to become a desiring subject in her own right.

Still another way of making this point, with direct reference to the case example: Is the patient's problem simply to suppress the discrepancy between the reality of her social competence and the feeling of inadequacy that keeps her attached to an unsatisfactory man? Or is the problem that she needs to be able to take a different approach to relationships with men in general?

CONCLUSION

Throughout this brief sketch for a discussion, two aspects of the same problem have been delineated. The first could be expressed as follows. Under what conditions can we articulate, in terms of the structural elements of psychic conflict, a valid critical analysis of cultural stereotypes that have been enshrined in psychoanalytic theory, if we grant that these structural elements are necessarily autonomous, transcultural, and transhistorical? (By this I mean that psychic conflicts connected with the demands of sexual and aggressive drives, sexed identifications, and the subject's access to desire involve cultural constraints elaborated upon by all societies.) How, according to what principle, can we untangle the permanent confusion between these two registers?

The question is, to begin with, theoretically crucial. For otherwise the critique of classical Freudian theory runs the risk of opening up into a psychosociology that, however generous, is incompatible with the solid nucleus of the analytic discovery. I admit that there is a major slippage, a widespread drifting, in the direction of confusing psychoanalysts with psychosociologists and thereby erasing the reality of the manifestations of the unconscious. Apparently anyone at all can decide to call himself a "psychoanalyst" even as he shows utter scorn for the unconscious, the drives, sexuality, and the division of the subject (these being no doubt Freudian, Viennese, European fantasies that are out of date in this time of self-service restaurants for the self?).

But Dr. Notman, of course, knows that it is not by means of such a misrecognition that we can easily resolve the issues that she raises, or, rather, that her patients raise for her. Promoting women's self-esteem by sustaining the positive side of aggression is a generous goal. But I think we can agree that such a goal should not conjure away the reality of relationships of desire and their connection to aggression. If not, I am afraid we are faced with a paradox. We may well wonder whether the promotion of the ego ideal of self-esteem, and perhaps even the issue of feminine aggression, would not have the following consequence: the question that is fundamental to us as psychoanalysts, namely that of the formation of desire in the girl and the woman, of her entry into the world of desire, would be eclipsed by the preoccupation with helping women to demonstrate their ability and to potentialize a sexually neutral aggression that men have thus far kept for themselves. This amounts to saying that both sexes would become equal in putting desire aside.

I think we can agree on two points. First, that sexual activity and relationships between men and women are in no way incompatible with esteem for oneself and for the other; and second, that they are most certainly not based on such esteem, but—as life would have it—on the possibility of being at the same time a desiring subject and the object of desire.

This brings me to my final point, which is itself twofold. I do not think it is enough, first of all, to present abstractly this tension—indeed, contradiction—that I have been trying to formulate between the question of self-esteem and the question of desire. I think that if, like Dr. Notman's colleagues in self psychology, she is led to privilege the question of self-esteem and the mother–daughter relation, it is because that is the way in which— if not in and through analysis, then perhaps as a psychoanalyst—she acknowledges both the transformations of the status of women in present-day society and the weight of a thousand years of relentless effort to *de*-symbolize the maternal by assuring the symbolic prevalence of the paternal and reducing woman's place in the symbolic order to her maternal role. Dr. Notman may be assured that along with other theoretical reference points, analysts in France can share this concern.

But, on the other hand, we may wonder what connection there may be between a certain way of manufacturing feminine identity and the social manufacture of minority identities. (Half of the population as a minority!) Do women have to identify themselves as a minority along with gays, lesbians, immigrant communities, and, no doubt soon, heterosexuals, sado-masochists, and so forth—and while we are at it, borderlines? Or, instead, should we set out, not from the sexual difference alone, but rather from relations between men and women and their mutual alienation?

Excerpts from the Discussion

Agnès Oppenheimer: Dr. Notman's rich and important paper brings up the concept of a separate feminine line of development, something Michel Tort and Jacques Hassoun also mentioned, and something that we in France have a lot of trouble accepting, since we believe that the human being develops in a dialectical process. Is this the same thing, or something different? I know that American theories emphasize sexual identity, and that's been the subject of a lot of research. But I think this involves a misunderstanding of Freud. Freud never spoke of sexual identity or gender identity—he spoke of woman in her sexual function in the *New Introductory Lectures*. The little girl who makes the transition from bisexuality to femininity isn't on the level of identity, or role, or gender, but what's in question is sexual function. I think it's a very good idea to round out what Freud says with a theory of sexuated identity that indicates the specificity of women and of men, of the two sides. But if we separate this from the sexual function, we lose precisely this relation to the Other that constitutes our fantasy of the other sex.

Monique David-Ménard: I completely agree with Michel Tort when he says that sexual relations don't depend on the question of self-esteem, or at any rate not essentially, but on the fact that both men and women are at the same time subjects of desire and objects of desire. What I'd like to ask Dr. Notman is this: Don't you think we could give a psychoanalytic description of the vicissitudes of the drives in women—which certainly aren't mapped onto male development, that is, the issue of the penis and the phallus isn't the only one that organizes development—without going so far as to exclude the sexual relationship of the woman to the man? I think that we can understand hysteria along those lines. What we analyze when we analyze women are the ways of relating to the mother that don't go only through penis envy, but that nevertheless do go through the masculine. But it's true, and here I completely agree with Agnès Oppenheimer, that we can't talk about feminine development apart from the relation of the sexes, and it's there that we don't see eye to eye, on the question of the separation that the Americans make between sex and gender. It makes no sense for us, as psychoanalysts, to think in terms of the feminine as an isolated category.

Anna Ornstein: Since so much has been said about sex in this paper, let me pick up the issue of aggression. I think we have plenty of problems with sex, but we have even more problems with aggression. I would say that in our formulations we're not using a refined affect theory; we're resorting to Freud's drive theory in this respect and reducing many affective experiences to the aggressive drive. I think that's what made it necessary for Dr. Notman to speak of "bad aggression" and "good aggression." If we were to take apart "aggression," a global word, and recognize that we have what we can call self-assertion, anger, narcissistic rage, destructive aggression, then we don't have to resort to one concept to refer to so many affective states.

(French Analyst): I feel that Dr. Notman does not go far enough in her suggestions. We should add that there is a feminine element in the man and consider how passivity and masochism affect his functioning, for example in fear of penetration, a feminine anxiety. If we have trouble approaching the topic of femininity, what Freud had to counter was Jung's theory of the Electra complex, since when the question of fidelity to the father arose for Electra the issue of her disorganization and psychosis arose at the same time. So we might well wonder whether castration puts in question a woman's deep identity, and this is relevant to the issue of borderline pathology. When your patient questions her self-image, doesn't this go beyond sexual identity and touch on a more profound level of disorder?

Malkah Notman: The issue of the penis versus the phallus is one on which I find myself in disagreement. I do understand that the phallus is used in Lacanian thinking as a symbolic concept, but I just wouldn't use that term. Why do you need the phallus, unless you're talking about the basic motivational forces having to do with the male point of view? The same is true of the use of the term "castration anxiety"; we're trained to use it conceptually, and we know it has different meanings for the female. But why use it? I don't have the fantasy that we can transform psychoanalytic language in one easy afternoon, but it does seem to me that it's important to ask where would we get if we shifted our language. It's like some of the language of drive theory: if you move away from drive theory, you do change your terminology.

Apropos language and Dr. Anna Ornstein's comment about using the language of affect, and the concept of affect, instead of speaking of aggression as a drive, I would agree that this would give us a much more complex and probably more accurate perspective, but I'm just not at that point yet. When this paper was written, we were trying to come to terms with some clinical phenomena that seemed more discussible in relation to the drive, but I do think it would be an advance to try to integrate drive theory with affect language. With regard to development, I may have abbreviated too much in implying that we, or I, see the primary developmental experience for the woman as being with the preoedipal mother. I certainly feel that the oedipal relationship is extremely important. This is something that feminist psychoanalysts in the States have been accused of—that in an attempt to focus on the preoedipal mother and the importance of the girl's relationship with her, they lose sight of the rest. But that really isn't our intent. The woman, the mother, as the subject and object of desire is very much part of the girl's development, as is identification with the woman who desires the man and is desired by him. I would see this as a pivotal identificatory move that replaces the rather thin understanding of motivation as based on deprivation of the penis, compared to the complexity of development that involves many of these themes.

Which brings me to the issue of sexual relationships. This may be a cultural difference. I would hate to think that sex is less important in the United States than in France, but nevertheless we don't tend to think of the sexual relationship as just sexual or genital; we think, in a more multifaceted way, of the sexual relationship as not being at the center. Not that the sexuality isn't critical, but what I would emphasize is the relationship and its gender and its power and its submission. When we were struggling in the 1970s and early 1980s to try to see what we thought about the psychoanalytic ideas we had in the face of the attacks, in the States, by the feminists of that time, I ran a workshop for about ten years within the Boston Psychoanalytic Institute and invited researchers and social scientists and analysts, and I remember our confusion with regard to the sexual relationship of the man and the woman as being the model of the social relationship—the passivity, the receptiveness, the actual sexual position and behavior. I think we moved away from that with a sense that it is too narrow a model.

10

Psychic Death and the
Generation of Meaning

ARNOLD H. MODELL, M.D.

Within that broad group of patients who suffer from something more than a neurosis, the so-called narcissistic character disorders
and borderline states, one can discern a subgroup whose main complaint
is that their lives are empty, futile, and meaningless. It is not only that they
perceive their lives to be empty; they also experience their sense of self to
be empty and dead and express the fear that if one probes beneath the
surface one will discover that there is nothing there. André Green (1986)
has referred to this phenomenon of emptiness as a *blank psychosis*; in extreme cases this represents the equivalent of a psychic suicide that has
already occurred. As you know, Fairbairn (1952) some years ago correctly
associated the sense of futility and emptiness with the schizoid personality. I would not limit this symptom to the schizoid or the privately psychotic, as I believe that it is present in a broad spectrum of personality
disturbances.

To be able to find meaning in life is equivalent to being psychically
alive. To be more precise, the traumatized person finds meaning in life but
the meaning is invariably a constricted one. For, in massively traumatized
individuals, experiences in real time are invariably invested with old meanings; the possibility of novelty is subverted through the imposition of old

meanings upon new experiences. There is evidently a selective process at work that disavows any percepts that are at variance with the original traumatic affective experience. In these severe cases, life becomes monotonous and extremely boring and invariably unhappy.

This inability to discover emergent meanings may have devastating consequences. If one is psychically dead, the affective core of the self is experienced as a "black hole," as if one's self has psychically imploded. In some cases such individuals are not suicidal for the reason that they simply do not care whether they are alive or dead—nothing matters.

We know that a given symptom may be arrived at by more than one pathway, for you will have recognized that the complaint that life has no meaning is also characteristic of depression. But the psychopathology and neurophysiological disturbances of depression are different from those of the narcissistic disorders and as such represent a separate subject that I will not consider here. Of course we know that depression may coexist with severe narcissistic disturbances.

As psychoanalysts we are, in our daily work, continually confronted with the problem of meaning and psychic aliveness, although we may not think in those particular terms. As we listen to our patients we are automatically attuned to what is meaningful. Meaning in a psychoanalytic context is different from the concept of meaning in philosophy and linguistics in that psychoanalysts search for private meanings. As you know, the relation between private and public meaning has been a problem for philosophers for centuries, but as psychoanalysts we are concerned with private meanings and private significance. Meaning in psychoanalysis always refers to what is significant for the analysand. Even when such meanings are arrived at through shared, that is, intersubjective experiences, they are always referred back to the analysand. This is not to suggest an identity or symmetry of meaning in these shared experiences, but the analyst's private experiences are placed in the service of the treatment. What gives an item significance (for both participants) in a psychoanalytic treatment is the extent to which speech or other forms of behavior are invested with feeling.

The analyst listens to the patient's speech and in addition observes the totality of the patient's behavior, including his posture, bodily movements, and silences. From these elements an affective charge is communicated that directs the analyst's attention and interest to what is meaningful to the patient. We customarily think of the analyst's empathy as analogous to a perceptual instrument, but in order to activate this instrument a certain quantum of affective charge is required. (I have discussed this topic in *Psychoanalysis in a New Context* [Modell 1984].) If the patient does not communicate feeling in speech, gestures, or other forms of behavior, the analyst is unable to enter into the patient's experience. Without the affective inflections of speech, all words become of equal significance and are shorn of their personal meaning.

Thus as we listen to our patients we select that which is meaningful because of the affects that are communicated to us. This paraverbal communication has been described as a metacommunication. We can assume that, automatically and unconsciously, we constantly monitor and select affective valences of speech. When meaningful communication is absent, we become bored, sleepy, or indifferent, so that boredom is a clue to psychic deadness. Of course it can be argued that the analyst's boredom may reflect the analyst's own internal psychic economy, such as a lack of interest that may have nothing to do with the patient. But, on the other hand, the analyst's boredom may reflect the fact that the patient is psychically "not there." If patients are completely walled-off within their private space, this invariably induces a counteraffective response in the analyst. We feel that such patients are not in the room with us. It would be unthinkable to have no response if one is in the continued presence of another human being who does not relate to us. This is not a question of the patient's being uncooperative or defiant, but it is an indication of the automatic defensive measures introduced in order to preserve private space. When our patients are encased within their private selves, their endopsychic experience is that of being in a cocoon or a plastic bubble. This may be a wonderfully safe retreat or a prison from which there is no escape.

We have arrived at the subject of Winnicott's false self, a defensive formation in which the individual is estranged from his or her central affective core, this inner core of the self that Winnicott (1971) has called the *true self* and that I have referred to as the *private self* (Modell 1993). The importance of this affective centering has long been noted. Its absence has been described as an alienation from the self, a decentering, a failure of indwelling. It is affective centering that enables one to feel real and alive, to feel that he or she is an entity with continuity in time and existence in space.

If we speak of decentering and alienation of the self, this assumes that at an earlier developmental stage the self has been more centered. When my patients declare that they are empty and have nothing inside of them, they also remain skeptical when I indicate to them that they really do possess an authentic self waiting to be found. My confidence in this assertion rests on the knowledge that most patients will establish better contact with their private self in the course of psychoanalytic treatment. If there were not any prior existence of an authentic self, it would be a nearly magical expectation to believe that the therapeutic process could bring it about.

Infant research suggests that the sense of agency of the self is related to an affective centering. Most infant observers believe that centering of the self is reinforced by the process of affective attunement or affective mirroring that occurs between the mother and child (Stern 1985). The mother who is able to match the infant or child's affects also enables that child to process his or her own affects. Conversely, a mother who is out of attunement with her child's affects may impede this process. If the mother's response mirrors the child's affects, this serves as affirmation of what the child is feeling. This is equivalent to the mother's naming the child's affects; the mother reaffirms the meaning of the child's affective state.

I believe that psychoanalysis may, in some cases, provide a second chance to repair a developmental deficit in this area, should one exist. There are some patients who require that the analyst identify, that is to say, name, the patient's affects. With regard to negative affects some patients experience only a vague sense of dysphoria—they are unable to name what they are feeling. By means of countertransference perceptions the analyst is able to identify affects that are unconsciously communicated by the patient. In such cases it is the psychoanalyst who names what the patient is feeling: "You are angry," "You are feeling anxious," "You are sad," and so forth. The therapist is in effect teaching such patients to name their own feeling states, and through this provision of meaning those affects are brought within the domain of the self.[1]

The question then arises: How did the self become alienated from itself? Where the child's private space is habitually violated, vital defenses are erected, such as the noncommunication of authentic affects. It seems, unfortunately, as if the defenses used against the intruder are turned upon the self. In accordance with Fairbairn's principle that traumatic relation-

---

1. It may be observed parenthetically that, according to linguists, in those cultures where there are no words to describe a specific affect state the individual cannot process that particular affect. For example, the Tahitians do not have a word for sadness, and consequently they have no way of coping with sadness and depression. They attribute sadness to something outside of the self and categorize it with sickness, fatigue, or the attack of an evil spirit.

ships between self and others are re-created within the self, *the means employed to protect private space against intrusion by others is also re-created within the self*. These individuals become estranged from their own affective core and are as false and inauthentic within themselves as they are with others. In the struggle to preserve private space they thus achieve a tragic pyrrhic victory. Ironically, the fight to protect the private self continues even after the individual has lost contact with it. It is as if a householder maintained a burglar alarm long after misplacing the jewels. *In closing oneself off from others, one inadvertently closes oneself off from oneself.*

If psychic aliveness requires this contact with one's inner affective core, then it is apparent that psychic aliveness is intimately connected with an internal communication of affects: one must be able to read one's own signals. Of course affects can be communicated unconsciously, as occurs in cases of projective identification. The conscious communication of affects is an aspect of object seeking. You will recall Fairbairn's aphorism that libido is object seeking; it is also true that if affects are communicated they are object seeking. Conversely, those patients who do not communicate authentic affects attempt to create the illusion that they are without desire, that is to say that they are self-sufficient. Winnicott thought this to be a sign of mental illness. When he was asked by mental-health counselors, "How do you distinguish someone who is mentally ill from someone who is basically healthy but only needs some counselling?" his reply was: "If a person comes and talks to you, and, listening to him, you feel he is *boring* you, then he is sick and needs psychiatric treatment. But if he sustains your interest, no matter how grave his distress or conflict, then you can help him alright" (1986, p. 1).

The communication of affects refers not only to object seeking but also to an internal scanning process that selects what is of interest in the world, what is needed, what is valued. In severe narcissistic disorders we may discover that such patients hate the world and everything in it. To express an interest in something may be felt to be dangerous: desire is experienced as enslaving, and accordingly one becomes panicked at the recognition of one's own interests and desires. As a consequence of such inhibition of desire the world becomes empty and boring. This sense of boredom and emptiness in the world is reinforced by a decentering from one's inner affective core. If one is out of touch with one's affective experience, one is unable to select what is desired, and as a result all thoughts are shorn of their affective content and thus become equally indifferent. If all thoughts have an equal affective valence one is unable to choose one thought in preference to another. Such patients not infrequently remark at the start of an hour that they have nothing to say. In extreme cases they experience a pervasive sense of blankness, as if their brain were damaged.

It is evident that what is of interest is meaningful and what is meaningful is of interest. Meaning and interest are reciprocal and driven by desire, which in turn determines what it is that is selected. Let us, for the moment, put to one side the repetition compulsion and the seeking of pain, and consider only positive interests; then interest in people and things can be thought of as a form of loving. This is only to repeat Freud's familiar concept of libidinal investment: what one invests with libido one invests with meaning. This equivalence of interest and love extends not only to persons but also to things, ideas, and activities—nearly anything can be invested with passionate interest. Thus in a larger sense the inability to find meaning in the world represents a withdrawal of love.

I have been discussing the experience of psychic aliveness in relation to affects and desire. There is a third component, which is of equal importance, and that is memory. From one perspective it can be said that the self is a structure whose function is to maintain a coherent model of past, present, and future. In health our memories of the past are continually updated and recontextualized, as Freud described by means of the concept of *Nachträglichkeit* (cf. Modell 1990, 1993). When one is psychically alive, one finds new meaning in experience, in contrast to the traumatized individual who cannot experience novelty and cannot recontextualize the original traumatic experience. When Freud still believed in the traumatic etiology of the neuroses, he had the deep insight that whether a traumatic event proved to be pathogenic depended on the individual's capacity to retranscribe memory. In a letter to Fliess dated December 6, 1896, we find the following:

> As you know, I am working on the assumption that our psychic mechanism has come into being by a process of stratification: the material present in the form of memory traces being subjected from time to time to a *rearrangement* in accordance with fresh circumstances—to a *retranscription*. Thus what is essentially new about my theory is the thesis that memory is present not once but several times over, that it is laid down in various kinds of indications. . . . I should like to emphasize the fact that the successive registrations represent the psychic achievement of successive epochs of life. At the boundary between two such epochs a translation of the psychic material must take place. I explain

the peculiarities of the psychoneuroses by supposing that this translation has not taken place in the case of some of the material which has
certain consequences. . . . [cited in Masson 1985, p. 207]

Pathogenesis thus represents a failure of translation from one developmental epoch to the next. Freud's theory of memory here is one of cyclic
time; health represents the capacity to retranscribe memory to form a model
of past, present, and future. I believe it is unfortunate that Freud later
deemphasized his theory of *Nachträglichkeit*. For, preoccupied as he was
in later years with instinct theory, he attributed the repetition compulsion
to the death instinct, suggesting a linear as opposed to a cyclic conception
of psychic time.

Freud's theory of *Nachträglichkeit* has recently received some unexpected support from contemporary neurobiology. It is very similar to a new
theory of memory proposed by the Nobel Prize laureate Gerald Edelman
(1992), who arrived at similar ideas independently in the course of pro-
posing a global theory of the mind–brain relationship. His basic idea is
that memory does not consist of a static record in the brain; instead it is a
dynamic reconstruction that is context bound and established by means
of *categories*. According to Edelman's theory, long-term memory consist of
categories of experiences awaiting activation. Although we do not yet possess firm scientific evidence concerning the way in which long-term memories are stored in the brain, Edelman suggests that what is retained in
memory is not a replica of an event, something that has a precise correspondence with the original experience, but instead a *potential* to general-
ize or to refind the category or class of which the event is a member.

The clinical application of these ideas can be seen in cases of trauma
resulting in a splitting and dissociation of parts of the self. Dissociation is
different from repression, but the end result is the same in that portions of
the self are outside of conscious awareness. The retranscription of memory,
the translation or recontextualization of the past in the context of current
experience, requires a relative coherence of the self. If portions of the self
are split off from each other and noncommunicative, this means that aspects of an individual's history are unavailable, and hence a retranscription
of memory cannot take place. If we think of the self as what reorganizes
our experience of time, then we can see how massive psychic trauma will
result in a telescoping of the past into the future and an obliteration of
present time. We know that in cases of massive trauma, experiences in

current time are meaningful only to the extent that such experiences are congruent with the traumatic past. From this perspective the repetition compulsion represents a disturbance in memory and not, as Freud believed, a disturbance in instinct. We also know that the effect of massive trauma can be passed to the next generation by means of a form of cultural inheritance. For example, children of the survivors of the Holocaust will not uncommonly incorporate their parents' experiences as if such events were part of their own past.

As Winnicott pointed out, the feeling of being psychically alive depends upon creative apperception or (in the language that I have used) upon the capacity to find new meanings in experience. This creative apperception, in turn, rests upon a measure of love of external reality and on the capacity to experience cyclic time. The opposite of creative apperception is psychic death. We know that there are some patients who actively seek psychic death as an alternative to the actual death of the body. These patients are among our most difficult therapeutic challenges. Therefore the more we understand of the processes that underlie their sense of emptiness and sense of futility, the more likely we are to be able to offer some help.

REFERENCES

Edelman, G. (1992). *Bright Air Brilliant Fire*. New York: Basic Books.

Fairbairn, W. R. D. (1952). *Psychoanalytic Studies of the Personality*. London: Tavistock.

Green, A. (1986). *On Private Madness*. Madison, CT: International Universities Press.

Masson, J., trans. and ed. (1985). *The Complete Letters of Sigmund Freud to Wilhelm Fliess*. Cambridge: Harvard University Press.

Modell, A. (1984). *Psychoanalysis in a New Context*. New York: International Universities Press.

——— (1990). *Other Times, Other Realities*. Cambridge: Harvard University Press.

——— (1993). *The Private Self*. Cambridge: Harvard University Press.

Stern, D. (1985). *The Interpersonal World of the Infant*. New York: Basic Books.

Winnicott, D. W. (1971). *Playing and Reality*. New York: Basic Books.

——— (1986). *Holding and Interpretation*. New York: Grove.

Meaning and the Direction of the Treatment: A Discussion of the Paper of Arnold H. Modell, M.D.

PROFESSEUR JOËL DOR

Arnold Modell's contribution calls for a general comment about what appears to be a fundamental difference between, on the one hand, the Freudian and Lacanian conception of transference dynamics and the general conduct of treatment, and, on the other, the pragmatic position implicit in Dr. Modell's clinical approach and in the therapeutic strategies it entails.

When we listen to our patients, Dr. Modell says, "we select that which is meaningful because of the affects that are communicated to us." This "technical" position[1] seems to me to sum up what analysts who base their work on Freud and Lacan have in common with Dr. Modell and his American colleagues, and also what separates us. When Dr. Modell tells us that the analyst's empathy is regarded as a perceptual instrument, this suggests

---

1. It is important to emphasize that Lacan did not set much store by the idea of "technique" in the sense in which Freud originated the use of the term. For him analysis was always a practice, and specifically a practice of truth. This truth, he says, speaks of itself and it is the analyst's task to "punctuate" its dialectics in the patient's discourse (see below on scansion).

Editor's note: In other words, there are no "recipes" in psychoanalysis. Only the patient's signifiers can serve as a guide to his truth, a truth that is always partly concealed by a discourse that obstructs it.

that he is looking and listening for formations of the unconscious in the patient. This is certainly true of our own work as well. But when American analysts focus their clinical activity on affect—since this is the basic feature underlying "insight" in their approach—then we part company theoretically and technically. Our activity is directly based on representation[2] and the signifier.

This difference becomes clear right away when Dr. Modell, in connection with the new kinds of symptoms that he calls psychic death and the inability to generate meaning, emphasizes that the analyst needs to give patients access to revised meanings through a technical approach basically governed by intuition and countertransference. As he says, "As we listen to our patients we are automatically attuned to what is meaningful. . . . [P]sychoanalysts search for private meanings. . . . [A]s psychoanalysts we are concerned with private meanings and private significance. Meaning in psychoanalysis always refers to what is significant for the analysand" (p. 186).

As far as the patient's words are concerned, these assertions leave in abeyance the position of the analyst and the status of his interventions and interpretations—if this distinction is taken into account in the first place. In fact, from this point of view it is as though there were not even a distinction between signifier and signification/signified, so we can understand why it is that affect, more than desire, becomes the analyst's sole guide. The question thus arises as to whether a listening stance essentially focused on the signifier apart from signification would not be better able to give these patients access to the truth of their desire and consequently to reverse the pathogenic mechanism of "psychic death" through analysis of the transference.

I want to be more precise about our understanding of such terms as *meaning* and *signifier/signified* when we use them in the context of ideas such as interpretation and transference analysis in contrast to insight and empathy.

Very early on in Freud's work the concept of *the royal road to the unconscious* clearly sets forth the connection that is presumed to exist between meaning and interpretation. Indeed, the aim of dream interpretation is to reveal the hidden meaning of the unconscious material: "to interpret a dream" is to indicate its "meaning" (Freud 1900).

---

2. *Editor's note*: "Representation" is used in the sense of the Freudian *Vorstellung*, a psychic inscription in the unconscious.

Just as interpretation is the primary modality of the therapeutic action, so, in this view, it is bound up in a causal subjection to the uncovering of a hidden meaning. Moreover, in connection with the distinction he makes between latent and manifest meaning, Freud does not hesitate to use metaphors such as the "analyst as detective," "riddle," "rebus," "investigation," and so forth. In short, Freud's original concept of interpretation is strictly confined to the domain of meaning.

But obviously, the connection between meaning and interpretation leads to certain problems of which Freud, too, was well aware. Because of the rule of free association the patient has the last word on the truth of his desire, but it is nevertheless the case that while the interpretation offered to him reveals a meaning, at the same time it closes off the question of the truth of that desire. The difficulty becomes even greater if we consider construction, which Freud presents as a systematic elaboration designed to mobilize the lifting of repression:

> Quite often we do not succeed in bringing the patient to recollect what has been repressed. Instead of that, if the analysis is carried out correctly, we produce in him an assured conviction of the truth of the construction which achieves the same therapeutic result as a recaptured memory. [1937, p. 265f.]

What is the truth Freud is speaking about here? He is referring to the truth of the construction taken as such, and thus the truth is part and parcel of its signifying structure. In this sense we can say that the truth of the construction places the interpretation in the context of a logic in which truth is presumed to be isomorphic with meaning. Now, is the truth of the subject's desire, as expressed in his discourse via free association, actually isomorphic with the truth of the analyst's interpretative utterance? There is nothing that would allow us to make this assumption *a priori*.

Let us take this questioning a little further by considering what Freud (1900) had to say about what he calls the secondary revision of unconscious material. With regard to dreams he indicates that secondary revision constitutes an initial interpretation on the part of the dreamer, designed to neutralize the dream's original absurdity and incoherence:

> Dreams occur which, at a superficial view, may seem faultlessly logical. . . . Dreams which are of such a kind have been subjected to a far-reaching revision by this psychical function that is akin to waking thought; *they appear to have a meaning, but that meaning is as far removed*

as possible from their true significance. They are dreams which might be said to have been already interpreted once, before being submitted to waking interpretation. [p. 490, emphasis added]

Here the difficulty is compounded. What could be the truth of the meaning of this initial interpretation? More generally, what we have here is the problem of the meaning of meaning, something of which, once again, Freud (1900) showed some awareness when he spoke of the navel of the dream. This issue of meaning really forces us to confront important questions: Is the meaning of the interpretation true? Even if it is, is it consistent with the truth of the desire that it presumably reveals?

We cannot, of course, claim the empirical evidence of the resolving of the symptom by way of proof. The objective disappearance of the symptom has never established any specific connection between the truth of the subject's desire and the truth of the meaning of its interpretation. At the very most we can say that there has been a displacement of the unconscious material.

Furthermore, the question of signification or of hidden meaning indirectly raises the issue of the boundary between interpretation and translation. To assume that the meaning uncovered by the interpretation is isomorphic with the truth of the desire is, in a certain sense, to assume that an interpretation corresponds to a translation. In that case the interpretation becomes a hermeneutic intervention. I will not dwell here on the numerous difficulties that arise in connection with the problem of hermeneutics, or on the interrogation of the meaning of meaning that it entails, or on the infinite regress of levels of truth.[3]

To consider desire and the possibility of "finding new meanings" from this perspective calls for a revision of the very concept of interpretation. Besides, Dr. Modell's paper makes such a revision all the more necessary if only to clarify his statement that "[m]eaning in psychoanalysis always refers to what is significant for the analysand." Nothing could be less certain. This is no doubt one of the reasons why Lacan, following Freud, distinguished between interpretation and intervention in analytic treatment and, consequently, between interpretation *in* the transference and interpretation *of* the transference.[4] He thereby threw wide open the question—in the sense

---

3. For a fuller discussion of this epistemological problem see Dor 1988, Chapter 4.

4. *Editor's note*: Here we have a fundamental difference between Lacanian and American psychoanalysis. Lacanians do not interpret transference (or conceptualize countertransference) in terms of the role in which the patient has placed the analyst (e.g., father, mother).

of calling for a critical interrogation—of the concept of countertransference and, *a fortiori*, of empathy.

Lacan points out an initial difference between intervention and interpretation as far as their respective aims are concerned. Intervention occurs in the context of fantasy, helping the patient to observe both how his fantasy is constructed and how it is gradually undone.[5] Its function is to bring into relief, little by little, the entire infrastructure of the imaginary representations that accompany the patient's discourse. In this sense intervention leads the patient to become aware of what Lacan calls his *misrecognition* (*méconnaissance*).[6]

For example, consider what we call *scansion*. This is an analytic intervention that punctuates certain sequences in a patient's utterances in order to highlight something that escaped his notice when he said it.[7] Scansion does not uncover meaning; it explains nothing. What it does is to isolate certain signifiers at the right moment. It does not undo the transference— on the contrary, it reinforces what underlies the transference, namely the patient's asumption that the analyst knows the truth about her or him (see Dor 1994, Chapters 2 and 3).[8] When all is said and done this type of intervention gradually enables the patient to define for himself, in his own discourse, the desire that is expressed in that discourse.

As opposed to intervention, interpretation is directed at the cause of desire. Therefore it can take place only at certain privileged moments during the analysis, in the domain of the transference. Yet it too does not contribute to the uncovering of a meaning. When interpreting, the analyst does not decipher a meaning that can be related to what the patient is saying.

---

5. *Editor's note*: A fantasy is an imaginary scenario that brings a series of conscious and unconscious representations onstage. It is simultaneously the effect of unconscious archaic desire and the matrix of current unconscious and conscious desires.

6. *Editor's note*: This concept expresses the tension between the subject's alienated ego and a perception that fundamentally eludes it. To the extent that the ego's perceptions are filtered through fantasy, it can never have access to objective reality. See the preface for further discussion of *méconnaissance*.

7. *Editor's note*: This may be done, for example, by breaking off the session at a moment when the patient is capable of understanding something in his discourse other than what he thought he was saying.

8. *Editor's note*: The transference is established because the patient attributes to the analyst knowledge about his own (the patient's) desire, knowledge that he himself does not have. At the end of the analysis the patient is able to unseat the analyst from this position of the one who is presumed to know. It is through interpretation of the transference that the patient becomes aware of his unconscious knowledge.

Interpretation is first and foremost citation (see Dor 1992, Chapter 11). The analyst in effect "cites" a sequence from the patient's utterance at a moment when the patient is misrecognizing his own text. The interpretation does not bear on the content of the utterance and it invents nothing. It brings to light a signifying sequence that is already present in the patient's discourse, that is to say an unknown piece of knowledge within what he knows. In this sense interpretation is above all a break. It brings apparently disconnected signifying components together in a single sequence, thereby actualizing an element of the truth of the desire that had escaped the subject's notice. To the extent that it brings in no supplementary meaning that could be attributed to the analyst's knowledge, it contrasts with intervention in that it selectively undoes the transference to the analyst as the one who is assumed to know: only the patient can know something about his own desire.

With these clarifications in mind, can we really make a clinical distinction isolating a subgroup of patients whose pathological uniqueness could be specified outside the framework of the psychic structures we normally encounter in our work? It is one thing to view the pathology of these patients as falling within the general category of "narcissistic disorders," another to set apart the particular kinds of cases Dr. Modell describes under symptomatic headings like psychic death and the inability to generate meaning. I would tend to hypothesize that these patients do not really represent distinctive symptomatic typologies but at most peculiarly heightened pathological aspects of common clinical pictures. To confirm this hypothesis, perhaps we ought to examine such clinical findings from the perspective of other metapsychological and technical reference points than the ones suggested by Dr. Modell.

REFERENCES

Dor, J. (1988). *L'a-scientificité de la psychanalyse, vol I: L'aliénation de la psychanalyse.* Paris: Editions Universitaires.

———— (1992). *Introduction à la lecture de Lacan*, vol. II. Paris: Denoël.

———— (1994). *Clinique psychanalytique*. Paris: Denoël.

Freud, S. (1900). The interpretation of dreams. *Standard Edition* 4/5:1–626.

———— (1937). Constructions in analysis. *Standard Edition* 23:257–269.

Excerpts from the Discussion

(A French analyst): I've come across patients who have nothing to say, whose deficits are so great that they can't say anything. What interests me in Dr. Modell's talk is that he offers an explanation for why this might be the case, and I found that valuable.

(A French analyst): If I understood Dr. Modell correctly, he is presenting a revised theory of trauma, though one that has a precedent in Ferenczi. These are traumas that can befall any of us at any time of life and that cause ruptures in symbolization. I'd like to say that in Nicolas Abraham's theory of the psychoanalytic symbol, as in Freud's first theory of symbolization, there isn't a neo-linguistic division into verbal language, vocality, physical gestures, and the potentiality for action. After all, we do have a global theory of the psychoanalytic symbol that integrates these four poles, don't we?

I regret the recent tendency in France to neglect the importance of affectivity in psychoanalysis, what André Green calls living speech, which includes what patients don't say along with what they say and takes into consideration emotions, feelings, affects. I grant that the interest in verbal language and the theory of the sign, the signifier, and the symbol has been an entirely positive trend, but I don't think we can separate off from psychoanalysis what belongs to affect and sense impressions. There is a sensori-affective-motor way of thinking that is in place from the outset and operates throughout life even though it is entirely transformed by verbal language. And as Dr. Modell suggested, even in the case of verbal language analysts pay just as much attention to vocal quality, tone, rhythm, intonation, and pauses as to the verbal content.

In connection with the transgenerational traumatic effects that Dr. Modell discusses, I want to add that many analysts of various theoretical persuasions in France are taking a look at this type of effect in the tradition of Nicolas Abraham and Maria Torok.

Daniel Widlöcher: I like the contrast you make between repetition compulsion and contextualization. But in contextualization there isn't only the *anti*-traumatic effect; there's also the secret of pleasure (*jouissance*). It's through contextualization and retroactivity that *jouissance* becomes linked to trauma, but when do these lead to *jouissance* and when is their effect *anti*-traumatic? I don't think we can set these over against each other. On the contrary, we have to ask ourselves whether, in these empty patients you mention, the emptiness isn't also the result of the fact that this contextualization by means of *jouissance* has somehow eluded them. And if so, Dr. Dor would object that this isn't something that we see only in major personality disorders, but that it's a psychopathological feature that we encounter all the time in our work.

Anna Ornstein: I understand that both affect and language are in the service of communication. And if we accept that, then for me, affect is the first form of communication. It retains its power, when we learn language, only to a certain degree. We know that language expresses as much as it hides; I think this is what I'm learning from the Lacanians. This is the reason why we have to analyze language, because it goes both ways. However, instead of seeing both language and affect as forms of communication, it seems that the Lacanians have given some kind of priority to language as communication, and then affect, naturally, would have a secondary place.

Did I understand correctly that Dr. Dor meant that we actually have to listen for what is being said, rather than look for what is being hidden? Because in that case there is a similarity between self psychology and the Lacanian position. We too believe that our path, our route, to the unconscious is not through learning the language of the unconscious, and therefore guessing at what the manifest language exposes, but through following the patient's lead with the manifest. That is the quickest way to the unconscious.

Paul Ornstein: I loved the passion with which Joël Dor approached the paper. It allows us to be more intense than we might otherwise have permitted ourselves to be.

I had the feeling that Arnold Modell was showing us not a new category but a way of cutting across categories that would enable us to get a deeper understanding of the phenomena he described. I missed a reference to the transference as a guide to understanding meaning, so in that regard I have some questions for Dr. Modell. Regarding Joël Dor's lack of comfort with empathy, I would like to ask: How do we know what we know in psychoanalysis? What is our way of finding out? What is the method whereby we can get, imaginatively, into the experience of the other and know how the other feels, if not via empathy?

Arnold Modell: I'll try to respond to Joël Dor's comments. I'm not talking about a syndrome, or a new group; I'm talking about an aspect of life that's present in all of us.

His comment about my "pragmatic" approach raises a question about my metapsychology. I'd say my own metapsychology is in transition. I have thought of myself as a Freudian. I no longer believe in Freud's theory of drives. My own work and interest at this point is trying to integrate some work in neurobiology with psychoanalytic concepts, and I think this may be very off-putting to many people in the audience who don't believe that psychoanalysis should have a biological underpinning. But that's a separate issue.

With regard to affect: affect, clearly, cannot be separated from speech. It is part of language. We all know Strachey's classic paper on the therapeutic effects of interpretation. He said that a transference interpretation is effective when it's given at the point of *affective* urgency. This means that there has to be some affective bond at the precise moment that the interpretation is given. So this role of affect in speech is part of our heritage.

Joël Dor: As a clinician listening to patients and as a researcher, Freud was initially interested in what the patient didn't say, what was hidden, what was manifest and what was latent. And Freud pursued this investigation quite far, only to realize that he could not sustain it. Even as he was continuing to explore this issue he found that what we really have to attend to as we listen is what the patient is saying. And what the patient is saying is not the meaning but the way in which the meaning is brought forth.

It's obvious that what is said by someone isn't necessarily exclusively verbal. I'm not reducing signifying or symbolic expression solely to an effect of language. The dimension of the symbolic isn't simply the verbal, the linguistic, the signifier, and the signified—it's really something a bit more important. It's a problem of representation. Freud saw this right away. This means that the question confronting the analyst at a given moment in his transferential relation to the patient is the relation he has not only to his own representations but to those that are evoked for him by the patient in *verbal*, or *extra-verbal*, or *infra-verbal* forms (to use these convenient and fashionable terms).

Now to come back to that classic issue, of course it's possible to caricature what is called Lacanian psychoanalysis, or Lacanians themselves. For my part, I appreciate Dr. Modell's explanation of the way he goes about freeing a patient from "psychic death." And until proved otherwise, even if I go about it differently I also have this concern. Though it's not easy, there are surely different ways of unlocking the process *with this kind of patient* (as with the kind of patient who says nothing), or *in this clinical situation*. I use these terms as opposed to "clinical profile" or "state," because I'm not quite sure that we are even dealing with a state—a situation, yes; pathological, certainly; but a state is something much more systematic. I'd just like to say that what Dr. Modell proposes in the name of empathy or affect raises some difficulties for me, quite apart from the terrorism of the silent Lacanians, which is something in which I don't recognize myself.

Arnold Modell: Let me be clear. I'm thinking about a severe state which is not a passing sense of having nothing to say. This is a state of deadness of the self, where nothing means anything and nothing gives pleasure, and so forth. It's a characterological issue. We call this a symptom, but it's also a problem of character.

Joël Dor: I'm completely in agreement with you there.

11

"Someday" and "If Only" Fantasies

SALMAN AKHTAR, M.D.

The "widening scope of indications for psychoanalysis" (Stone 1954) has led, over the last three decades, to an enormous growth in the psychoanalytic literature on severe character pathology. This literature, far from being uniform, contains many controversies of both a theoretical and a technical nature. In the realm of theory, the most prominent controversies involve (1) the sufficiency of structural theory (Abend et al. 1983, Arlow and Brenner 1964) versus the need for new approaches to the understanding of severe psychopathology (Balint 1968, Kernberg 1975, 1984, 1992, Kohut 1971, 1977, Searles 1986); (2) the applicability of the conflict model to such conditions (Abend et al. 1983, Kernberg 1975, 1992) versus the need to conceptualize them in terms of deficit (Adler 1985, Kohut 1977, Winnicott 1965); and (3) the usefulness of the developmental perspective provided by separation-individuation theory (Kramer 1980, Mahler 1968, 1971, 1972, Mahler et al. 1975, Parens 1991, Settlage 1977, 1991, 1993) as opposed to that of self psychology (Kohut 1977; Kohut and Wolf 1978, Wolf 1994) in shedding light on the ontogenesis of severe personality disorders. In the realm of technique, the most prominent controversies involve (1) the differential emphasis upon a searching and skeptical listening attitude (Abend et al. 1983, Kernberg 1975, 1984) versus a credulous and affirming one (Balint 1968, Kohut 1977); and (2) the relative role of interpretive intervention (Kernberg 1975, 1984, 1992, Volkan 1976, 1987, Yeomans et al. 1992) as opposed to the "holding," containing, and empathic functions of the analyst (Balint 1968, Casement 1991, Khan 1974, 1983, Kohut 1984, Lewin and Schulz 1992, Winnicott 1965) in the treatment of these conditions.

Caught on the horns of such dilemmas are attempts to elucidate the affective experiences of individuals with these disorders. Their envy, rage, and hatred have received multiple, often contradictory, explanations. What is more important for the purposes of this paper is that the focus of psychoanalytic literature has remained largely upon these patients' bitterness, pessimism, and vulnerability to despair. Less attention has been paid to their heedless optimism (Kernberg 1967), their "unshakable determination to get on" (Balint 1968, p. 19), and their tenacious, though often covert, attitude of waiting. The descriptions of "primitive idealization" (Kernberg 1967) and "idealizing transference" (Kohut 1971) did address this area of their inner experience. However, subsequent elaborations of these views became trapped in polemic, such idealization being seen as either a residual developmental need (Kohut 1977, Kohut and Wolf 1978, Wolf 1994) or an instinctualized defense against deep-seated rage (Kernberg 1975b, 1992, Volkan 1976, 1987). This polarization, with the inevitable pressure to amass "evidence" for one or the other position, has caused inattention to other aspects of this idealization, including the existence of unconscious fantasies related to it. My paper seeks to fill this lacuna in the psychoanalytic literature.

I will describe two fantasies, "someday . . . " and "if only . . . ," which seem not only to be important vehicles of idealization but also to be related to each other in intricate ways. I will highlight their phenomenological characteristics, especially their relationship to optimism and nostalgia, and their deleterious effects upon the temporal continuity of the self-experience. I will then elucidate their metapsychological substrate and trace their origin through various phases of psychic development. Having described the clinical, metapsychological, and developmental aspects of the two fantasies, I will conclude with their implications for the technique of psychoanalysis and psychoanalytic psychotherapy. It seems advisable, however, to delineate the potential pitfalls in such conceptualization at the very outset.

SOME CAVEATS

> *Caveat:* (L. *caveat*, let him beware, 3rd pers. sing. pres. subj. of *cavere*, to beware, take heed): a warning, admonition
> —*Webster's New Universal Unabridged Dictionary*, 2nd Edition, 1983

> Books must be read as deliberately and reservedly as they are written.
> —Thoreau 1854

First and foremost, the fantasies I am about to describe should not be taken as literally representing the ideational events of early infantile life. While the feelings and wordless thoughts of infancy do form the building blocks of these fantasies, their specific content, requiring greater cognitive maturity, seems derived from later childhood. In a fashion analogous to writing a song on a preexisting tune, the experiences and images of later childhood give form to the nebulous residues of the preverbal period (Burland 1975, Frank 1969, Isakower 1936, Spitz 1965). Freud's (1918) designation of notions involving intrauterine life as "retrospective phantasying" (p. 103) is an apt reminder here.

Second, the manner in which these fantasies are communicated (by the patient) and deciphered (by the analyst) precludes certainty about them. Patients fail to put them into words satisfactorily[1] and often resort to metaphors, while the analyst finds himself relying on his own affective experience to a greater than usual extent (Burland 1975). The ground is murky and the risks attendant upon excessive reliance on empathy (Akhtar 1989, Rubovits-Seitz 1988, Wallerstein 1983), including countertransference intrusions, loom large in such an interpretive undertaking.

Third, it should not be overlooked that the origin of these fantasies is often multilayered and their intrapsychic purposes complex. Longings implicit in them usually arise as a result of unresolved separation-individuation, but such desires may also be mobilized by the developmentally later conflicts of the phallic-oedipal phase.

Fourth, caution should be exercised in assigning diagnostic significance to such fantasies. In subtle and subterranean forms, these fantasies are ubiquitous. It is only when they are tenacious, serve major defensive

---

1. The meagerness of free-associative data has resulted in my resorting to a composite sketch of such individuals rather than specific case illustrations.

and discharge functions, and encroach upon the executive functions of the ego that these fantasies become pathological.

Finally, it should be remembered that these fantasies may have an idiosyncratic relevance for a given patient. For instance, the "someday" fantasy of a patient might be based upon an identification with a parent who had such a fantasy. Another patient's excessive optimism might be carrying out, in an ironic fashion, the parental demand to think only good thoughts, be cheerful, and not complain. Keeping such diverse determinants in mind will facilitate discovery and enrich reconstructions in this area.

THE "SOMEDAY . . . " FANTASY

> Some people are dominated by the belief that there will always be some kind person—a representative of the mother, of course—to care for them and to give them everything they need. This optimistic belief condemns them to inactivity.
>
> —Abraham 1924

> Only by remaining a hope does hope persist.
>
> —Bion 1961

> When hope attains ascendency over desire, future time takes on a correspondingly magnified importance. If hope is to be maintained against the erosions of hopelessness and desire, time needs to be conserved and preserved—the more so since the pleasures attendant upon gratification of desire are not present to console or compensate for the loss of hope.
>
> —Boris 1976

Like Balint (1968), who was led to choose the term *basic fault* because that was "exactly the word used by many patients to describe it" (p. 21), I am guided by my patients in calling this fantasy "someday." This is precisely how these individuals refer to a certain kind of expectation from themselves, from their analyses, from life in general. They undertake treatment with gusto, religiously keep their appointments, arrive punctually, pay their bills promptly, and, from all appearances, seem good patients. Most of them talk copiously, offering well-thought-out formulations regarding their maladies. They earnestly express the hope of overcoming this or that inhibition, resolving this or that symptom, and achieving this or that life goal. They often stir up much redemptive enthusiasm in the analyst as well, especially during the opening phase of the analysis. Gradually, however, a different picture that challenges the assumed industriousness of these patients begins to emerge. They seem to be taking on too much, putting things off, never finishing anything. Whenever they run into difficulties, "road-blocks," or "too much hassle," they withdraw. This withdrawal gives a superficial appearance of their being flexible and realistic. Actually the case is just the opposite, since their withdrawal is not caused by accepting realistic difficulties and the resultant mourning but is intended to negate the impact of such limits on their vision. It is a behavioral counterpart of denial. After a brief lull in their optimistic pursuits, they begin all over again. They do not truly look for alternatives for anything, since they never accept defeat in the first place. They overlook discordant realities, cut ethical corners, and perpetually "shelve things away." Their secret hope is that "someday" all problems will vanish or they will be strong enough to deal with them.

The unrealistic optimism of these patients caricatures the "confident expectation" (Benedek 1938) or "basic trust" (Erikson 1950) that results from a satisfactory infant–mother relationship. These normatively inclined concepts illustrate a long-held tendency in psychoanalysis to regard optimism, even when excessive, in relatively positive terms. This tendency was set into motion by Freud's (1917) well-known correlation of "confidence in success" with being mother's "undisputed darling" (p. 156), and by Abraham's (1924) linking "imperturbable optimism" (p. 399) with an overly gratifying oral phase. Glover (1925) repeated that profound oral gratification leads to an "excess of optimism which is not lessened by reality experience" (p. 136). Later contributions (French 1945, French and Wheeler 1963, Menninger 1959) also remained focused upon the positive aspects of hope and optimism. In an exception to such thinking, Angel (1934) noted that excessive optimism is often a defensive development.[2] She described five patients with chronic, unrealistic hope (*Wunderglauben*) of a magical event that would improve their lots. She traced the origin of her three female patients' undue hopefulness to a denial of their lack of a penis and associated feelings of inferiority. Angel offered a different explanation for undue optimism in the two men. They had been prematurely and painfully deprived of their infantile omnipotence and were seeking its restoration by a

---

2. Nearly 200 years before this, Voltaire (1759) had declared optimism to be "a mania for maintaining that all is well when things are going badly."

fantasied regressive oneness with their mothers. Their optimism contained the hope that such longings would be realized.

Over the sixty years following Angel's significant paper, only a few contributions commented upon the defensive functions of excessive optimism. First, Searles (1977) noted that realistic hope needs to be distinguished from "unconscious-denial-based, unrealistic hopefulness" (p. 484). The former emanates from a successful integration of prior disappointments. The latter results from an "essentially manic repression of loss and despair" (p. 483). In contrast to healthy hopefulness, which is a source of support and gratification for oneself and others, excessive hope serves sadomasochistic aims. Searles outlined two connections between such inordinate hope and sadism:

> First, one of the more formidable ways of being sadistic toward the other person is to engender hope, followed by disappointment, in him over and over. Second, the presenting of a hopeful demeanor under some circumstances can constitute, in itself, a form of sadism toward the other person, for it can be expressing, implicitly and subtly, cruel demands upon him to fulfill the hopes written upon one's face. [p. 485]

Following Searles' contribution, Amati-Mehler and Argentieri (1989) described two cases in which "pathological hope" (p. 300) represented "the last and unique possible tie with the primary object, giving [which] up would mean the definite downfall of illusion and the admission that it is really, truly lost" (p. 302). Then, highlighting the effects of unresolved separation-individuation and impaired object constancy, I (Akhtar 1991, 1994a) briefly outlined the "someday" and "if only" fantasies discussed here in detail. Finally, Potamianou (1992) asserted that excessive hope can serve as a character armor that keeps reality at a distance. In normal and neurotic conditions, hope sustains a link with the good object and makes waiting bearable. In borderline conditions, however, hope serves as an expression of the patient's narcissistic self-sufficiency; waiting is made bearable only by recourse to infantile omnipotence. For such individuals, the present has only secondary importance. They can tolerate almost any current suffering in the hope that future rewards will make it all worthwhile.[3] Potamianou emphasized that excessive hope, besides fueling (and

---

3. Boris (1976) has proposed a "fundamental antagonism between hope and desire" (p. 141): possession of hope acts as a restraint upon desire and loss of hope is followed by a burgeoning of desire.

being fueled by) narcissism, strengthens and prolongs the hidden masochistic suffering of these individuals.

In addition to these descriptions of pathological optimism, there exists the view of "independent" British analysts that hope, even when expressed through pathological behavior, is essentially healthy and adaptive. Winnicott (1956) declared that "the antisocial act is an expression of hope" (p. 309) insofar as it seeks a redress for an early environmental deprivation. Khan (1966) extended Winnicott's ideas to certain narcissistic and schizoid individuals who seemed uncannily capable of creating special and exciting experiences for themselves, experiences from which they nonetheless withdrew and which left them basically unchanged.[4] It is as if they had hoped for something ("someday"?) but did not find it. More recently, Casement (1991) related "unconscious hope" to the repetition compulsion through which unconscious conflicts continue to generate attempts at solutions which do not actually work. At the same time, patients do contribute in various ways, and "hopefully" (p. 301), to finding the clinical setting needed by them.

In sum, the psychoanalytic literature on hope can be grouped into three broad categories emphasizing (1) its normative, healthy aspects; (2) its employment as a defense against early loss and defective object constancy as well as its covert narcissistic and masochistic aims; and (3) its adaptive role in seeking redress, including redress through pathological behavior, of early environmental loss. The "someday" fantasy described here subsumes all these aspects of hope and optimism.

Returning from this detour into the literature, one notes that patients vary greatly in the extent to which they provide details of their hopes for "someday." Often they feel puzzled, uncomfortable, ashamed, and even angry upon being asked to elaborate on their "someday." This is especially so if they are asked what would happen *after* "someday." It is as if "someday," like God, is not to be questioned. Some patients use metaphors and/or visual images to convey the essence of "someday," while others remain silent about it. Frequently, the analyst has to fill in the blanks and surmise the nature of their expectations. In either case, it is the affective texture of "someday" that seems its most important feature. Basically, "someday" refers to a time when one will be completely peaceful and conflict free. Every-

---

4. Much earlier, Eissler (1950) had pointed out that the "addiction to novelty" (p. 154) among antisocial personalities actually consists of a monotonous repetition of essentially similar experiences. True novelty scares them and they vehemently avoid it.

thing will be available, or nothing will be needed. Motor activity will be either unnecessary or effortless. Even thinking will not be required. There will be no aggression from within or from outside.[5] Needless to say, such a universe is also oblivious to the inconvenient considerations of the incest taboo and the anxieties and compromises consequent upon the oedipal situation.

A complex set of psychodynamic mechanisms helps to maintain the structural integrity of "someday." These include (1) denial and negation of sectors of reality that challenge it; (2) splitting-off of those self- and object-representations that mobilize conflict and aggression; (3) a defensively motivated feeling of inauthenticity (Gediman 1985, Loewald 1979) in those areas of the personality where a healthier, more realistic, compromise-formation level of mentality and functioning has been achieved;[6] and (4) a temporal displacement, from past to future, of a preverbal state of blissful unity with the "all-good" mother of the symbiotic phase (Mahler 1972, Mahler et al. 1975). The speculation that this fantasy, at its core, contains a longing for a luxurious (and retrospectively idealized) symbiotic phase gains strength from the inactivity, timelessness, wordlessness, thoughtlessness, unexcited bliss, and absence of needs implicit in "someday."

This genetic backdrop is supported by my observation that individuals who tenaciously cling to "someday" had often been suddenly "dropped" from maternal attention during their second year of life (at times due to major external events, for example, birth of a sibling, prolonged maternal hospitalization). However, other factors including early parent or sibling loss, intense castration anxiety, and problematic oedipal scenarios also play a role in the genesis of the "someday" fantasy. Boys who were excessively close to their mothers, especially if they also had weak or absent fathers, may continue to believe that "someday" their oedipal triumph can actually be consummated; Chasseguet-Smirgel's (1984) delineation of "perverse character" is pertinent in this context. Girls who were "dropped" by their mothers and valiantly rescued by their fathers in childhood persist in the hope of "someday" finding an all-good mother/father combination in adult life.

---

5. Echoes of the "oceanic feeling" (Freud 1930) of psychic infancy, during which the self-absorbed infant experiences all of space and time as coextensive with his ego, are unmistakably present here.

6. In an extension of Winnicott's (1960) terminology, the situation here can be described as a "pseudo-false-self" organization.

As a rule only the focal and externalized derivatives of "someday" are conscious. The infantile fused self- and object-representations powerfully invested with "primitive idealization" (Kernberg 1967) emerge only after considerable analytic work has been accomplished. The adaptive functions of the "someday" fantasy involve its fostering optimism, perseverance, and a "search for an environmental provision" (Winnicott 1956, p. 310). The idealized "someday" is a defensive structure against the affective turmoil, including rage, consequent upon inadequate availability of the mother, especially during the rapprochement subphase of separation-individuation (Mahler 1971). However, it might also defend against anxieties consequent upon the realization of the anatomical differences between the sexes (Freud 1925), and of oedipal boundaries and limits (e.g., "someday" I will have a penis; "someday" I will be the romantic partner of my mother/father).[7] The excessive hope implicit in "someday" fantasy serves both narcissistic and masochistic aims. In an attempt to establish a link between narcissistic and masochistic character types, Cooper (1989) emphasized that "pathological narcissistic tendencies are unconscious vehicles for obtaining masochistic disappointment; and masochistic injuries are an affirmation of distorted narcissistic fantasies" (p. 551).[8]

On the behavioral level, the manner in which patients strive to reach "someday" varies greatly (Akhtar 1992b). Those with a narcissistic personality seek to bring "someday" to life by devoting themselves to hard work and social success. Those with an antisocial bent seek similar magic through swindling, gambling, and other get-rich-quick schemes. Paranoid individuals focus on the obstacles in their path to "someday." Borderline individuals frantically look for this "someday" through infatuations, perverse sexu-

---

7. Among the growing ego's attempts to hold on to illusions of omnipotence, Dorn (1967) includes the "when I grow up . . ." incantation of childhood. Such motivating idealizations are already an advance over the earlier, more magical, state of infantile omnipotence.

8. States of addiction and "codependency" also depict the masochistic dimension of excessive hope. The addict continues to be self destructive while hoping that the drug will somehow magically solve intrapsychic problems, and the codependent individual remains relentlessly optimistic that a terrible relationship will somehow become all right. The connection between pathological hope and masochism becomes blatant when the longed-for "someday" involves death. Patients with this configuration manifest a chronic attitude of waiting for death, with or without suicidal acts. Such incorporation of self destructiveness into the ego ideal usually speaks for a guarded prognosis (Kernberg 1975).

ality, and mind-altering drugs. Schizoid individuals adopt a passive stance and wait for a magical happening, a windfall, or a chance encounter with a charismatic guru. All individuals with a severe personality disorder—be it narcissistic, antisocial, paranoid, borderline, or schizoid—seem to be seeking a "fantasied reversal of a calamity that has occurred" (Renik 1990, p. 244) and a restitution of an inner homeostasis that was disturbed years ago. All are in chronic pursuit.[9]

This relentless pursuit of the "all-good" mother of symbiosis occasionally gets condensed with positive oedipal strivings. Condensation of the "good" mother-representation with that of the desired oedipal partner gives rise to intense longings experienced as unquestionable "needs" (Akhtar 1992b, 1994a). The parallel amalgamation of the "bad" mother-representation with the oedipal rival creates vengeful hostility, which is often split-off, denied, displaced onto others, or enacted in a contradictory but unassimilated manner towards the analyst. During analytic treatment, such "malignant erotic transference" (Akhtar, 1994b)[10] often turns out to be an upward defense against faulty self- and object constancy.

Four aspects of this transference are: (1) predominance of hostility over love in the seemingly erotic overtures, (2) intense coercion of the analyst to indulge in actions, (3) inconsolability in the face of the analyst's depriving stance,[11] and (4) the absence of erotic counterresonance in the

---

9. To borrow terms used by Settlage and colleagues (1991) in a different context, it seems that all patients with severe character pathology are stuck in the appeal phase of the infantile "appeal cycle" (adaption-distress-appeal-interaction), only the manner of their appeal varies. Perhaps these stylistic differences contain remote echoes of early infantile experiences. Spitz (1953) points out that, when separated, an infant "first becomes weepy, demanding and clinging to everybody who approaches it; it looks as though attempts are made by these infants to regain the lost object with the help of their aggressive drive. Later on, visible manifestations of the aggressive drive decrease" (p. 133). Could the various phenotypic variations of severe character pathology (e.g., borderline, narcissistic, schizoid) at least partly be due to their different locations on this spectrum of affectomotor responses of a betrayed child?

10. The choice of the adjective "malignant" to describe such "erotized" (Blum 1973) transference is intended to highlight these aggressive and coercive features and to extend the context in which this adjective has been used in the psychoanalytic literature; for example, "malignant regression" (Balint 1968), "malignant narcissism" (Kernberg 1984).

11. Freud (1915) referred to such patients as "children of nature who refuse to accept the psychical in place of the material" (p. 166). In his experience, most such patients were "women of elemental passionateness who tolerate no surrogates" (p. 166). Such greater frequency of malignant erotic transference in women seems to have many explanations:

analyst, who experiences the patient's demands as intrusive, controlling, and hostile. In such cases, "the preeminent oral insatiability, the vulnerability to disappointment and detachment, the underlying sadomasochism soon become apparent" (Blum 1973, p. 69). In the throes of such intense erotic transference (see also Eickhoff 1987, Joseph 1993, Wallerstein 1983), the patient can become convinced that the analyst should (or will) "someday" actually consummate their relationship and marry her. Here the emergence of the "someday" fantasy shows a beginning loss of reality testing and is therefore a cause for alarm. Conversely, in patients who, in a near-psychotic version of such a transference, are insistent that the analyst marry them right now, a movement towards "someday" implies the dawning capacity to tolerate postponement of desire. It might constitute the first evidence of a strengthened capacity to mourn and renounce omnipotent claims on reality.

THE "IF ONLY" FANTASY

> The first two years of life, in which external "omnipotent" persons took care of us, protected and provided us with food, shelter, sexual satisfaction, and reparticipation in the lost omnipotence, gave us a feeling of being secure in a greater unit, while, at the same time losing our own individuality. This memory establishes in every human being a capacity for nostalgia for such a state whenever attempts at active mastery fail. [Fenichel 1945, p. 561]

> [T]he reiterative declarations of uselessness, failure and lack of hope made by our patients are placed in a non-temporal dimension in which the idea of failure is fictitious, since all energies are pathologically directed to a past that needs to be kept immobile and therefore inca-

---

(1) more intense reproaches in the female child towards the mother; (2) the extra burden on the female child's ego of mourning the "loss" of the penis; and (3) the actual experience, in the background of many such patients, of being "picked up" by their fathers after having been "dropped" by their mothers. This last-mentioned factor, while saving the child from a schizoid or suicidal breakdown, robs her of a fundamental prototype of mourning; instead, she learns that what is lost ("all-good" mother) can indeed be found (an overindulgent father). The fact that such rescues are usually quite instinctualized contributes to sadomasochistic sexual fantasies and a perverse defiance of oedipal limits in later, adult life.

pable of becoming "history." [Amati-Mehler and Argentieri 1989, pp. 300–301]

Individuals with an "if only" fantasy lack interest in the future and constantly wring their hands over something that happened in the past. They insist that "if only" this had not taken place, everything would have turned out all right. Life before that event is glossed over or retrospectively idealized. When a childhood event, for example, parental divorce, gets involved in the "if only" fantasy, an elaborate "personal myth" (Kris 1956) tends to develop that, with its seductive logic, may even go unquestioned during analytic treatment (e.g., my case of Mr. A, in Kramer and Akhtar 1988). The "screen" nature of such "if only" formulations is, however, clearer when the trauma, relentlessly harped on, is from the recent past. Individuals who remain tormented year after year by the memories of a failed romance from college days, a psychotherapist who moved out of town, or an extramarital lover who withdrew his or her affection often give histories of having been painfully "dropped" from maternal attention during early childhood.

A concomitant of the "if only" fantasy is intense nostalgia. The wish to recapture an idealized past stirs up a poignant mixture of "mental pain" (Freud 1926, p. 171) and joy. Pain is evoked by the awareness of separation from the now idealized object and joy by a fantasied reunion with it through reminiscences. "It is the subtlety, iridescence, and ambivalence of these feelings that gives nostalgia its inimitable coloration" (Werman 1977, p. 393). While often attributed to a loss during adult life, this characteristically "bitter-sweet pleasure" (Kleiner 1970, p. 11) has its origin in the incomplete mourning of a traumatic disruption of the early mother–child relationship. Sterba (1940) was the first to correlate "home-sickness" with a longing for the maternal breast. Fenichel (1945) also explained nostalgia as a wish to return to the preoedipal mother. Fodor (1950) went so far as to correlate nostalgic yearnings with a deep-seated longing for the undisturbed prenatal state.[12] However, these references to prenatal bliss, the maternal breast, and the preoedipal mother, and so forth, are better regarded as largely metaphorical. Much takes place between a premature traumatic rupture of infantile bliss and its alleged counterpart in adulthood. Hartmann's (1964) warning regarding the *genetic fallacy* must be heeded

---

12. Chasseguet-Smirgel's (1984) notion of the pervert's "nostalgia for primary narcissism" (p. 29) seems related to this view.

here. Recall of such early events is questionable, fantasies involving them are retrospective creations, and the idealization is intended to keep aggressively tinged self- and object-representations in abeyance.[13] It is, however, unmistakable that the nostalgic individual is looking for a completely untroubled state. Such a person is looking not only for the lost object but for an idealized object, and, what is even more important, for the time before the object was lost. This covert element of search in nostalgic hand-wringing is a clue to the psychodynamic kinship between the "if only" and "someday" fantasies.

The metapsychological structure of the "if only" fantasy is indeed similar to that of the "someday" fantasy. It too involves splitting, denial, and primitive idealization. It too serves defensive purposes and reflects incomplete mourning for preoedipal traumas (premature loss of adequate maternal attention) as well as oedipal and narcissistic traumas (being excluded from the parents' mutually intimate life, painful awareness of being vulnerable). Under normal circumstances, mourning such traumas goes hand in hand with the ego's renunciation of infantile omnipotence. "The experiencing of hopelessness is thus a part of normal development and is necessary for the attainment of a more reality-oriented sense of psychic self" (Schmale 1964, p. 300). Klein's (1940) "depressive position" and Mahler's (1968) "object constancy" are both contingent upon renunciation of omnipotence, development of the capacity for ambivalence, and a certain diminution in optimism about the self and others. The "if only" fantasy, in contrast, is, at its core, a product of incomplete mourning over the loss of the all-good mother of symbiosis. It expresses a position in which the idealized primary object is neither given up through the work of grieving nor is assimilated into the ego through identification. Instead, the object is retained in psychic limbo by a stubborn "nostalgic relationship" (Geahchan 1968) which is

characteristically indeterminate in its representations, and by its imaginary nature the subject is able to maintain separateness from the object. This leads to an indefinite and indefinable quest—and if an object should appear that seems to correspond to the nostalgic desire, it is promptly rejected, it becomes demythologized; it is not what it promised to be: the subject's projection of what it should be. The subject can

---

13. Awareness of the resulting "screen" functions of such nostalgia has led to the distinction between "normal and pathological" (Werman 1977) or "true and false" (Sohn 1983) types of nostalgia. The former is supposed to reflect a continuation of mourning and the latter its idealized blockage.

thus only enjoy the search and never the possession. [Werman 1977, p. 391]

At the same time, the displaced derivatives of this "loss" are harped upon ad infinitum. Here splitting mechanisms also play a significant role, since the aggressively tinged representations of the lost object are totally repudiated and/or displaced onto other objects.

Similarities between the "someday" and "if only" fantasies do not end with the dynamics of insufficient mourning. Their form might differ, but their message is essentially the same. Indeed, the two together can be labeled as "the fantasies of ideal times" (Juan-David Nasio, 1994, personal communication). The "someday" fantasy says: "A day will come when I will recapture the lost mother of symbiosis and also overcome the oedipal barrier." The "if only" fantasy says: "I wish the day had not come when I was dropped from maternal attention, nor the day when I become aware of oedipal limitations." Another similarity between the two fantasies involves their pronounced sadomasochistic aims. In the "someday" fantasy, these are evident in the destruction of all here-and-now satisfactions. This destruction may be either an angry denigration of the available satisfactions or a defense against superego accusations for not having done better. In the "if only" fantasy, much hateful blaming of self and others underlies the preoccupation with an "unfortunate" external event.

> Those with ferocious superegos and masochistic inclinations are involved in endless self-condemnation: if only I had said this; if only I had done that, etc. These fantasies are a way of paying back one's conscience without really intending to do anything different in the future. They are mea culpas: "I have confessed to being guilty, and now we can close the books on this episode." Then there are the "if only" fantasies that blame others: "If only so-and-so had chosen to behave decently towards me; if only people could see the real me and realize how wonderful I am," and so on. In other words, whatever catastrophe has befallen me, it is not my fault. It would not have happened had others not denied me my due or maliciously gotten in my way. [Cooper, personal communication 1995]

Yet another element common to "someday" and "if only" fantasies is the quest for a lost object and, behind it, for a lost self-experience. Moreover, the psychic ointment of idealization is used by both "someday" and "if only" fantasies. It serves a self-soothing purpose and helps to deny aggression towards the unavailable, frustrating object held responsible for the narcissistic disequilibrium. These "advantages" of idealization are matched by its deleterious effect upon the temporal dimension of self-experience. In the "someday" fantasy, the future is idealized, leading to excessive hope and a search for ideal conditions. In the "if only" fantasy, the past is idealized, leading to nostalgia and self-pity. Individuals with the former fantasy live in the future and those with the latter in the past; both are alienated from the present.[14] In other words, both fantasies cause a "temporal discontinuity in the self experience" (Akhtar 1984, 1992b). Frequently, the two fantasies coexist and form a tandem theme: "if only this had not happened, life would be all right, but someday this will be reversed and life will (again) become totally blissful." This tandem theme is all too frequently found in religious motifs, literary productions, and various cultural institutions and rituals.

SOCIOCULTURAL VICISSITUDES

> In our nostalgia for the major freedom of animal life we remember a Golden Age, a Garden, a time before sin. The sacred does not beckon to us from up ahead, urging us forward toward higher spiritual realms. The sacred lies behind us. It blocks the way back to the freedom of our prehuman past. The sacred and the forbidden are one.
> —Wheelis 1994

The Christian notion of the "original sin," a transgression that brought the idyllic existence of mankind's mythic forebears to an abrupt end, embodies a parricidal oedipal theme (Freud 1913) as well as a scenario of separation and loss of omnipotence. Together the two yield an "if only" fantasy of cosmic proportions. Counterposed to this fall from grace is the possibility of "someday" returning to it in the form of heaven. Judaism, while not subscribing to the "original sin" idea, does hold that a Messiah will arrive "someday" and bring eternal peace upon earth. Islam, like Christianity, subscribes to the notion of heaven, and certain of its sects, for example the Shiites, also contribute to the notion of the return of the Mes-

---

14. I have elsewhere (Akhtar 1995) highlighted such temporal fractures of the psyche and the associated role of "someday" and "if only" fantasies in the lives of immigrants, a group of people especially vulnerable to such experiences.

siah (*Mahdi*). Hinduism holds that after numerous reincarnations the soul will ultimately be relieved of the anguish of corporeal existence. Achieving *moksha* (freedom), the individual *atma* (soul) will become one with *paramatma* (the supreme soul, Brahma, the creator). Thus, in one form or the other, themes of being "dropped" and "expelled" from a blissful existence and of return to it exist in all the major religions of the world.

This human desire to return to an earlier ideal (idealized!) state of total freedom from conflict finds nonreligious expressions as well. The deep love of nature in some persons and the yearning for a reunion with it seem to have roots in a nostalgia of the kind described above. Themes of pining for a lost paradise (often displaced to its derivatives, e.g., bygone youth, cities and nations left behind, past lovers) have created some of the most powerful literary pieces in history. Kleiner (1970) and Werman (1977), in their papers on nostalgia, give many evocative examples of this sort, including that of Marcel Proust whom Werman aptly calls "the most famous *grand nostalgique*" (p. 394). Hamilton's (1969) essay on Keats is also in the same vein. Art, too, frequently capitalizes on nostalgia; examples of this extend from Giorgio de Chirico's preoccupation with Italian landscapes (Krystal 1966) to the more plebeian themes of Norman Rockwell's popular paintings. The recent attempt to resurrect Woodstock may also have betrayed a yearning to recapture the spirit and feeling of a past, now idealized, place and time. It is with such longing that individuals with "someday" and "if only" fantasies arrive at the psychoanalyst's doorstep.

TECHNICAL IMPLICATIONS

> Nostalgic tendencies are seen as associated with an inability to mourn in early life, and later, an unwillingness to do so. Only after the search for unification with infantile objects is given up is the nostalgic able to accept meaningful substitutes. [Kleiner 1970, p. 29]

> To firmly undo the idealization, to confront the patient again and again with the unrealistic aspects of his transference distortion, while still acknowledging the positive feelings that are also part of this idealization, is a very difficult task because underneath that idealization are often paranoid fears and quite direct, primitive aggressive feelings toward the transference object. [Kernberg 1975, pp. 97–98]

Having acknowledged the ubiquitousness of "someday" and "if only" fantasies in human mental life, I have, by implication, conceded that all individuals entering psychotherapy or psychoanalysis bring such attitudes with them. The hope and idealization implicit in these fantasies serve, in most patients, as a therapeutic incentive that sustains the interpretive enterprise and makes treatment possible. Their hope has a realistic quality that contributes to the development of a therapeutic or working alliance (Friedman 1969, Gitelson 1962, Greenson 1965). "Someday" and "if only" fantasies do not become an explicit focus of analytic inquiry in these patients. Themes of disillusionment and loss of omnipotence appear mostly during the termination phase of their treatment.

Other patients are different.[15] Their entire psychic lives are governed by "someday" and "if only" fantasies; in their case, these fantasies reflect not only an inner organizing element of central importance but also an outer relational paradigm. In the analytic situation, the "someday" fantasy of many such patients gives rise to an attitude of perpetual waiting. This may be expressed nakedly through protracted silences, or cloaked by superficial compliance, even verbal excess. Other patients develop a malignant erotic transference and try to coerce the analyst into having sex with them or marrying them. All patients with a "someday" fantasy hope that analysis (or the analyst) will somehow magically solve all their problems. However, excessive optimism impedes realistic hope and paves the way for hopelessness. Consequently, such patients oscillate between inordinate optimism and a bruised sense of futility.[16]

The "if only" fantasy manifests in the analytic situation either as an abysmal preoccupation with an adult-life loss to the exclusion of other associations, or as a slow emergence of a "personal myth" (Kris 1956) involving a childhood trauma. The individual with a "someday" fantasy waits

---

15. In his discussion of this paper (this volume), Juan-David Nasio distinguishes the "someday" and "if only" fantasies of the neurotic and the borderline patients on two grounds: (1) the neurotic postpones castration anxiety by temporally displacing his wishes while the borderline avoids self-disintegration by hiding behind the hope or "memory" of absolute bliss, and (2) the neurotic attributes to the analyst the power to fulfill his needs while the borderline excludes the analyst and awaits no promise. Nasio's first notion is more agreeable to me than the second. In my experience, the narcissist (seemingly) excludes the analyst and waits for nothing, the borderline attributes to the analyst the power to realize his hope, and the neurotic retains an awareness of the illusory nature of his excessive optimism.

16. Killingmo (1989) has also noted such oscillation between "desperate hope and resignation" (p. 73). According to him, when this happens, the clinical material at hand is based primarily on a deficit-driven sector of the personality and not on the sector governed by conflict.

or coerces, and the one with an "if only" fantasy laments, seeks to convince, or pleads for validation of a particular viewpoint. Issues of narcissistic vulnerability, shaky object constancy, repudiated aggression, and inconsolability are prominent in both. Secretly or openly, both types of individual are given to intense idealization which betrays both unmet "growth needs" (Casement 1991) of childhood *and* a defense against aggression. It is to the treatment of such patients that the following technical suggestions apply.

Before I proceed further, however, a brief return to the developmental perspective on these issues seems necessary. Both Winnicott (1951) and Mahler (1972) trace a developmental line from illusion to disillusion during childhood. Initially, in Winnicott's (1951) terminology, "omnipotence is nearly a fact of life" (p. 238). Later the transitional object appears, when the mother is in transition from the state of being undifferentiated from the infant to the state of being perceived as a separate object. In Mahler's terminology, it is during the rapprochement subphase that the child realizes that his wishes and those of the mother do not always coincide. Unable to sustain the magic of symbiosis, "the child can no longer maintain his delusion of parental omnipotence" and also "must gradually and painfully give up the delusion of his own grandeur" (Mahler et al. 1975, p. 79). Adding a significant nuance to Freud's (1911) outlining of the gradual replacement of the pleasure principle by the reality principle, both Winnicott and Mahler regard this journey from illusion to disillusion as necessary for psychic growth.[17] And it is this movement from illusion to disillusion that is the central task in the treatment of individuals with tenacious "someday" and "if only" fantasies. Being able to take this agonizing step is what transforms their pathological hope to realistic expectation and their idealization to a mature, post-ambivalent object investment. For them to make such an advance, however, the treatment must offer both illusion and disillusionment.[18]

---

17. This similarity should not lead one to overlook the fact that significant conceptual differences exist in the theories of Winnicott and Mahler (see Wolman 1991).

18. Technical approaches in this realm have leaned either towards providing and sustaining illusion (Adler 1985, Balint 1968, Kohut 1977, Lewin and Schulz 1992) or toward interpretive dissolution of such illusion (Abend et al. 1983, Kernberg 1975, Volkan 1976, Yeomans et al. 1992). Elsewhere (Akhtar 1992b), I have attempted a broader synthesis of these two trends related to the "romantic" and "classic" visions of psychoanalysis (Strenger 1989).

First and foremost, therefore, the analyst must provide a psychological atmosphere of trust, emotional security, and acceptance, attributes akin to the early maternal care of the child. Modell (1976) has spelled out those elements in the analyst's technique that facilitate the development and maintenance of such "holding environment" (Winnicott, 1960):

> [T]he analyst is constant and reliable; he responds to the patient's affects; he accepts the patient, and his judgment is less critical and more benign; he is there primarily for the patient's needs and not for his own; he does not retaliate; and he does at times have a better grasp of the patient's inner psychic reality than does the patient himself and therefore may clarify what is bewildering and confusing. [Modell 1976, p. 291]

To be sure, all this is important in the conduct of any analysis. However, in patients with "someday" and "if only" fantasies these ingredients acquire a much greater significance insofar as they help to mobilize, and temporarily sustain, the patient's illusion that hope can be fulfilled and lost objects found. However illusory such goals might be, the patient does need to be able to feel and think them valid before seeing them as fantasies, with regressive aims and defensive functions. Volkan's (1981) observation that attuned listening and containment of emotions often constitute the only interventions for quite some time before any interpretive work can be done with individuals suffering from pathological grief is pertinent here. Also important is Amati-Mehler and Argentieri's (1989) caution that, before the patient's excessive hope is frustrated either directly or by way of interpretation,

> the patient ought to experience for a sufficient length of time and at different levels the soundness of the therapeutic rapport, the security of being understood, the benefit of a careful and thorough working through of the transference, and a relational structure that enables him or her to contain the comprehension and the elaboration of the disruption of the transference play. [p. 303]

Second, the analyst must be comfortable with the use of "affirmative interventions" (Killingmo 1989). These comprise "an objectifying element" (which conveys the sense to the patient that the therapist can feel what it is to be in the former's shoes), "a justifying element" (which introduces a cause-and-effect relationship), and "an accepting element" (which imparts a historical context to the current distress by including the mention of similar experiences from the patient's childhood). Affirmative interventions often necessitate that the analyst deliberately restrict the scope of his interventions, yet such "superficiality," paradoxically, prepares the ground for unmasking, interpretive interventions. The issue at hand, however, extends beyond matters of "tact" (Poland 1975) and "optimal distance" (Akhtar 1992a, Escoll 1992) from the depths of the patient's psyche. Considerations of actual time are involved here. For instance, when a patient endlessly laments the loss of a loved one, it is better, for a long while, to "agree" with the patient and to demonstrate one's understanding of the nature and the conscious sources of the patient's agony. Balint (1968) emphasizes that, under such circumstances, the analytic process "must not be hurried by interpretations, however correct, since they may be felt as undue interference, as an attempt at devaluing the justification of their complaint and thus, instead of speeding up, they will slow down the therapeutic processes" (p. 182). To point out discrepancies and contradictions in the patient's story, to bring up the defensive nature of this idealization, and to analyze the potentially masochistic aspects of such continued pain, are tasks that must be left for much later.

Third, the analyst must help the patient unmask what underlies his waiting attitude. This will pave the way for the two of them to face squarely the idealization inherent in "someday" and "if only" fantasies. For instance, to a patient who, after four years of analytic work, continued to complain bitterly about the ineffectiveness of psychoanalysis with regard to his short stature (a disguised but close version of his actual complaint), I once responded by saying the following: "You know, the pained disbelief in your voice and the intensity with which you berate me about this issue make me wonder if you really believe that analysis could or should lead to your becoming taller. Do you?" The patient was taken aback but, after some hesitation, did acknowledge that all along he had believed that he might become taller as a result of hard work.

Once such omnipotent expectations are brought to the surface, the analyst can attempt to interpret their defensive aims against aggression in the transference and, behind that, towards the early objects (Kernberg 1975). He might also help the patient bring forth the narcissistic and masochistic gratifications derived from these fantasies, which keep the patient's existence in a grand, suffering limbo. He might now point out to the patient the illusory nature of his "someday" fantasy and the "screen functions" of the nostalgia (Freedman 1956, Sohn 1983, Werman 1977) inherent in his "if only" fantasy. However, even during this phase, the analyst must remain respectful of the patient's psychic soft spots and be affectively and conceptually prepared to oscillate between affirmative interventions, when thwarted growth needs and ego deficits seem to dictate the transference demands, and interpretive interventions, when more traditional conflict-based transferences are in the forefront (Akhtar 1992b, 1994a, b, Killingmo 1989, Strenger 1989). Such "oscillations in strategy" (Killingmo 1989, p. 75) would necessitate a conceptual freedom on the analyst's part to view the patient's idealization as both a thwarted developmental need (Kohut 1977) and a pathological defense (Kernberg 1975), that is, as a psychic configuration requiring both empathic and interpretive handling.

Fourth, failing to engage the patient in such an interpretive undertaking, the analyst must be prepared to rupture the patient's inordinate hope. Clearly, many analysts would question the need ever to "rupture" the patient's excessive hope. They would suggest that simply understanding its origins and functions and letting the usual analytic approach take its course will lead to the transformation of such fantasies. This does happen in milder cases. However, in those stubbornly fixated on "someday" and "if only" fantasies, a more "ruthless"[19] intervention is indicated. Basically it comes down to "having to state that neither analysis nor analyst [are] omnipotent rescuers, as the patients in their illusion needed to believe" (Amati-Mehler and Argentieri 1989, p. 301). In a case of malignant erotic transference, such an intervention would translate into the analyst's explicit declaration that he will never marry the patient. With those endlessly lamenting a long dead parent, the analyst might have to literally confirm the irreversibility of the situation. A less dramatic, but essentially similar, example is of the patient who "kept crying and saying, 'I can't help it', and the analyst [who] said: 'I am afraid I can't help it either'" (Amati-Mehler and Argentieri 1989, p. 296).

Such interventions can be subsumed under the broad rubric of "optimal disillusionment" (Gedo and Goldberg 1973), which requires that the analysand learn to give up magical thinking. They are neither conventional nor risk free. They disrupt the transference dynamics and, therefore, are inevitably traumatic to the patient. Indeed, when their "dosage" or timing is inappropriate—and this may not be entirely predictable—the resulting despair and psychic pain may lead the patient to become seriously suicidal. This puts the analysis to a most severe test. Temporary departures from neutrality may now become unavoidable, and adjunct, stabilizing measures

---

19. I am using the word in the paradoxically benevolent sense outlined by Mayer 1994.

may have to be employed. On the other hand, interventions of this sort may constitute a turning point of the analytic process in less complicated circumstances, provided, of course, that the analyst's holding functions are in place, and that the effects of such an intervention can be analyzed. Rupture of pathological hope is a necessary precondition for mourning that is otherwise blocked in these patients.[20] At the same time, the analyst

> must convey to the patient not only the direction he wants the patient to move in, but also confidence that the movement is inherent in the patient, which means that what the uncured patient wants is indeed a representation, however distorted, of what the cured patient will get. [Friedman 1969, p. 150]

In other words, the analyst must make sure (to the extent it is possible) that the consequence of his intervention is not a transition from pathological hope to hopelessness but one from pathological hope to realistic hope. This movement is facilitated if the analyst has faith in the patient's capacity in this regard, a proposition reflecting Loewald's (1960) outlining of the childhood need to identify with one's growth potential as seen in the eyes of one's parents.

Fifth, the analyst, at this stage, must cautiously undertake actual reconstructions. The word "actual" here is used not to denote their historical accuracy but to distinguish them from the historical dimension of the "affirmative interventions" made earlier during the course of analysis; the latter largely exert the psychotherapeutic effect of "inexact interpretations" (Glover 1931). It is only after the defensive and drive-related nature of idealization has been brought under analysis—an event that sometimes does not occur until the patient's hope has been actively ruptured—that meaningful reconstructions are possible. Since the core problems involved in

---

20. Beginning with Freud's injunction that phobics face their feared objects (quoted in Alexander and French 1946) and his (1918) setting an end-point to the Wolf Man's analysis, the psychoanalytic literature is replete with unconventional measures in the service of facilitating analytic work. Kolansky and Eisner (1974), for instance, speak of the "spoiling" of preoedipal developmental arrest in impulse disorders and addictions in order to stir up a relatively more analyzable intrapsychic conflict, a notion extended to the treatment of sexual perversions by Socarides (1991). In Eissler's (1953) terminology, these are "parameters." However, since the publication of his paper, it has become increasingly evident that analytic technique includes not only interpretation but preparation for interpretation as well.

tenacious "someday" and "if only" fantasies usually date back to early preverbal levels, such reconstructive attempts are fraught with pitfalls. Blum's (1981) astute observations regarding preoedipal reconstruction must be kept in mind here.

Finally, throughout this work, the analyst must be highly vigilant toward his own emotional experience. The informative potential of countertransference in such cases is considerable. Since the idealization inherent in "someday" and "if only" fantasies is not easily verbalized by the patient, the analyst often has to decipher it through his own feelings. Within the transference, the analyst is invested by these patients with the task of preserving an illusion. This puts pressure on the analyst. On the one hand, there is the temptation to actively rescue the patient. On the other hand, there is the allure of quickly showing the patient that his expectations are unrealistic and serve defensive aims. Cloaked in the guise of therapeutic zeal, hasty attempts of this sort often emanate from the analyst's own unresolved narcissism and infantile omnipotence. "The determinedly optimistic therapist coerces . . . his patients into experiencing the depression which he is too threatened to feel within himself" (Searles 1977, p. 483). Clearly, both extremes (rescue and rejection) are to be avoided. In this context, the issue of the analyst's own hope is pertinent (see also Mitchell 1993 in this regard). While he does envision an ego more free of conflicts in the patient's future (Loewald 1960), his hope must not become an unrealistic one whereby he keeps waiting for a day ("someday"!) when a patient who appears increasingly unanalyzable will suddenly become analyzable. An analyst–analysand collusion around such waiting is a certain recipe for an interminable analysis. Winnicott (1971) states that in such cases

> the psychoanalyst may collude for years with the patient's need to be psychoneurotic (as opposed to mad) and to be treated as psychoneurotic. The analysis goes well, and everyone is pleased. The only drawback is that the analysis never ends. It can be terminated, and the patient may even mobilize a psychoneurotic false self for the purpose of finishing and expressing gratitude. But, in fact, the patient knows that there has been no change in the underlying (psychotic) state and the analyst and the patient have succeeded in colluding to bring about a failure. [p. 102]

Yet another aspect of the countertransference important in such cases is the analyst's becoming restlessly aware of the passage of time while the patient seems oblivious of the months and years that have gone by with relatively little change in his situation. The analyst's dawning awareness of time suggests approaching termination (Akhtar 1992a) in most other analyses. In the case of patients with "someday" and "if only" fantasies, however, the situation is just the opposite. The analyst's awareness of passing time is reflective of the fact that termination is nowhere in sight and the analysis has bogged down. Indeed, in cases where "someday" and "if only" fantasies are deep and subtle, this countertransference experience may be the first clue to their existence. Interestingly, such an entry of "the fatal limits of real time" (Boris 1976, p. 145) in the analytic situation might itself yield a technical intervention. The analyst might announce that much time has passed and that the patient seems totally oblivious to it. This might be a catalyzing intervention for the analysis and, under fortunate circumstances, might be the only comment needed to "rupture" the patient's illusory stance.

In sum, the six tasks outlined above seem of considerable importance in working with individuals with "someday" and "if only" fantasies. Keeping these guidelines in mind without turning them into a rigid strategy, and maintaining a firm allegiance to the "principle of multiple function" (Waelder 1930), will help the analyst develop a clinically responsive technique and avoid the conceptual dichotomies mentioned in the very beginning of this paper. An "informed eclecticism" (Akhtar 1992c, p. 44; see also Pulver 1993) of this sort seems the best approach to ameliorate the troubled and troubling existence associated with "someday" and "if only" fantasies.

SUMMARY

> [H]ope in the paranoid-schizoid position . . . is easy, a longing for a magical, omnipotently controlled, easily exchangeable object. Hope in the depressive position requires great courage, a longing for an all-too human, irreplaceable object, outside of one's control. [Mitchell 1993, p. 212]

Fantasies whose core is constituted by the notions of "someday" and "if only" are ubiquitous in the human psyche. In severe character pathology, however, these fantasies have a particularly tenacious, defensive, and ego-depleting quality. The "someday" fantasy idealizes the future and fosters optimism, and the "if only" fantasy idealizes the past and lays the groundwork for nostalgia. The two fantasies originate in the narcissistic disequilibrium consequent upon the early mother–child separation experiences, though the oedipal conflict also contributes to them. Both can be employed as defenses against defective self- and object constancy as well as later narcissistic and oedipal traumas. This paper attempts to highlight the metapsychology and behavioral consequences of these fantasies as well as their unfolding in the treatment situation. It suggests six tasks to be especially important for analytic work with such patients: (1) providing and sustaining a meaningful holding environment, (2) employing affirmative interventions, (3) helping the patient to unmask these fantasies and interpreting their defensive, narcissistic and sadomasochistic aspects, (4) rupturing the patient's excessive hope, analyzing the effects of such rupture, and facilitating the resultant mourning, (5) reconstructing the early scenarios underlying the need for excessive hope, and (6) paying careful attention to countertransference feelings throughout such work.

REFERENCES

Abend, S. M., Porder, N. S., and Willick, M. S. (1983). *Borderline Patients: Psychoanalytic Perspectives*. New York: International Universities Press.

Abraham, K. (1924). The influence of oral erotism on character formation. In *Selected Papers of Karl Abraham, M.D.*, pp. 393–406. New York: Brunner/Mazel.

Adler, G. (1985). *Borderline Psychopathology and Its Treatment*. New York: Jason Aronson.

Akhtar, S. (1984). The syndrome of identity diffusion. *American Journal of Psychiatry* 141:1381–1385.

——— (1989). Kohut and Kernberg: a critical comparison. In *Self Psychology: Comparisons and Contrasts*, ed. D. W. Detrick and D. P. Detrick, pp. 329–362. Hillsdale, NJ: Analytic Press.

——— (1991). Three fantasies related to unresolved separation-individuation: a less recognized aspect of severe character pathology. In *Beyond the Symbiotic Orbit: Advances in Separation-Individuation Theory—Essays in Honor of Selma Kramer, M.D.*, ed. S. Akhtar and H. Parens, pp. 261–284. Hillsdale, NJ: Analytic Press.

——— (1992a). *Broken Structures: Severe Personality Disorders and Their Treatment*. Northvale, NJ: Jason Aronson.

——— (1992b). Tethers, orbits and invisible fences: clinical, developmental, sociocultural, and technical aspects of optimal distance. In *When the Body Speaks: Psychological Meanings in Kinetic Clues*, ed. S. Kramer and S. Akhtar, pp. 21–57. Northvale, NJ: Jason Aronson.

———— (1992c). Review of *Between Freud and Klein: The Psychoanalytic Quest for Knowledge and Truth*, by Adam Limentani. *Psychoanalytic Books* 3:43–49.

———— (1994a). Object constancy and adult psychopathology. *International Journal of Psycho-Analysis* 75:441–455.

———— (1994b). Needs, disruptions, and the return of ego instincts: some explicit and implicit aspects of self-psychology. In *Mahler and Kohut: Perspectives on Development, Psychopathology, and Technique*, ed. S. Kramer and S. Akhtar, pp. 97–116. Northvale, NJ: Jason Aronson.

———— (1995). A third individuation: immigration, identity, and the psychoanalytic process. *Journal of the American Psychoanalytic Association*.

———— (in press). "Someday . . . " and "if only . . . " fantasies: pathological optimism and inordinate nostalgia as related forms of idealization. *Journal of the American Psychoanalytic Association*.

Alexander, F., and French, T. M. (1946). *Psychoanalytic Therapy*. New York: Ronald Press.

Amati-Mehler, J., and Argentieri, S. (1989). Hope and hopelessness: a technical problem? *International Journal of Psycho-Analysis* 70:295–304.

Angel, A. (1934). Einige Bemerkungen über den Optimismus. *International Journal of Psycho-Analysis* 20:191–199.

Arlow, J. A., and Brenner, C. (1964). *Psychoanalytic Concepts and the Structural Theory*. New York: International Universities Press.

Balint, M. (1968). *The Basic Fault: Therapeutic Aspects of Regression*. London: Tavistock.

Benedek, T. (1938). Adaptation to reality in early infancy. *Psychoanalytic Quarterly* 7:200–214.

Bion, W. R. (1961). *Experience in Groups*. New York: Basic Books.

Blum, H. P. (1973). The concept of erotized transference. *Journal of the American Psychoanalytic Association* 21:61–76.

———— (1981). Object constancy and paranoid conspiracy. *Journal of the American Psychoanalytic Association* 29:789–803.

Boris, H. N. (1976). On hope: its nature and psychotherapy. *International Review of Psycho-Analysis* 3:139–150.

Burland, J. A. (1975). Separation-individuation and reconstruction in psychoanalysis. *International Journal of Psychoanalytic Psychotherapy* 4:303–335.

Casement, P. J. (1991). *Learning from the Patient*. New York: Guilford.

Chasseguet-Smirgel, J. (1984). *Creativity and Perversion*. New York: Norton.

Cooper, A. M. (1989). Narcissism and masochism: the narcissistic-masochistic character. *Psychiatric Clinics of North America* 12:541–552.

———— (1995). Personal communication.

Dorn, R. N. (1967). Crying and weddings (and) "When I Grow Up." *International Journal of Psycho-Analysis* 48:298–307.

Eickhoff, F. W. (1987). A short annotation to Sigmund Freud's "Observations on Transference-Love." *International Review of Psycho-Analysis* 14:103–109.

Eissler, K. R. (1950). Ego psychological implications of the psychoanalytic treatment of delinquents. *Psychoanalytic Study of the Child* 6:97–121. New York: International Universities Press.

——— (1953). The effect of the structure of the ego on psychoanalytic technique. *Journal of the American Psychoanalytic Association* 1:104–143.

Erikson, E. H. (1950). *Childhood and Society*. New York: Norton.

Escoll, P. J. (1992). Vicissitudes of optimal distance through the lifecycle. In *When the Body Speaks: Psychological Meanings in Kinetic Clues*, ed. S. Kramer and S. Akhtar, pp. 59–87. Northvale, NJ: Jason Aronson.

Fenichel, O. (1945). *The Psychoanalytic Theory of Neurosis*. New York: Norton.

Fodor, N. (1950). Varieties of nostalgia. *Psychoanalytic Review* 37:25–38.

Frank, A. (1969). The unrememberable and the unforgettable: passive primal repression. *Psychoanalytic Study of the Child* 24:48–77. New York: International Universities Press.

Freedman, A. (1956). The feeling of nostalgia and its relationship to phobia. *Bulletin of the Philadelphia Association for Psychoanalysis* 6:84–92.

French, T. M. (1945). The integration of social behavior. *Psychoanalytic Quarterly* 14:149–168.

French, T. M., and Wheeler, D. R. (1963). Hope and repudiation of hope in psychoanalytic therapy. *International Journal of Psycho-Analysis* 44:304–316.

Freud, S. (1911). Formulations on the two principles of mental functioning. *Standard Edition* 12:213–226.

——— (1913). Totem and taboo. *Standard Edition* 13:1–161.

——— (1915). Observations on transference love. *Standard Edition* 12:159–171.

——— (1917). A childhood recollection from *Dichtung und Wahrheit*. *Standard Edition* 17:145–157.

——— (1918). From the history of an infantile neurosis. *Standard Edition* 17:1–122.

——— (1925). Some psychical consequences of the anatomical distinction between the sexes. *Standard Edition* 19:243–258.

——— (1926). Inhibitions, symptoms and anxiety. *Standard Edition* 20:77–174.

——— (1930). Civilization and its discontents. *Standard Edition* 21:57–146.

Friedman, L. (1969). The therapeutic alliance. *International Journal of Psycho-Analysis* 50:139–153.

Geahchan, D. (1968). Deuil et nostalgie. *Revue Française de Psychanalyse* 32:39–65.

Gediman, H. K. (1985). Imposture, inauthenticity and feeling fraudulent. *Journal of the American Psychoanalytic Association* 33:911–936.

Gedo, J. E., and Goldberg, A. (1973). *Models of the Mind*. Chicago: University of Chicago Press.

Gitelson, M. (1962). The curative factors in psychoanalysis. *International Journal of Psycho-Analysis* 43:194–205.

Glover, E. (1925). Notes on oral character formation. *International Journal of Psycho-Analysis* 6:131–153.

————— (1931). The therapeutic effect of inexact interpretation. *International Journal of Psycho-Analysis* 12:397–411.

Greenson, R. R. (1965). The working alliance and the transference neurosis. *Psychoanalytic Quarterly* 34:155–181.

Hamilton, J. W. (1969). Object loss, dreaming, and creativity: the poetry of John Keats. *Psychoanalytic Study of the Child* 24:488–531. New York: International Universities Press.

Hartmann, H. (1964). *Essays on Ego Psychology*. New York: International Universities Press.

Isakower, O. (1936). A contribution to the pathopsychology of phenomena associated with falling asleep. *International Journal of Psycho-Analysis* 19:331–345.

Joseph, B. (1993). On transference love: some current observations. In *On Freud's "Observations on Transference-Love,"* ed. E. S. Person, A. Hagelin, and P. Fonagy, pp. 102–113. New Haven, CT: Yale University Press.

Kernberg, O. F. (1967). Borderline personality organization. In *Borderline Conditions and Pathological Narcissism*, pp. 1–47. New York: Jason Aronson, 1975.

————— (1975). *Borderline Conditions and Pathological Narcissism*. New York: Jason Aronson.

————— (1984). *Severe Personality Disorders: Psychotherapeutic Strategies*. New Haven, CT: Yale University Press.

————— (1992). *Aggression in Personality Disorders and Perversions*. New Haven, CT: Yale University Press.

Khan, M. (1966). Role of phobic and counterphobic mechanisms and separation anxiety in schizoid character formation. In *The Privacy of the Self*, pp. 69–81. New York: International Universities Press, 1974.

————— (1974). *The Privacy of the Self*. New York: International Universities Press.

————— (1983). *Hidden Selves*. New York: International Universities Press.

Killingmo, B. (1989). Conflict and deficit: implications for technique. *International Journal of Psycho-Analysis* 70:65–79.

Klein, M. (1940). Mourning and its relation to manic depressive states. In *Love, Guilt and Reparation and Other Works, 1921–1945*, pp. 344–369. New York: Free Press.

Kleiner, J. (1970). On nostalgia. *Bulletin of the Philadelphia Association for Psychoanalysis* 20:11–30.

Kohut, H. (1971). *The Analysis of the Self*. New York: International Universities Press.

————— (1977). *Restoration of the Self*. New York: International Universities Press.

————— (1984). *How Does Analysis Cure?* Chicago: University of Chicago Press.

Kohut, H., and Wolf, E. (1978). The disorders of the self and their treatment: an outline. *International Journal of Psycho-Analysis* 59:413–425.

Kolansky, H., and Eisner, H. (1974). *The psychoanalytic concept of preoedipal developmental arrest*. Paper presented at the Fall Meetings of the American Psychoanalytic Association, December.

Kramer, S. (1980). The technical significance and application of Mahler's separation-individuation theory. In *Psychoanalytic Explorations of Technique: Discourses on the Theory of Therapy*, ed. H. Blum, pp. 240–262. New York: International Universities Press.

Kramer, S., and Akhtar, S. (1988). The developmental context of internalized preoedipal object relations: clinical applications of Mahler's theory of symbiosis and separation-individuation. *Psychoanalytic Quarterly* 57:547–576.

Kris, E. (1956). The personal myth: a problem in psychoanalytic technique. *Journal of the American Psychoanalytic Association* 4:653–681.

Krystal, H. (1966). Giorgio de Chirico: ego states and artistic production. *American Imago* 23:210–226.

Lewin, R. A., and Schulz, C. (1992). *Losing and Fusing: Borderline Transitional Object and Self Relations*. Northvale, NJ: Jason Aronson.

Loewald, H. W. (1960). On the therapeutic action of psychoanalysis. *International Journal of Psycho-Analysis* 41:16–33.

——— (1979). The waning of the Oedipus complex. *Journal of the American Psychoanalytic Association* 27:751–755.

Mahler, M. S. (1968). *On Human Symbiosis and the Vicissitudes of Individuation*. Vol. I: Infantile Psychosis. New York: International Universities Press.

——— (1971). A study of the separation and individuation process and its possible application to borderline phenomena in the psychoanalytic situation. *Psychoanalytic Study of the Child* 25:403–424. New Haven, CT: Yale University Press.

——— (1972). Rapprochement subphase of the separation-individuation process. In *The Selected Papers of Margaret S. Mahler, vol 2*, pp. 131–148. New York: Jason Aronson, 1979.

Mahler, M. S., Pine, F., and Bergman, A. (1975). *The Psychological Birth of the Human Infant*. New York: Basic Books.

Mayer, E. (1994). Some implications for psychoanalytic technique drawn from analysis of a dying patient. *Psychoanalytic Quarterly* 63:1–19.

Menninger, K. (1959). Hope. *American Journal of Psychiatry* 116:481–491.

Mitchell, S. A. (1993). *Hope and Dread in Psychoanalysis*. New York: Basic Books.

Modell, A. (1976). The holding environment and the therapeutic action of psychoanalysis. *Journal of the American Psychoanalytic Association* 24:285–307.

Nasio, J.-D. (1994). Personal communication.

Parens, H. (1991). Separation-individuation theory and the psychosexual theory. In *Beyond the Symbiotic Orbit: Advances in Separation-Individuation Theory— Essays in Honor of Selma Kramer, M.D.*, ed. S. Akhtar and H. Parens, pp. 3–34. Hillsdale, NJ: Analytic Press.

Poland, W. S. (1975). Tact as a psychoanalytic function. *International Journal of Psycho-Analysis* 56:155–162.

Potamianou, A. (1992). *Un bouclier dans l'economie des etats-limites: l'espoir*. Paris: Presses Universitaires de France.

Pulver, S. (1993). The eclectic analyst, or the many roads to insight and change. *Journal of the American Psychoanalytic Association* 41:339–357.

Renik, O. (1990). Comments on the clinical analysis of anxiety and depressive affect. *Psychoanalytic Quarterly* 59:226–248.

Rubovits-Seitz, P. (1988). Kohut's method of interpretation: a critique. *Journal of the American Psychoanalytic Association* 36:933–959.

Schmale, A. H. (1964). A genetic view of affects: helplessness and hopelessness. *Psychoanalytic Study of the Child* 19:287–310. New York: International Universities Press.

Searles, H. F. (1977). The development of mature hope in the patient-therapist relationship. In *Countertransference and Related Subjects: Selected Papers*, pp. 479–502. New York: International Universities Press, 1979.

———— (1986). *My Work with Borderline Patients*. Northvale, NJ: Jason Aronson.

Settlage, C. F. (1977). The psychoanalytic understanding of narcissistic and borderline personality disorders: advances in developmental theory. *Journal of the American Psychoanalytic Association* 25:805–833.

———— (1991). On the treatment of preoedipal pathology. In *Beyond the Symbiotic Orbit: Advances in Separation-Individuation Theory—Essays in Honor of Selma Kramer, M.D.*, ed. S. Akhtar and H. Parens, pp. 351–367. Hillsdale, NJ: Analytic Press.

———— (1993). Therapeutic process and developmental process in the restructuring of object and self constancy. *Journal of the American Psychoanalytic Association* 41:473–492.

Settlage, C. F., Bemesderfer, S., Rosenthal, J., et al. (1991). The appeal cycle in early mother-child interaction: the nature and implications of a finding from developmental research. *Journal of the American Psychoanalytic Association* 39:987–1014.

Socarides, C. W. (1991). The specific tasks in the psychoanalytic treatment of well-structured sexual deviations. In *The Homosexualities and the Therapeutic Process*, vol. 2, ed. C. W. Socarides and V. D. Volkan, pp. 277–291. New York: International Universities Press.

Sohn, L. (1983). Nostalgia. *International Journal of Psycho-Analysis* 64:203–211.

Spitz, R. (1953). Aggression. In *Drives, Affects, Behavior*, ed. R. M. Loewenstein, pp. 126–138. New York: International Universities Press.

———— (1965). *The First Year of Life*. New York: International Universities Press.

Sterba, E. (1940). Homesickness and the mother's breast. *Psychiatric Quarterly* 14:701–707.

Stone, L. (1954). The widening scope of indications for psychoanalysis. *Journal of the American Psychoanalytic Association* 2:567–594.

Strenger, C. (1989). The classic and romantic visions in psychoanalysis. *International Journal of Psycho-Analysis* 70:595–610.

Thoreau, H. D. (1854). *Walden*. New York: Random House, 1971.

Volkan, V. D. (1976). *Primitive Internalized Object Relations*. New York: International Universities Press.

———— (1981). *Linking Objects and Linking Phenomena*. New York: International Universities Press.

———— (1987). *Six Steps in the Treatment of Borderline Personality Organization*. Northvale, NJ: Jason Aronson.

Voltaire. (1759). *Candide*. New York: Random House, 1992.

Waelder, R. (1930). The principle of multiple function. *Psychoanalytic Quarterly* 5:45–62.

Wallerstein, R. S. (1983). Self psychology and "classical" psychoanalytic psychology: the nature of their relationship. In *The Future of Psychoanalysis*, ed. A. Goldberg, pp. 19–63. New York: International Universities Press.

———— (1993). On transference love: revisiting Freud. In *On Freud's "Observations on Transference-Love,"* ed. E. S. Person, A. Hagelin, and P. Fonagy, pp. 57–74. New Haven: Yale University Press.

Webster's New Universal Unabridged Dictionary, 2nd Edition. (1983). New York: Simon & Schuster.

Werman, D. S. (1977). Normal and pathological nostalgia. *Journal of the American Psychoanalytic Association* 25:387–398.

Wheelis, A. (1994). *The Way Things Are*. New York: Baskerville.

Winnicott, D. W. (1951). Transitional objects and transitional phenomenon. In *Through Paediatrics to Psychoanalysis*, pp. 229–243. London: Hogarth, 1978.

———— (1956). The antisocial tendency. In *Through Paediatrics to Psychoanalysis*, pp. 306–315. London: Hogarth, 1978.

———— (1960). Ego distortion in terms of true and false self. In *The Maturational Processes and the Facilitating Environment*, pp. 140–152. New York: International Universities Press, 1965.

———— (1965). *The Maturational Processes and the Facilitating Environment*, New York: International Universities Press.

Wolf, E. (1994). Selfobject experiences: development, psychopathology, treatment, pp. 65–96. In *Mahler and Kohut: Perspectives on Development, Psychopathology and Technique*, ed. S. Kramer, and S. Akhtar. Northvale NJ: Jason Aronson.

Wolman, T. (1991). Mahler and Winnicott: some parallels in their lives and works. In *Beyond the Symbiotic Orbit: Advances in Separation-Individuation Theory—Essays in Honor of Selma Kramer, M.D.*, ed. S. Akhtar and H. Parens, pp. 35–60. Hillsdale, NJ: Analytic Press.

Yeomans, F. E., Selzer, M. A., and Clarkin, J. F. (1992). *Treating the Borderline Patient: A Contract Based Approach*. New York: Basic Books.

The Borderline Patient and His Relation to the Present Moment: Response to the Paper of Salman Akhtar, M.D.

JUAN-DAVID NASIO, M.D.

I would like to thank Salman Akhtar for this vivid account of a clinical situation. Both in his case examples and in the ideas he puts forward about the fantasies of past time and future time, Dr. Akhtar has brought us right onto the privileged ground of psychoanalysis, namely clinical practice. Practice is our common ground because, over the years, the raw material of Freudian theory—the patient's suffering and our undertaking to hear it—has remained the essential bond among analysts regardless of their style, their language, or their training.

Needless to say, this raw material of clinical facts exists only insofar as the theoretician gives it a name—the name brings the event into being. This is exactly what Dr. Akhtar has done by means of that intuition, unique to theorists, that consists in isolating different clinical phenomena and then collecting them under a single name (that is, conceptualizing them) and bringing them into existence as a clinical reality. Again I want to emphasize that clinical reality exists only to the extent that it is named by a concept, one that is rigorously attached to other concepts of psychoanalytic theory.

Dr. Akhtar has in effect created a new clinical reality. He has succeeded in classifying and formulating our confused idealizations of time into two precise fantasies: "someday . . . ," which idealizes the future, and "if only

. . . ," which idealizes the past. From now on we analysts will have to detect this new clinical reality, confirm it in our patients' reports, and develop it theoretically. Just a few days after becoming aware of this contribution, I found myself noting these two fantasies in my analysands' material and wondering about their very different defensive functions in borderline as opposed to neurotic cases.

We can all agree that Dr. Akhtar's paper is rich in clinical, theoretical, and technical considerations. What I would like to do is to focus on the implicit core of the paper, namely the relation of the borderline patient to the present moment. I shall also attempt to compare neurotic and borderline conditions with regard to their encounter with time.

Let me begin by recalling that, like all fantasies, those that Dr. Akhtar has outlined—an impetus towards the future and a yearning for the past—entail a setting, a movement, and a function. The setting is an imaginary and idealized one that brings narcissistic satisfaction. The movement is a movement towards identification: The ego identifies with an ideal object and loves itself as an ideal ego. As for the function, it is to protect the ego against being overwhelmed by the drives.

This much can be said for fantasies in general. But what is distinctive about the fantasies of an ideal past and future, whether in neurotics or borderlines, is their role in protecting the ego against the danger of instinctual overload feared as the danger represented by the present moment. They are a screen against present time. Whether with the persistent hope of one day attaining absolute happiness or with obsessive nostalgia for a happiness that is lost, the analysand avoids the anxiety of living in the present.

But why turn away from the present; what is it that the ego finds so threatening? In order to reply, I must first define the present not as the ego imagines and fears it, but as it is conceived by psychoanalysis. Here, then, is the definition I propose. In analytic treatment, in the midst of the transference, the present is the time of the event, the time of a word, a gesture, or an emotion that occurs, surprises us, and transforms us. When the event arises it causes us to lose a part of ourselves, and in so doing it creates us. I am created as a subject in the unexpected present of partial losses and painful gaps. This subject, born of the event, is what we call the subject of the unconscious, and the moment of its appearance is the time of the unconscious. We can say, then, that the present is the tense of the unconscious, while the idealized past and future are the tenses of the ego.[1]

---

1. *Translator's note:* In French, *le temps* means both "time" and "grammatical tense."

But it would be a mistake to reduce Dr. Akhtar's theoretical contribution to a mere rationalization of our twofold relation to time, the thrust towards the future and the regret for the past. When I say that with his concept of fantasy Dr. Akhtar formalizes our twofold relation to time, I primarily want to emphasize that he introduces an essential element between time and us, one that is specific to psychoanalysis, namely the absolute satisfaction of desire. He introduces what we, in our terminology, call absolute *jouissance*, the hypothetical and impossible absolute *jouissance* of a promised time or a lost one, what Dr. Akhtar characterizes as the state in which one is completely at peace and without conflict, in which everything is available without prohibition or desire, aggression or anxiety. It is precisely because this is a matter of *jouissance* that we can conceptualize the impetus towards the future or the desire for the past as a fantasy, instead of considering it to be a vague reverie. Fantasized time is always the time of a *jouissance*, of a happiness to come or one that is already lost. It is *jouissance* that is the true object of the fantasy, time being only its outward appearance.

At this point I must add another feature of the general structure of all fantasies whatsoever. Fantasy is a psychic formation resulting from the conjunction of the ego and the object of its quest. In the present case, the two fantasies described by Dr. Akhtar are the products of an ego identified with the hypothetical absolute happiness that it supposedly knew at one time and hopes to experience again. Fantasy is the work of an ego that feels itself to be as absolute and ideal as the happiness it seeks. When the subject is nostalgic for perfect happiness or hopes to find it again, he is really expressing nostalgia for himself as being perfect, or he is hoping to be as perfect, someday, as the sought-for happiness.

When all is said and done, the object of the fantasy is the ego itself as an ideal object. This is the narcissism inherent in all fantasy. Essentially, what I love is not the object lost in my past but the past itself—and, further, myself as a child in the past. The two fantasies of ideal time conceptualized by Dr. Akhtar are above all fantasies of an ideal ego once lost or yet to come. In a remarkable passage, Freud (1914) defines nostalgia and hope as two forms of narcissism:

> man has . . . shown himself incapable of giving up a satisfaction he had once enjoyed. He is not willing to forgo the narcissistic perfection of his childhood; and . . . he seeks to recover it in the new form *of an ego ideal*. What he projects before him as his ideal is the substitute for the lost narcissism of his childhood in which he was his own ideal. [p. 94]

The metapsychological structure of fantasy thus has three components: the ego, the ideal object (that is, the *jouissance* of future or past time), and the identificatory movement of the ego towards the object. Narcissism and idealization are therefore aspects of one and the same movement.

To return to our initial question about why the ego becomes anxious in the present, what danger it senses there, the answer depends on whether we are dealing with a neurotic patient or a borderline one. Although both have recourse to the same fantasy of ideal time, the ego of the neurotic and the ego of the borderline interpret the danger of the present moment in dissimilar ways. In neurosis, the ego experiences the present as the time of action, choice, and decision, as the time of an imminent test in which the risk of losing a part of himself is falsely interpreted as the threat of losing everything. For the neurotic, the present is the time in which he is vulnerable to the loss of all his power. It is here that the ego experiences castration anxiety, the anxiety that impels the ego to evade the present and take refuge in the ideal of an unreachable future or past.

For the borderline patient, on the other hand, the imminence of the present is experienced in an entirely different way. The present moment is not the time of loss or of castration anxiety; instead it is the time of a much more radical danger, one that is certainly less fictitious than that of the neurotic. It is the danger of acting. In acting I can destroy others or myself. I can explode and destroy what is outside, or implode and destroy what is inside me. While the neurotic fears an excess of the sexual instincts, the borderline is vulnerable to the excess of the death instincts. But whether the violence is directed outward or inward, the present is experienced by the borderline as what Pierre Fédida has called the psychotic moment, the dreaded time of collapse, of dissolution of one's being. Here there is no anguish or even anxiety. The immediacy of an action to be performed arouses in the borderline patient a deep feeling of unbearable abandonment. We may add that once this distress is in place the fantasy of ideal times dissolves and disappears, only to reappear eventually, when the crisis is over, as a means of lessening the rupture and reconsolidating one's being.

As Dr. Akhtar has shown very well, the borderline patient, like the neurotic, avoids the present moment by taking shelter behind the hope of an absolute happiness or the nostalgia for a happiness in the past. However, the fantasies that distract the borderline from the dangerous present and reassure him about the coherence of his being are different, for example in the way in which they are communicated to the analyst. When the neurotic sets forth his hope or confides his nostalgia, he implicitly attributes to the analyst the power to respond to his expectations. For neurotic fantasies are in effect nothing but expectations, and the transference neurosis is nothing but the promise that these expectations will be satisfied one day. In contrast, when the borderline conveys the same fantasies of ideal time to the analyst, he attributes to him no ability to respond and as a rule expects no commitment. The borderline patient's fantasies, though forged in the glow of the transference, are not addressed to the analyst. These fantasies arise, to be sure, by virtue of the practitioner's listening, but the practitioner is excluded from them.

In conclusion, I would like to mention briefly several of the issues that, in order to keep within the framework of Dr. Akhtar's thinking, I was not able to address:

—The distinctive feature of fantasies of ideal time in borderline patients is that they consist of phrases that are often uttered without the support of an imaginary scene.
—Does the structure of the fantasy of ideal time correspond to the structure of unconscious fantasies? What difference might there be between unconscious fantasy and the conscious reveries of borderline patients?
—We must recognize that these fantasies are very fragile borderline defenses.
—Finally, what are the fluctuations in appearance and disappearance of these fantasies in the borderline patient?

In this commentary I have chosen to respond to Dr. Akhtar's paper not from the outside, by comparing it to other theoretical conceptions, but from the inside, from within his own conceptual universe. In focusing on what causes the borderline patient's flight from the present moment I have attempted to enlarge the theoretical field opened up by our colleague, thanks to whose work we now have before us the task of investigating more fully the different relations to time of neurosis, psychosis, perversion, and borderline states.

REFERENCE

Freud, S. (1914). On narcissism: an introduction. *Standard Edition* 14: 69–102.

Excerpts from the Discussion

Paul Ornstein: I strenuously object to prescriptions for treatment that require the puncturing of the optimism of the patient. When I began my analysis, many years ago, I recall one of the things I told my analyst on the first day is that I would not let him tamper with my incurable optimism. He understood this and it led to very interesting developments. From a self-psychological point of view, the analysis is supposed to lead to belated structure building, to the strengthening of the fragmentation-prone self. Once the self is revitalized and made more stable and cohesive, the fantasies that otherwise are maladaptive become unnecessary. There is no need to puncture that fantasy; instead we must accompany the patient, as you said, in the initial phase. But I don't think there is ever any need to take out the knife. The psychoanalyst should leave the knife at home, or he should not have one. What he needs is a constant effort at understanding, and at articulating this understanding, with a hope that at times—I agree—will never be fulfilled. I also agree that not everybody is analyzable and not every structure can be belatedly strengthened.

Michel Feher: Dr. Akhtar, you presented a nice symmetry between the "someday" fantasy, in which the future prevents the present from taking on substance, and the "if only" fantasy, where the past prevents the present from doing so. But the "someday" may also have another symmetry, an inverse one in which an unending present prevents the future from emerging. This would be the "as soon as" fantasy; for example, "as soon as I finish classifying the books in my library, I'll be able to get to work." It is my belief that such procrastination is commonly linked with neurosis, especially obsessional neurosis, but I wonder whether you find any heuristic value in this strictly inverse symmetry.

Janine Chasseguet-Smirgel: Paul Ornstein's remarks about technique bring up a general point relating to criteria for analyzability. Freud says that we can never give up a satisfaction we once enjoyed, that we can only exchange one satisfaction for another. When it comes to leading the patient from a state of illusion to disillusionment I cannot agree with Paul Ornstein, because this is what analysis is about, though of course it has to be done without leaving the patient feeling abandoned and possibly suicidal. And when we're dealing with patients who are not neurotic but borderline or perverse, we should keep in mind this criterion for analyzability, namely whether we are able to help them exchange the satisfaction they derive from their illnesses, from the solutions they've found for their conflicts and their suffering, for something else that is closer to the reality principle.

One last point: I wonder whether the state of being in love temporarily resolves the "someday" and "if only" fantasies.

Jacques Hassoun: Whenever two boatmen meet each other on the Nile they greet one another and say, "Come and have coffee." Clearly they will never, but never, stop to have coffee, but it is also the case that never will their paths cross without their saying, "Come and have coffee," and in Arabic this is called a boatman's invitation. To pick up on what Paul Ornstein said, is it possible, as an analyst, to say, "Let's disembark now and have some coffee," or "I'm going to stop being a boatman," or "Coffee has become so expensive that I'm not going to invite you any more"?

As far as being in love is concerned, I like to quote something Marina Tsvetayeva said. She was deeply in love with a man, but then she lost all interest in him and barely recognized him when their paths crossed. When he asked what had happened, she replied that when a woman loves a man she sees him as God created him, when she doesn't love him she sees him as his parents created him, and when she no longer loves him she sees a table or a chair instead of him. Now what we need to know is what kind of table or chair we have the right to reveal in the transference.

(French analyst): With regard to analyzability, it's a funny thing, but in my experience, after trying and trying, the minute you say that you have to give up and abandon the fantasy of thinking "someday" about a potential analysand, he suddenly becomes analyzable.

Radmila Zygouris: I wouldn't want this conference to end without a single mention of Harold Searles. Many of us here in France owe a great deal to his book on the treatment of borderline patients. And in connection with the "someday" fantasy I recall how in one of his earlier books he related that, in the course of an analysis with a woman patient who was not analyzable according to traditional criteria, she kept asking him to go with her on a romantic trip to Miami. Of course he resisted this "someday" fantasy of hers, but then one day he understood and told her, "Ah, but it's just in imagination—well, if it's just imaginary we can go wherever you want." And the patient replied, "It's taken you a long time to make progress."

Salman Akhtar: I have the greatest respect for Dr. Searles, and his name is in my paper in the bibliography. He also has written about turning pathological hope into mature hope. The experience of giving up hope and then finding that the patient has become analyzable is very common. You know the Kris Study Group monograph on borderline patients—almost all patients began to get better when the analyst gave up. It is not that the patient becomes analyzable because the analyst was waiting, but that the act of the analyst's giving up constitutes the rupture of pathological hope. What I was saying is that the analyst cannot just sit back and optimistically hope for the patient to become analyzable. This is a definitive intervention; the analyst's giving up hope is a surgical intervention and in that sense you and I are in agreement.

Dr. Ornstein, I was not at all surprised that you would be vehemently opposed to what I have to say in this regard. I disagree with your statement that the analyst should not have a knife. If we compare the conduct of psychoanalysis to a surgical operation, I think that the psychoanalyst has three kinds of instruments. One is a retractor for removing the tissues, the second is an artery forceps—that is, when we cut an artery we have to clamp it to stop the bleeding—and the third is the scalpel. The retractor is like affirmative intervention and inexact interpretation: "Mmm, I know it hurts," "Tell me more," "What happened then?," "Mmm, so you thought that." The artery forceps is what in self psychology is called the mending of the disruption.

But if a surgeon performs only with the retractor and the artery forceps, than how is he going to cut? I think psychoanalysis must have surprises. Something new must take place, and for that unmasking, that unveiling, cutting through a layer is essential. You must understand what I am saying about the rupture of pathological hope. If the interpretative technique does not work, then the analyst has to do this, but it is an unusual dimension and I am also aware that it is traumatizing for the patient. But, after all, we raise children and we sometimes traumatize them. We do so for a good purpose, and I don't think that the fact that the analyst hurts the patient makes this an inappropriate intervention. That is getting too afraid of aggression.

Michel Feher's comment about the "as soon as" fantasy makes a very good point. In the various character organizations that I mentioned—schizoid, narcissistic, antisocial, schizotypal, transsexual, borderline—I forgot to mention one, and that is the hypomanic organization. In the hypomanic organization the "one day maybe" is supposed to have arrived, and as a result the person is constantly bubbling with confidence. Sometimes we need to induce a dimension of futurity in the patient.

Psychoanalysis began with an interest in the past, with the archeological metaphor of Freud, and then it got interested in the present with the here and now and transference. One thing psychoanalysis has been weak about is the dimension of the future, and this is something I am working to correct. The element of the future enters in from the moment the patient comes for treatment—in the assessment of analyzability, in the hope, the dream, the vision that the analyst has about how the patient would be if he lost the perversion, the neurosis, and so forth. Now I know it may rub some people the wrong way when I say that the analyst can have a vision about the patient. But I think this would be like saying that a mother should not have a vision about her child, and we can disagree over this. But your point is well taken that in some patients we will need to induce the future. I think the point about obsessional neurosis is also very well taken.

In connection with the issue of analyzability, I recall hearing of an anecdote in which someone said to Freud,

A friend of mine has some problems, and he asked me whether he should be in analysis. I told him, "Why not? If it doesn't help, at least it won't hurt." Freud got very upset and said, "Did you tell him it won't hurt, that it is a harmless procedure?" And then in his characteristic triumphant way he said, "I predict that a day will come when psychoanalysis will be considered as a legitimate cause of death."

The point I am trying to make is that it is naive, and also disrespectful of psychoanalysis, to believe that it can do everything. It cannot help everybody. There are people who have very defective egos, who for instinctual reasons have very tenacious fixations, people who, because of their experiences, have large stakes in staying sick. There are people who are not capable of this kind of metaphorical dialogue because for cultural reasons they don't have a sufficient degree of self-observing ego. And so forth. I believe that not everybody can be analyzed.

Part III

The Subject and the Self: Conclusions

PROFESSEUR MICHEL TORT

This conference developed out of an exchange with Judith Feher Gurewich, a meeting in which neither of us knew exactly what sort of event the conference would be, or who all the participants were, or how much pleasure there would turn out to be in this coming together. We exchanged names. We brought some people together, and did so on the basis of a clear division: these were to be people who, as a rule, spoke with each other but not with those in the other group. Our aim was—precisely—to get everyone to speak with one another.

In one of Alain Tanner's films a man comes into a café. There is only one person sitting there. The man sits down opposite this person, at the same table. The seated man is surprised, since there's plenty of room elsewhere and he doesn't know the newcomer. The man who came in replies: "Precisely."

We knew that the two groups had good, long-standing reasons for remaining more or less actively unaware of each other, but we felt they would be bound to have a lot to talk about. We had chosen people clearly established within their own communal identities or "selves," not merely American and French, but Americans on one theoretical side and Lacanians across the theoretical border. And so it seemed most appropriate to choose borderline conditions, the realm of boundaries, as the theme of the conference.

Each of us here has been aware of the opposing forces in the air. These are by no means just measured intellectual differences in doctrine, theory, even practice. Instead, expressed through these intellectual viewpoints, there have been violent tensions sometimes erupting into arguments. These tensions have been overt. They were spoken aloud and they returned in the form of rumors, but always as violence. Yet how strange it is for psychoanalysts to relate this way to affect—this contained, subtle, discreet, or impassioned violence! Diffuse and circumscribed, it did not characterize all the contributions. Each of you perceived the calmness, the particular tone and affect, of our American colleagues and a tone that was, from time to time, different on the French side.

I shall try to describe it, to name it, just as some of our American colleagues have spoken of the naming of affects. In so doing I don't think I'm getting away from our theme, for as it happens this goes right to the heart of the question of borderline states. This tone, *sui generis*, is a combination of several elements: an indulgent confidence ("I don't have to remind you of the evidence . . . "); rigor, which is also an affect; the jubilant, repeated declaration of allegiance to the Master's formula, slipped in subtly but inexorably; the allergy to the words of the other ("Did you hear what s/he said?!")

Dr. Kouretas presented an outline of the conflicts within American psychoanalysis that was eloquent enough to allow us to realize that elsewhere, too, in other forms, the same question has arisen, but perhaps in another tone, one that is in accordance with the Americans' contributions to the conference. These contributions were expressed in a relaxed, nonpolemical manner, and—what is most important—they referred in various ways to empathy, affect, recognition, mutuality, symmetry.

There must be some connection there. We must take note of the allergy to empathy, affect, understanding, and so forth, take it seriously, but not as a merely theoretical question, just a difference in point of view. Instead, the question is: What is the passion that is expressed in an anti-affect theory?—not a particular individual's passion, but the originary passion that is conveyed along with a certain theoretical modality and tone, and whose repercussions have been very noticeable here.

This is a question that unites us and separates us, that holds us. To the extent that we haven't managed to resolve it here, at future meetings we will have trouble hearing each other. And that is perhaps the virtue of the presence and the speech of that Other whom the stranger can represent: to help us to hear and understand this shared symptom.

At the end of his presentation Dr. Kouretas offered a hypothesis about the function of "borderline conditions" in the United States. I'd like to go in the same direction, for before asking all the relevant questions about where we are to locate these conditions, there is a kind of preliminary question: How, with what predisposition, should we approach them? What is it that we are putting in order, and what order, since, like psychosis, borderline states throw *us* into disorder? It is clear, for example, that the entire effort of someone like Kernberg is aimed at placing beyond the border what he cannot bear and thus designates as the cause—archaic, pregenital oral aggression. Obviously our American colleagues who are here with us, and a number of others, are more peaceful, much less combative, with regard to their analysands' aggression. The main problem, it seems to me, is really not placing our analysands into our three compartments—neurosis, psychosis, perversion—or inventing a special compartment. What we need to do is ask ourselves why we have such a great love of compartmentalization.

What brings us together today, then, and divides us, is what I would call the borderline condition of psychoanalysis itself: its splitting, its denial, its narcissistic disorders, its theory-compartments, its concept-missiles. We have all witnessed this strange dialogue between analysts who talk about communicating and analysts who reply that there is always a misunderstanding, that is, that it should be clearly understood that there is inevitably misunderstanding. So I'll end these preliminary remarks with a question. Since we have gotten together, what is it that has brought us together, misunderstanding or the desire to understand nevertheless? For there has been another movement on both sides, a way of saying, not "What an awful idea!", but "If I put this another way, in my language, does this mean something to you?" or "You've said this, and I'd like to tell you what it brings up for me in my experience, and then we'll see where we are."

There has been a crossing over, a building of bridges. You know what is at stake with a bridge or a tunnel, and the discussions they stir up. There are those who, basically, are afraid that the passage will be too easy, that there will be all sorts of crossing over and communicating, and others who are happy about crossing. Here, then, are some attempts at crossing, round trip.

It seems to me that the misunderstanding and confrontation have four aspects: first, the ways in which we construe psychic functioning; second, clinical reference points and the status of borderline conditions; third, strategies of treatment and handling of the transference; fourth, the relation of the preceding points to conditions external to psychoanalytic theory and practice.

THE CONSTRUAL OF PSYCHIC FUNCTIONING

I would like to start by repeating Judith Gurewich's characterization of the basic divergence as being between a position in which alienation from the Other is considered to be accidental and one in which it is considered to be structural. Surely borderline conditions offer a favorable opportunity for a meeting of minds, since, in their own way, they illustrate the division and the alienation of the subject, or—in another language—of the self. How, then, can we formulate the work that has been carried out under these diverging assumptions?

Our American colleagues who adopt the perspective of self psychology (and also many others outside this theoretical framework who refer to the self or to identity more vaguely, less systematically) begin by positing a reality that they call the self, which either is recognized and supported or is subjected to various destructive processes on the part of its primary objects. Does this mean that there is a self that, from the outset, is not reducible to the Other? The answer to this question must be nuanced. Their idea seems to be that what comes first is, instead, a kind of recognition by the Other as a self, which permits a self to be constituted—the self that, however it may otherwise have been treated, will address the analyst in the transference. This recognition has taken place, or else there would be no demand for it, but it was mishandled. From this perspective all of the oedipal processes are seen as being preceded by the recognition that naturally takes as its model the so-called mother–child relationship (cf. Dr. Paul Ornstein on mirroring). The point of view that Lacan developed, following Freud, is based on a somewhat similar intuition, that of an original subjection of the subject to the Other.[1]

Several of the discussants noted the difficulty of separating a line of development of the self from the developmental lines of fantasies and of the structure of desire. But the conclusions to be drawn from this observa-

---

1. *Translator's note:* The word *assujettissement* has the primary meaning "subjection," but it is also related to *subjectivation*, the process of becoming a subject, which, as the author will go on to say, is of primary importance in Lacanian thought.

tion can be quite different indeed. One way of presenting them would emphasize that every original mother–child dyad is an idealizing fiction, that the self/subject is already inscribed in the innumerable antecedent strategies of desire of the first Others, strategies in which the subject functions as the object of fantasmatic processes and not simply as a recognized subject. The observations presented during this conference do not disconfirm such a view, so that if we are to speak of "recognition," it is, in a sense, recognition of this substantial and unavoidable fact prior to any specification of clinical structure.

But—and here I turn to a very different way of formulating the same fact—if subjection to the Other were not also a process permeated by symbolization and entailing modes of recognition of a subject by a subject, how could we hope to transform modes of subjection in analysis? Thus, in the case presented by Dr. Anna Ornstein, when Dr. White takes his anger out on his own children he is certainly subjected to fantasies in which he reproduces the manner in which he was seduced by his father, but this procedure makes no sense unless it is carried out on subjects to be dominated, seduced, deceived.

The paradox is that recognition takes the form of a subjection, just as the communication of what was experienced takes, in analysis, the form of a seduction and an appeal.

We should, then, modify our disagreement and express it as follows. Analysts in France who have been receptive to Lacan's theory have privileged the aspect of subjection because it allows full scope to the problem of the relation to the Other in a non-idealized way. *The Other is in no way an intrapsychic object, good or bad, but rather the symbolic condition of there being an object, a subject, and a relationship.*

But this involves the risk of misconstruing the element of recognition accompanying subjection. For the question of symbolic recognition is right at the center of Lacan's thought, even before the Rome Discourse[2] where it is fully formulated. What is at issue is this: Are Lacan's various accounts of what he calls the paternal function the final word on the question of the symbolic that he himself poses? Or, instead, are these accounts characterized by a series of shifts, the point of which is to assimilate the law to the so-called law of the father and to desymbolize the maternal so that it enters via this father-law into symbolization?

---

2. *Translator's note*: This is the seminal paper entitled "The Function and Field of Speech and Language in Psychoanalysis," delivered in 1953. A translation may be found in Lacan 1977, pp. 30–113.

If we don't clarify this point, the argument advanced by Judith Feher Gurewich—namely that borderline states are an excellent illustration of the division of the subject and can therefore form a bridge between American and Lacanian viewpoints—might be turned around in a dangerous way. We might feel justified in thinking that a theory of the subject emphasizing its division and its alienation implied a typical "borderline" presentation.

In the Lacanian view of the subject and his desire there is a relation to independence, or rather to nondependence, separation. This idea of nondependence could certainly be criticized as a form of refusal of primary recognition, but in the concept of the independence of the subject's unique desire there is, I think, something that accords with the experience of the "self." Yet let us not minimize the remaining differences in perspective but instead try to locate them precisely:

—The idea of a new paradigm offered by selfobject functions and selfobject experiences aims at a general reformulation of the process of subjectivation, of becoming a subject; it is basically opposed to the primacy of the drives. In this sense, as a number of people have observed, it does not affect the Lacanian view of subjectivation. On the contrary, we might even consider it to be a way of reopening the question of the subject.

—On the other hand, if this paradigm implies achieving a cohesive and well-structured self it definitely presents a twofold problem for analysts whose frame of reference is the Lacanian theory of the subject. The cohesive, well-structured self may appear to be a variant of the well-adjusted, adapted ego of American ego psychology, and, furthermore, the paradigm is scarcely compatible with the Lacanian idea of the division of the subject. Taking note of this division in no way prevents us from offering the subject, in analysis, the possibility not so much of reconstituting a structured self as of affirming himself in the singularity of his desire.

CLINICAL REFERENCE POINTS AND THE STATUS OF BORDERLINE CONDITIONS

Here, too, we have perhaps managed to clarify certain misunderstandings.

1. A clear formulation of the problem of the status of borderline conditions must try to characterize these conditions without presup-

posing that they represent new forms of pathology that have appeared in conjunction with the present era. We must, instead, characterize them intrinsically and then ask how and why it is that they present themselves to the analyst as new forms.

2. It is obvious, on the other hand, that their autonomy as a separate clinical entity is highly dependent on two significant and related facts. The first of these is the establishment, in the various forms of the *DSM*, of an empirical, extra-analytical classification in terms of symptoms. One has only to look at the time someone like Kernberg devotes to the prolonged discussion of this classification and at the way in which he reproduces it, with all its entailments, in clinical practice. The second fact, which Dr. Kouretas set forth so well, is the struggle between the American trends of ego psychology and self psychology and what that struggle implies.

3. As soon as we consider that the conditions of becoming a subject are governed by the same symbolic data, by the same structure of human desire, the question of borderline states takes on another aspect. Can we still regard these states as a separate category? It all depends on what we mean.

—If we mean that there are, alongside neurosis, psychosis, and perversion, clinical entities with other identifying features, then the answer is clearly no. However, this is not a flat, abstract refusal; it is an invitation to reconsider—for example in the case presented by Dr. Anna Ornstein—whether we have truly exhausted the resources of sadomasochism, of perversion, before relegating them to a clinical category at the "border." From this point of view we would have to pay careful attention to the fact that the inflation of the borderline category goes hand in hand with the disappearance in *DSM* of hysteria, and with an excessively narrow conception of perversions, one that retains only the so-called "serious" cases.

—If, however, we understand "borderline" to refer to clinical cases that, while clearly assigned to one of the divisions neurosis/psychosis/perversion, include "border zones," then, if we wish, we may speak of borderline cases. Here we can find the makings of an agreement. The position suggested by Dr. Modell, when he connects "psychic death" to psychotic or schizoid states as well as to other pathologies, suggests that there is no absolute need to regroup these states into a separate category. It is possible to consider that borderline states may arise, as forms of symptomatology, on the foundation of all psychic structures.

Having said that, I think we can go further and locate some positive connections among apparently divergent points of view. Certain aspects of Dr. Akhtar's paper, for example, clearly provide a basis for such connections. For example, why should we see a contradiction between the role of early losses and the role of the oedipal period? Wouldn't it be preferable to juxtapose them in accordance with Freud's extensive exploration of the concept of retroactive effect? From this perspective early losses take effect in the context of the oedipal dialectic, and that dialectic is formed in relation to possible early traumas. This is the direction in which Dr. Akhtar is heading, it seems to me, when he defines condensation by explaining that the pursuit of the good mother of symbiosis is condensed with positive oedipal desires.

TRANSFERENCE AND STRATEGIES OF TREATMENT

The third item is the transference and strategies of treatment. In a conference planned as a debate on clinical issues, this is, clearly, the most decisive and the most difficult point. In all justice we must not lose sight of the fact that, in this first encounter, we on the French side have been much less precise, less willing to take risks, in setting forth our procedures.

It seems to me that the outcome of the discussions is all the more fruitful because it presents contrasts. The main issue is that of understanding and of the need for communication in the analytic setting, with the modes of interpretation or intervention that they imply. Here we can discern two quite different reactions.

1. The first of these is a reminder, on the part of some of the discussants, of Lacan's critique of certain post-war trends. This critique, quite independent of self psychology, was aimed at the utilization of affect, which it represented as an obstacle to the understanding of signifying forms of fantasy. With regard to this coherent theoretical position, the work of our American colleagues has perhaps invited us to ask questions—which, as it happens, has already been taking place here in France. Of course communication cannot be taken for granted, misunderstanding is inevitable, and silence is

golden. But we must restore to these statements the ambiguity of what they are stating. Misunderstanding can be cleared up, but it can also be cultivated sadistically; it is one thing not to gratify the patient's demand, another to turn this rule into a perverse mantra.

2. The other position that was maintained is perhaps even better suited to taking into account both what our American colleagues have described to us and the Lacanian theory of fantasy. It corresponds to our experience, not only of "borderline" cases, but doubtless also of many more clear-cut cases of neurosis and, obviously, of psychosis or perversion. It seems to me more apposite from the strategic point of view. What I am referring to is the presupposition that analysis, strictly speaking, involves a kind of preliminary task, a shoring up, a bringing together of the elements of fantasy, without which interpretations of fantasy are at best ineffective and often persecutory, indeed traumatic. This is the perspective from which Dr. Blevis discussed Dr. Anna Ornstein's case. It is consistent with Dr. Akhtar's belief that, however illusory the patient's objects, he must experience them as true before he can admit that they are fantasies with regressive aims and defensive functions.

Can we go further and suggest that many misunderstandings, many counterarguments, would be resolved if we were mindful of the time given by and for the analysis, and of the strategic ordering of intervention and interpretation within this time? Perhaps. But it is not certain that differences of opinion concerning the transference and its analysis would then disappear. What we would have to do in order to go further is, in fact, to concern ourselves with technical questions, for example to go deeper into the implications of certain modes of intervention. I'm thinking here of what Dr. Akhtar defined as malignant transference. None of our French colleagues could fail to recognize the difficulty of the situations he describes, and none would claim that such situations can be handled easily. But the price the analyst pays for simultaneously trying to prolong the illusion of the good mother and trying to undo this illusion seems too high, from our point of view, when it comes to his having to declare explicitly to a patient that he will never marry her.

Beyond the discussions concerning the phases of the transference as set forth in the theory of the self (for example the progression from the idealizing to the mirror transference), there emerges a decisive question about interpreting sexuality. Dr. Paul Ornstein himself notes what he calls the perversity of the disturbances, but clearly there are different ways of locating this perversity. If we maintain that the perverse is a kind of appeal for the interpretation of sexuality (a trap into which the analyst must avoid falling), questions arise. Is this all that is necessary to transform the relation of the subject to his objects and to the father? Is the sexual a "content," a sort of indifferent material of the subject's actions? So one might think if the paradigm of the self replaces the primacy of the drives (which are also completely abstract).

In exaggerated form the issue would be as follows: Sexuality is perhaps not reducible to a secondary datum, linked to an Oedipus complex represented as secondary. What is the meaning of a certain *desexualization* of psychoanalytic processes? In characteristic fashion, Dr. Paul Ornstein spoke of sexualization. An image comes to my mind here: It is as if the sexual were a kind of colorization of the psychic black and white, or one operation, among others, of the self. What we seem to have here is a positioning of sexuality that is in strong opposition to the Freudian (and Lacanian) view of the determinative nature of sexuality, of the whole matter of sex.

This observation naturally brings me back to the question I asked Dr. Notman about the relationship between the conceptions of feminine development and the cultural and multicultural problematics of identity in the United States. This question leads to my final point. What is the relationship of psychoanalysis with the arts of loving that are at the heart of Western history? Perhaps the attachment to sexual difference has something to do with courtly love, with the libertines' thought and their practice of desire; and perhaps love has followed different paths on the other side of the Atlantic.

CONDITIONS EXTERNAL TO THE STRUCTURE OF DESIRE

Because we chose to have this conference center around an exchange of views on clinical cases, we can distinguish the points of difference and agreement on conceptions of psychic reality and the treatment we assign to them, as well as the relationship between these conceptions and techniques on the one hand and our external realities on the other.

Dr. Kouretas' historical presentation had the great merit of pointing out how these two levels have become entangled to form, among other things, that amorphous grouping known as borderline states. It also had the merit of disentangling them neatly. The notion of the false self (following on the notion of the "as if" personality) and the recourse to the self of self psychology are examples of a clinical intuition that perhaps raises problems of harmonizing these discourses with one another and with what we call the subject and others think of as the ego or self. But we certainly have here an empirical arena for psychoanalytic confrontation, be it about the borderline states or not. What Dr. Kouretas showed so well from the outset is that this confrontation is dependent on a *systematization* that is more a collective group phenomenon of recognition and rejection than it is a real debate. With the ego you do ego psychology and gain a following. With the object you do object relations. With the self you do self psychology. I would add that with the subject you also do subject theory.

Dr. Kouretas pointed out genuine paradoxes, for example that the most obvious result of the triumph of ego psychology is that subjectivity was relegated to the sidelines. He shed light on the relationship between tendencies that on the surface appear to be purely internal to psychoanalysis, and societal trends on the largest scale—in the present case those of American society—where they develop through psychoanalysis, but also, and first, through psychiatry. It would of course be appropriate to undertake the same exercise with regard to the "subject French style."

In a sense, then, what we have had to do in this conference is to make allowance for these national flags and practices. But while such putting into perspective can be hurtful to group narcissism, it enables the discussion to go forward. I would hope that what I have described as conversations—and perhaps they turned out to be just that—will continue in the same spirit of truth that can sometimes arise unexpectedly from a good conference.

REFERENCE

Lacan, J. (1977). *Écrits: A Selection*. Trans. A. Sheridan. New York: Norton.

Index

Made in the USA
San Bernardino, CA
20 January 2016